Full-Stack Web Development with Vue.js and Node

Build scalable and powerful web apps with modern web stack: MongoDB, Vue, Node.js, and Express

Aneeta Sharma

BIRMINGHAM - MUMBAI

Full-Stack Web Development with Vue.js and Node

Commissioning Editor: Kunal Chaudhari
Acquisition Editor: Nigel Fernandes
Content Development Editor: Jason Pereira
Technical Editor: Leena Patil
Copy Editor: Safis Editing
Project Coordinator: Sheejal Shah
Proofreader: Safis Editing
Indexer: Pratik Shirodkar
Graphics: Jason Monteiro
Production Coordinator: Shantanu Zagade

First published: May 2018

Production reference: 1100518

Published by Packt Publishing Ltd.
Livery Place
35 Livery Street
Birmingham
B3 2PB, UK.

ISBN 978-1-78883-114-7

www.packtpub.com

`mapt.io`

Mapt is an online digital library that gives you full access to over 5,000 books and videos, as well as industry leading tools to help you plan your personal development and advance your career. For more information, please visit our website.

Why subscribe?

- Spend less time learning and more time coding with practical eBooks and Videos from over 4,000 industry professionals

- Improve your learning with Skill Plans built especially for you

- Get a free eBook or video every month

- Mapt is fully searchable

- Copy and paste, print, and bookmark content

PacktPub.com

Did you know that Packt offers eBook versions of every book published, with PDF and ePub files available? You can upgrade to the eBook version at `www.PacktPub.com` and as a print book customer, you are entitled to a discount on the eBook copy. Get in touch with us at `service@packtpub.com` for more details.

At `www.PacktPub.com`, you can also read a collection of free technical articles, sign up for a range of free newsletters, and receive exclusive discounts and offers on Packt books and eBooks.

Contributors

About the author

Aneeta Sharma is a software engineer from Kathmandu, Nepal who has been in the tech industry for more than seven years. She started her career as a Web Designer, before becoming a PHP Developer and then a Ruby on Rails engineer. She has been working on both frontend and backend aspects of web application development since she started her career and has been developing web applications professionally since 2009.

She likes to explore new technologies and has learned to work with lots of them over the years. Most recently, she has been working with full-stack solutions with Ruby on Rails, along with frontend frameworks such as Vue.js and React.js.

I am grateful to Packt Publishing for giving me the opportunity to write this book. I am thankful to the team with whom I worked and everyone who contributed to this book. Thank you all for spending your precious time in ensuring the quality of this book. I loved working with you.

I am thankful for my family and friends, as well as my colleagues who supported and encouraged me on this journey. Thank you for being an inspiration.

About the reviewer

Anton de Regt is a programmer and blogger with a passion for making life better, faster, and easier. After graduating with a bachelor's degree in Embedded Systems and Automation, he worked in the Netherlands, China, and the USA as a programmer and database admin. Anton now develops apps for small business owners to help them focus on the things that matter and make their impact bigger.

On his tech blog, he writes about a variety of subjects, ranging from cybersecurity and data science, to hackathons and socially responsible programming.

Packt is searching for authors like you

If you're interested in becoming an author for Packt, please visit `authors.packtpub.com` and apply today. We have worked with thousands of developers and tech professionals, just like you, to help them share their insight with the global tech community. You can make a general application, apply for a specific hot topic that we are recruiting an author for, or submit your own idea.

Table of Contents

Preface

JavaScript has become one of the most important languages of today and tomorrow. The rise of JavaScript in the past few years has been so drastic that it has become a powerful language in the development of modern web applications.

MEVN is one of the stacks for developing modern web applications in addition to MEAN and MERN. This book provides a step by step way of building a full-stack web application using the technology in MEVN, which is MongoDB, Express.js, Vue.js, and Node.js.

The book will provide the basic concepts of Node.js and MongoDB, continuing with building an Express.js application and implementing Vue.js.

In this book, we'll cover the following things:

- Learning about the technology stack—MongoDB, Node.js, Express.js, and Vue.js
- Building an Express.js application
- Learning what REST APIs are and how to implement them
- Learning to use Vue.js as the frontend layer in the Express.js application
- Adding an authentication layer in the application
- Adding the automation scripts and tests

Who this book is for

This book is designed for web developers who are interested in learning how to build a full-stack application with only one programming language as JavaScript using the technology stack: Mongo DB, Express.js, Vue.js, and Node.js.

This book is suitable for beginners and intermediate developers with a basic knowledge of HTML, CSS, and JavaScript. If you are a web or full-stack JavaScript developer JavaScript developer and has tried hands on the traditional stacks, such as LAMP, MEAN, or MERN, and wish to explore a new stack with modern web technologies, then this book is for you.

What this book covers

Chapter 1, *Introduction to MEVN*, gives an introduction to the MEVN stack and the installation of different tools required to build the foundation for the application.

Chapter 2, *Building an Express Application*, provides an introduction to Express.js, an idea of what **Model**, **Views**, **Controller** (**MVC**) structure is, and shows you how to set up an application using Express.js and MVC structure.

Chapter 3, *Introduction to MongoDB*, focuses on the introduction of Mongo and its queries, introduction to Mongoose and performance of **Create**, **Read**, **Update**, and **Delete** (**CRUD**) operations using Mongoose.

Chapter 4, *REST APIs*, gives an idea of what REST architecture is and what RESTful APIs are. This chapter also gives an idea of different HTTP verbs and developing REST APIs.

Chapter 5, *Building the Real Application*, introduces Vue.js and shows you how to build a fully working dynamic application using all technologies in MEVN.

Chapter 6, *Authentication with Passport.js*, deals with what Passport.js and describes how to implement JWT and local strategy to add an authentication layer in the application.

Chapter 7, *Passport.js OAuth Strategies*, gives idea about what OAuth strategies and guides you through the implementation of Facebook, Twitter, Google, and LinkedIn Passport.js strategies.

Chapter 8, *Introduction to Vuex*, gives an idea about core concepts of Vuex – states, getters, mutations, and actions. It also describes how you can implement them in the application.

Chapter 9, *Testing an MEVN Application*, explains what unit tests and end-to-end tests are and guides you through writing both unit tests and automation tests for the different aspects of the application.

Chapter 10, *Go Live*, explains what Continuous Integration is, guiding you through how to set up a Continuous Integration service with the application and deploy the application on Heroku.

To get the most out of this book

This book will be of most benefit if you have the following skills:

- A knowledge of HTML, CSS, and JavaScript
- A knowledge of Vue.js and Node.js is a plus
- A knowledge on how to build web applications using MEAN and MERN stacks is a plus

Download the example code files

You can download the example code files for this book from your account at www.packtpub.com. If you purchased this book elsewhere, you can visit www.packtpub.com/support and register to have the files emailed directly to you.

You can download the code files by following these steps:

1. Log in or register at www.packtpub.com.
2. Select the **SUPPORT** tab.
3. Click on **Code Downloads & Errata**.
4. Enter the name of the book in the **Search** box and follow the onscreen instructions.

Once the file is downloaded, please make sure that you unzip or extract the folder using the latest version of:

- WinRAR/7-Zip for Windows
- Zipeg/iZip/UnRarX for Mac
- 7-Zip/PeaZip for Linux

The code bundle for the book is also hosted on GitHub at https://github.com/ PacktPublishing/Full-Stack-Web-Development-with-Vue.js-and-Node. In case there's an update to the code, it will be updated on the existing GitHub repository.

We also have other code bundles from our rich catalog of books and videos available at https://github.com/PacktPublishing/. Check them out!

Conventions used

There are a number of text conventions used throughout this book.

`CodeInText`: Indicates code words in the text, database table names, folder names, filenames, file extensions, pathnames, dummy URLs, user input, and Twitter handles. Here is an example: "A module is something that can be loaded by Node.js with a `require` command and has a namespace. A module has a `package.json` file associated with it."

A block of code is set as follows:

```
extends layout

block content
  h1= title
  p Welcome to #{title}
```

When we wish to draw your attention to a particular part of a code block, the relevant lines or items are set in bold:

```
var index = require('./routes/index');
var users = require('./routes/users');

var app = express();

// Require file system module
var fs = require('file-system');
```

Any command-line input or output is written as follows:

```
$ mkdir css
$ cd css
```

Bold: Indicates a new term, an important word, or words that you see onscreen. For example, words in menus or dialog boxes appear in the text like this. Here is an example: "Just hit **Continue** until the installation completes."

Warnings or important notes appear like this.

 Tips and tricks appear like this.

Get in touch

Feedback from our readers is always welcome.

General feedback: Email `feedback@packtpub.com` and mention the book title in the subject of your message. If you have questions about any aspect of this book, please email us at `questions@packtpub.com`.

Errata: Although we have taken every care to ensure the accuracy of our content, mistakes do happen. If you have found a mistake in this book, we would be grateful if you would report this to us. Please visit `www.packtpub.com/submit-errata`, selecting your book, clicking on the Errata Submission Form link, and entering the details.

Piracy: If you come across any illegal copies of our works in any form on the Internet, we would be grateful if you would provide us with the location address or website name. Please contact us at `copyright@packtpub.com` with a link to the material.

If you are interested in becoming an author: If there is a topic that you have expertise in and you are interested in either writing or contributing to a book, please visit `authors.packtpub.com`.

Reviews

Please leave a review. Once you have read and used this book, why not leave a review on the site that you purchased it from? Potential readers can then see and use your unbiased opinion to make purchase decisions, we at Packt can understand what you think about our products, and our authors can see your feedback on their book. Thank you!

For more information about Packt, please visit `packtpub.com`.

Introducing MEVN
1

Mongo, Express, Vue.js, and Node.js (MEVN) is a collection of JavaScript technologies just like **MongoDB**, **Express**, **Angular**, and **Node.js** (MEAN), and like **MongoDB**, **Express**, **React**, and **Node.js** (MERN). It is a full-stack solution for building web-based applications that use MongoDB as data storage, Express.js as the backend framework (which is built on top of Node.js), Vue.js as the JavaScript framework for the frontend, and Node.js as the main engine for the backend.

This book is for web developers who are interested in learning to build a full-stack JavaScript application using MongoDB, Express.js, Vue.js, and Node.js. It is suitable for beginners and intermediate developers with a basic knowledge of HTML, CSS, and JavaScript.

The term MEVN may be new, but the technologies used in it are not new. The only new technology that is being introduced here is Vue.js. Vue.js is an open source JavaScript framework, and its popularity is growing rapidly. There's not much of a learning curve with Vue.js and it is also a fierce competitor of other JavaScript frameworks such as AngularJS and ReactJS.

Modern web applications need to be fast and easily scalable. In the past, JavaScript was used in web applications only when there was a need to add some visual effects or animations that normal HTML and CSS could not achieve. But today, JavaScript has changed. Today, JavaScript is used in almost every web-based application, from small- to large-scale apps. JavaScript is chosen when the application needs to be much faster and more interactive.

Building a full-stack application using JavaScript as the sole programming language has its own benefits:

- If you are just starting out and learning how to program, you only have to master one language: JavaScript.
- Full-stack engineers are high in demand. Becoming a full-stack developer means that you have an idea of how databases work, you know how to build both the backend and the frontend, and you also have the skills for UI/UX.

In this book, we will build the application using these technology stacks.

We will cover the following topics in this chapter:

- An introduction to the MEVN technology stack
- An introduction to Node.js and its installation on Windows, Linux, and macOS
- An overview of npm and its installation
- An introduction to MongoDB and its installation and a few basic commands used in MongoDB
- An introduction to GitHub version control and how it helps software engineers in terms of easy access to code history and collaboration

Evolution of the technology stack in JavaScript

JavaScript is one of the most important programming languages today. Founded by Brendan Eich in 1995, it has done superbly well, not only in maintaining its status, but also in rising above all other programming languages.

The popularity of JavaScript is ever growing with no end in sight. Building web applications with JavaScript as the sole programming language has always been popular. And with this fast growing pace, the need for software engineers to have knowledge of JavaScript is only increasing. No matter what programming language you choose to excel at, JavaScript always crawls its way in to get involved with other programming languages as well, one way or the other.

There are a lot of technologies to choose from for the frontend and backend while developing an application. While this book uses Express.js for the backend, there are other frameworks as well, which you can learn if you want.

The other available backend frameworks are **Meteor.js**, **Sails.js**, **Hapi.js**, **Mojito**, **Koa.js**, and many others.

Similarly, for the frontend, the technologies include **Vue.js**, **React**, **Angular**, **Backbone**, and many more.

For databases, the options, other than MongoDB, are **MySQL**, **PostgreSQL**, **Cassandra**, and others.

Introducing MEVN

JavaScript frameworks are rising day by day, both in terms of numbers and their usage. JavaScript used to be implemented only for the client-side logic but, over the years, it has seen significant growth and now it is used both on frontends and backends.

Express.js in the MEVN stack is used to manage all the backend-related stuff and Vue.js handles all the view-related stuff. The advantages of using an MEVN stack are as follows:

- One language is used throughout the whole application, which means the only language you need to know is JavaScript
- Understanding the client side and server side is very easy with one language
- Its very fast and reliable application with the non-blocking I/O of Node.js
- Its a great way to keep updated on the growing ecosystem of JavaScript

Installing Node.js

To get started, we need to add all the dependencies that are required for an MEVN stack application. We can also refer to the documentation on the official website (https:// nodejs.org/) for details on how to install Node.js in any operating system.

Installing Node.js on macOS

There are two ways to install Node.js on macOS: using the installer or using the bash.

Installing Node.js using the installer

To install Node.js using the installer, perform the steps:

1. Install the installer: We can download the installer for macOS from the official website's download page (`https://nodejs.org/en/#download`). We will be installing the latest `node` version, which is `10.0.0`. You can install any `node` version you want, but the application that we will be building in this book will require the `node` version `>= 6.0.0`. Run the installer and follow the instructions given. When we download and run the installer, we will be prompted with the following dialog box:

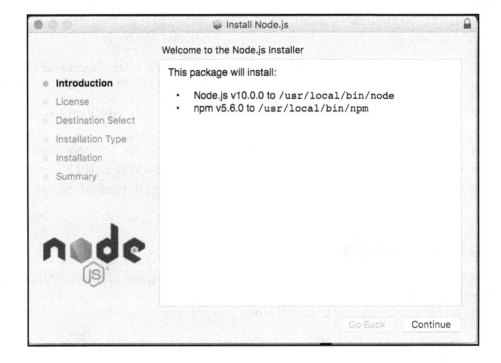

2. Just hit **Continue** until the installation finishes. Once the installation is complete, we will be able to see the following dialog box:

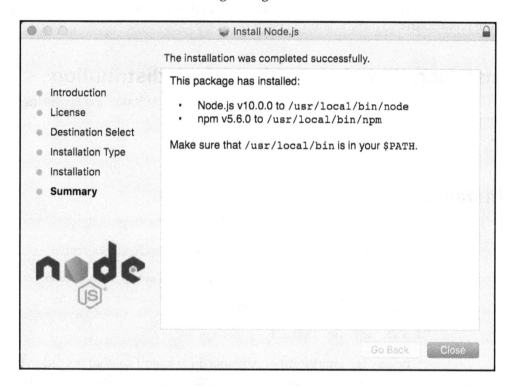

Just hit **Close** and we will be done.

Installing Node.js using the bash

Node.js can be easily installed using Homebrew in macOS. Homebrew is a free and open source software package manager that is used to install software on macOS. I personally prefer Homebrew because it makes it very easy to install different software on Mac:

1. To install Homebrew, type the following command:

```
$ /usr/bin/ruby -e "$(curl -fsSL
https://raw.githubusercontent.com/Homebrew/install/master/install)"
```

2. Now, use Homebrew to install Node.js with the following command:

```
$ brew install node
```

Installing Node.js on Linux

For Linux, we can either install the default distribution of Node.js or we can download it from NodeSource to use the latest version.

Installing Node.js from the default distribution

To install from the default distribution, we can install Node.js on Linux by using this command:

```
$ sudo apt-get install -y nodejs
```

Installing Node.js from NodeSource

To install Node.js from NodeSource, perform the following steps:

1. First download the latest version of Node.js from NodeSource:

    ```
    $ curl -sL https://deb.nodesource.com/setup_9.x | sudo -E bash
    ```

2. Then, install Node.js with the command:

    ```
    $ sudo apt-get install -y nodejs
    ```

 The `apt` is a short form of Advanced Package Tool that is used to install software on Debian and Linux distributions. Basically, this is equivalent to the Homebrew command in macOS.

Installing Node.js on Windows

We can install Node.js on Windows by following these steps:

1. Download the Node.js installer from the official website (https://nodejs.org/en/download/).
2. Run the installer and follow the given instructions.
3. Click on the **Close/Finish** button.

Installing Node.js for Windows via an installer is almost the same as on macOS. Once we download and run the installer, we will be prompted with a dialog box. Just click on **Continue** until the installation completes. When we finally see a dialog with a confirmation, we hit **Close**. Node.js will be installed!

Introducing NVM

NVM stands for **Node Version Manager**. NVM keeps track of all the node versions that we installed and also lets us switch between different versions. This is handy when the application that we built for one version of Node.js does not become compatible with the other versions, and we need that specific node version to make things work. NVM allows us to manage these versions easily. This is also very helpful when we need to upgrade or downgrade the node versions.

Installing Node.js from NVM

1. To download NVM, use the following command:

```
$ curl -o-
https://raw.githubusercontent.com/creationix/nvm/v0.33.0/install.sh
| bash
```

2. We can also use the following command:

```
$ wget -qO-
https://raw.githubusercontent.com/creationix/nvm/v0.33.6/install.sh
| bash
```

3. Check whether nvm has successfully installed using the following command:

```
$ nvm --version
```

4. Now, to install node via nvm, use this command:

```
$ nvm install node
```

Introducing npm

The npm is the acronym for **Node Package Manager**. Basically, it is a tool that takes care of all the packages that we install for Node.js. We can find all the existing packages on the official website (https://www.npmjs.com/). npm makes it easy for developers to keep their code updated and to reuse code shared by many other developers.

Developers are often confused by the terms package and modules. However, there is a clear distinction between these two.

Module

A module is something that can be loaded by Node.js with a require command and has a namespace. A module has a package.json file associated with it.

Package

A package is just a file, or group of files, that is capable of functioning on its own. Every package also has a package.json file that contains all the metadata-related information that describes that package. A combination of modules makes up a node package.

Installing npm

When we install Node.js from the installer itself, npm is installed as a part of the node. We can check whether npm is installed or not by using the following command:

```
$ npm --version
```

If npm is not installed, the command displays an error, whereas if installed, it just prints out the version of the installed npm.

Using npm

npm is used to install different packages in our application. There are two ways to install packages: locally and globally. When we want to install a certain package specific to our application, we want to install that package locally. However, if we want to use a certain package as a command-line tool or be able to access it outside our application as well, we will want to install it as a global package.

Installing an npm package locally

To install a package specific to our application only, we can use this command:

```
$ npm install <package_name> --save
```

Installing an npm package globally

To install a package globally, we can use this command:

```
$ npm install -g <package_name>
```

Introducing package.json

All the node packages and modules consist of a file called package.json. The main function of this file is to carry all the meta information associated with that package or module. A package.json file requires the content to be a JSON object.

As a minimum, a package.json file consists of the following things:

- **name**: The name of the package. This is an important part of a package.json file as it is the main thing that distinguishes it from other packages and, hence, it is a required field.
- **version**: The version of the package. This is also a required field. To be able to install our package, the name and version fields need to be given.
- **description**: A short summary of the package.

- **main**: This is the primary entry point used to look for the package. Basically, it is a file path, so when a user installs this package, it knows where to start looking for the modules.
- **scripts**: This field consists of commands that can be run for various states in the application. It has a key-value pair. The `key` is the event at which the command should be run and the `value` is the actual command.
- **author/contributors**: The author and contributors are the people. It contains an identifier of the person. An author is a single person, whereas contributors can be a group of people.
- **license**: The license field, when provided, makes it easy for the users to use our package. This helps in identifying the permissions and restrictions when using the package.

Creating a package.json file

We can manually create a `package.json` file and specify the options ourselves, or we can use a command to create it interactively from the command prompt.

Let's go ahead and initialize a sample application with a `package.json` using npm.

First, create a folder in your projects directory using the command:

```
$ mkdir testproject
```

To create a `package.json` file, run the following command in the application that we created:

```
$ npm init
```

Running this command will ask us a bunch of questions that we can answer interactively from the command line:

```
~/P/testproject git⁆master ⟩⟩⟩ npm init
This utility will walk you through creating a package.json file.
It only covers the most common items, and tries to guess sensible defaults.

See `npm help json` for definitive documentation on these fields
and exactly what they do.

Use `npm install <pkg>` afterwards to install a package and
save it as a dependency in the package.json file.

Press ^C at any time to quit.
package name: (testproject)
version: (1.0.0)
description: A test project
entry point: (index.js)
test command: npm run test
git repository:
keywords:
author: get.aneeta@gmail.com
license: (ISC)
About to write to /Users/aneetasharma/Projects/testproject/package.json:

{
  "name": "testproject",
  "version": "1.0.0",
  "description": "A test project",
  "main": "index.js",
  "scripts": {
    "test": "npm run test"
  },
  "author": "get.aneeta@gmail.com",
  "license": "ISC"
}


Is this OK? (yes)
~/P/testproject git⁆master ⟩⟩⟩ |
```

In the end, it will create a `package.json` file, which will have the following content:

```
package.json — testproject

EXPLORER                    {} package.json  ×

OPEN EDITORS                 1   {
    package.json             2       "name": "testproject",
TESTPROJECT                  3       "version": "1.0.0",
    package.json             4       "description": "A test project",
                             5       "main": "index.js",
                             6       "scripts": {
                             7         "test": "npm run test"
                             8       },
                             9       "author": "get.aneeta@gmail.com",
                            10       "license": "ISC"
                            11   }
                            12
```

Installing MongoDB

MongoDB is the first part of the technology in the MEVN stack. MongoDB is a free and open source document-based database published under a GNU license. It is a NoSQL database, meaning it is a non-relational database. Unlike relational databases, which use tables and rows to represent data, MongoDB uses collections and documents. MongoDB represents the data as a collection of JSON documents. It provides us with the flexibility to add fields in whatever way we want. Each document in a single collection can have a totally different structure. Aside from adding fields, it also provides the flexibility to change the fields from document to document in whatever way we want, something that is a cumbersome task in relational databases.

The benefits of MongoDB compared to Relational Database Management Systems (RDBMS)

MongoDB offers a lot of benefits compared to Relational Database Management Systems:

- Schema-less architecture: MongoDB does not require us to design a specific schema for its collections. A schema for one document can vary, with another document being totally different.

- Each document is stored in a JSON-structured format.
- Querying and Indexing the MongoDB is very easy.
- MongoDB is a free and open source program.

Installing MongoDB on macOS

There are two ways to install MongoDB. We can either download it from the official MongoDB website (`https://www.mongodb.org/downloads#production`) or we can use Homebrew to install it.

Installing MongoDB by downloading

1. Download the version of MongoDB you want from `https://www.mongodb.com/ download-center#production`.

2. Copy the downloaded gzipped to the root folder. Adding it to the root folder will allow us to use it globally:

   ```
   $ cd Downloads
   $ mv mongodb-osx-x86_64-3.0.7.tgz ~/
   ```

3. Unzip the gzipped file:

   ```
   $ tar -zxvf mongodb-osx-x86_64-3.0.7.tgz
   ```

4. Create a directory that will be used by Mongo to save data:

   ```
   $ mkdir -p /data/db
   ```

5. Now, to check if the installation was done successfully, start the Mongo server:

   ```
   $ ~/mongodb/bin/mongod
   ```

Here, we have successfully installed and started the mongo server.

Installing MongoDB via Homebrew

To install MongoDB in macOS from Homebrew, follow these steps:

1. With Homebrew, we just need a single command to install MongoDB:

   ```
   $ brew install mongodb
   ```

2. Create a directory that will be used by Mongo to save data:

   ```
   $ sudo mkdir -p /data/db
   ```

3. Start the Mongo server:

   ```
   $ ~/mongodb/bin/mongod
   ```

Hence, MongoDB is finally installed.

Installing MongoDB on Linux

There are two ways to install MongoDB on Linux as well: we can either use the apt-get command or we can download the tarball and extract it.

Installing MongoDB using apt-get

To install MongoDB using apt-get, perform the following steps:

1. Run the following command to install the latest version of MongoDB:

   ```
   $ sudo apt-get install -y mongodb-org
   ```

2. Verify if mongod has been successfully installed by running the command:

   ```
   $ cd /var/log/mongodb/mongod.log
   ```

3. To start the mongod process, execute the following command in the Terminal:

   ```
   $ sudo service mongod start
   ```

4. See if the log file has a line that denotes that the MongoDB connection was made successfully:

   ```
   $ [initandlisten] waiting for connections on port
   <port>
   ```

5. To stop the mongod process:

```
$ sudo service mongod stop
```

6. To restart the mongod process:

```
$ sudo service mongod restart
```

Installing MongoDB using tarball

1. Download the binary file from https://www.mongodb.com/download-center?_ga=2.230171226.752000573.1511359743-2029118384.1508567417. Use this command:

```
$ curl -O https://fastdl.mongodb.org/linux/mongodb-linux-x86_64-3.4.10.tgz
```

2. Extract the downloaded files:

```
$ tar -zxvf mongodb-linux-x86_64-3.4.10.tgz
```

3. Copy and extract to the target directory:

```
$ mkdir -p mongodb
$ cp -R -n mongodb-linux-x86_64-3.4.10/ mongodb
```

4. Set the location of the binary in the PATH variable:

```
$ export PATH=<mongodb-install-directory>/bin:$PATH
```

5. Create a directory to be used by Mongo to store all database-related data:

```
$ mkdir -p /data/db
```

6. To start the mongod process:

```
$ mongod
```

Installing MongoDB on Windows

Installing MongoDB from the installer is as easy as installing any other software on Windows. Just like we did for Node.js, we can download the MongoDB installer for Windows from the official website (https://www.mongodb.com/download-center#atlas). This will download an executable file.

Once the executable file is downloaded, run the installer and follow the instructions. Just go through the dialog box, reading the instructions carefully. When the installation is complete, just click on the **Close** button and you are done.

Using MongoDB

Let's dive a little deeper into MongoDB. As mentioned earlier as well, Mongo consists of a database with collections (tables/groups of data) and documents (rows/entries/records). We will use a few commands provided by MongoDB to create, update, and delete the documents:

First, start the Mongo server with this command:

```
$ mongod
```

Then, open the Mongo shell with this command:

```
$ mongo
```

Creating or using a MongoDB database

This is the place where we can see all of our databases, collections, and documents. To display the list of databases that we have, we can use the following:

```
> show dbs
```

Now, this command should list all the existing databases. To use the database that we want, we can simply run this command:

```
> use <database_name>
```

But if there is no database listed, don't worry. MongoDB provides us with a functionality where, when we run the preceding command, even if that database does not exist, it will automatically create a database with the given name for us.

So, if we already have a database that we want to use, we simply run that command and, if there are no databases yet, we create one using this command:

```
> use posts
```

When we run this command, a database named posts will be created.

Creating documents

Now, let's quickly review the commands used in MongoDB. The `insert` command is used to create new documents in a collection in MongoDB. Let's add a new record to the database that we just created called `posts`.

Here as well, in order to add a document to a collection, we first need a collection, which we don't have yet. But MongoDB allows us to create a collection easily by running the `insert` command. Again, if the collection exists, it will add the document to the given collection and, if the collection does not exist, it will simply create a new collection.

Now, in the Mongo shell, run the following command:

```
> db.posts.insertOne({
    title: 'MEVN',
    description: 'Yet another Javascript full stack technology'
});
```

The command will create a new collection called `posts` in the `posts` database. The output of this command is:

```
> db.posts.insertOne({
...     title: 'MEVN',
...     description: 'Yet another Javascript full stack technology'
... });
{
    "acknowledged" : true,
    "insertedId" : ObjectId("5ac0c73d157a03498d12f147")
}
>
```

It will return a JSON object that has the ID of the document that we just created in the `insertedId` key and a flag that the event was received as `acknowledged`.

Fetching documents

This command is used when we want to fetch the records from a collection. We can either fetch all the records or a specific document by passing parameters as well. We can add a few more documents to the `posts` database to better learn the command

Fetching all documents

To fetch all the records from the `posts` collection, run the following command:

```
> db.posts.find()
```

This will return all the documents that we have in the `posts` collection:

```
● ● ●                          3. mongo (mongo)
> db.posts.find()
{ "_id" : ObjectId("5aeb14e94c86bbb5a2c94952"), "title" : "MEVN", "description
" : "Yet another Javascript full stack technology" }
>
```

Fetching a specific document

Let's find a post where the title is MEVN. To do that, we can run:

```
> db.posts.find({ 'title': 'MEVN' })
```

This command will return only those documents whose title is MEVN:

```
● ● ●                          3. mongo (mongo)
> db.posts.find({ 'title': 'MEVN' })
{ "_id" : ObjectId("5aeb14e94c86bbb5a2c94952"), "title" : "MEVN", "description
" : "Yet another Javascript full stack technology" }
>
```

Updating documents

This command is used when we want to update a certain part of a collection. Let's say we want to update the description of a post whose title is `Vue.js`; we can run the following command:

```
> db.posts.updateOne(
    { "title" : "MEVN" },
    { $set: { "description" : "A frontend framework for Javascript
programming language" } }
  )
```

The output for this command will be:

```
> db.posts.updateOne(
...        { "title" : "MEVN" },
...        { $set: { "description" : "A frontend framework for Javascript programming language" } }
... );
{ "acknowledged" : true, "matchedCount" : 1, "modifiedCount" : 1 }
>
```

We can see here that the `matchedCount` is 1, which means that as regards the parameter that we sent to update the record with the title `MEVN`, there was one document in the `posts` collection that matched the query.

The other key called `modifiedCount` gives us the count of the documents that got updated.

Deleting documents

The `delete` command is used to remove documents from a collection. There are several ways to delete a document from MongoDB.

Deleting documents that match a given criteria

To remove all the documents with certain conditions, we can run:

```
> db.posts.remove({ title: 'MEVN' })
```

This command will remove all the documents from the `posts` collection whose titles are MEVN.

Deleting a single document that matches the given criteria

To delete only the first record that satisfies the given criteria, we can just use:

```
> db.posts.deleteOne({ title: 'Expressjs' })
```

Deleting all records

To delete all the records from a collection, we can use:

```
> db.posts.remove({})
```

Introducing Git

Git is a version control system for tracking the code changes in our application. It is a free and open source software used to track and coordinate multiple users when building an application.

To start using this software, we need to install it first. There is a very easy way to install it on every OS.

Installing Git on Windows

We can find the installer for Git for Windows at `https://gitforwindows.org/`.

Download the executable installer file for Windows and follow the step-by-step instructions accordingly.

Installing Git on Mac

We can easily install Git on Mac via Homebrew. Just type the following command in the command line to install Git on Mac:

```
$ brew install git
```

Installing Git on Linux

Installing Git in Linux is as easy as installing Git on macOS. Just type the following command and hit Enter to install Git on Linux:

```
$ sudo apt-get install git
```

Introducing GitHub

GitHub is a version control service. It is a source code management tool specifically designed to track changes to our code. GitHub also provides features of social networking, such as adding comments, and displaying feeds, which makes it even more powerful because multiple developers can collaborate at the same time in a single application.

Why GitHub?

GitHub is a savior for software engineers. There are several advantages that GitHub provides that make it worthwhile to use. A few benefits that are provided by GitHub are listed here:

- **Tracking code changes**: GitHub helps track changes to the code, which means it maintains a history of our code. This enables us to view revisions of our code base made during any time period.
- **Documentation**: GitHub provides features for adding documentation, Wikis, and so on to our code bases, and these can be written using the simple markdown language.
- **Graphs and reporting**: GitHub provides insight into various metrics, including how many additions and deletions were made to the code, who the top contributors were, and who has the most commits.
- **Bug tracking**: Since GitHub tracks all the activities made at every point in time, when something breaks, we can easily backtrack to the point that broke the code. We can also integrate third-party tools such as Travis for continuous integration, which helps us to track and identify bugs easily.
- **Collaboration is easy**: Github tracks every activity done by every collaborator working on the project and also sends email notifications about the same. It also provides social media features, such as feeds, comments, emojis, and mentions.

- **Hosting our own website**: We can also host our own website with GitHub using a feature called GitHub pages. We just need to create a repo for our own project and host it using Github pages, which will then make the website applicable to the URL: `https://<username>.github.io`.

Using GitHub

GitHub is very easy to use. However, to get started using GitHub, we need to least know about a few terminologies that are used in GitHub:

- **Repository/Repo**: A repository is a place where all of our code bases are stored. A repository can be either private or public.
- **ssh-key**: ssh-key is a way to authorize in GitHub. It stores our identities.
- **Branch**: A branch can be defined as multiple states of a repository. The primary branch of any repository is the `master` branch. Multiple users can work in parallel on different branches.
- **Commit**: A commit makes it easy to distinguish between different states of a file at a given time. When we make a commit, a unique identifier is assigned to that commit so what it's easy to check what changes were made in that commit. A commit takes a message as a parameter to describe the type of change that is being made.
- **Push**: A push sends the commit that we made back to our repository.
- **Pull**: As opposed to pushing, pulling fetches the commit from the remote repository to our local project.
- **Merge**: Merging is basically done between multiple branches. It is used to apply changes from one branch to another.
- **Pull requests**: Creating a `pull request` is basically sending the changes that we made to our code base for the approval of other developers. We can start discussions on a `pull request` to check the quality of code and ensure that the changes don't break anything.

To learn more about the vocabulary used in GitHub, visit `https://help.github.com/articles/github-glossary/`.

Setting up a GitHub repository

Now that we know the basics of GitHub, let's get started creating a GitHub repository for the project we want to build:

1. First, create a folder for the application in the root folder. Let's name this application `blog`:

   ```
   $ mkdir blog
   ```

2. Create an account on GitHub at `https://github.com/`.
3. Go to your profile. Under the **Repositories** tab, click **New** as follows:

4. Name this repository `blog`.
5. Now, on the Terminal, go to the location of this application and initialize an empty repository with this command:

   ```
   $ cd blog
   $ git init
   ```

6. Now, let's create a file called `README.md` and write a description for the application and then save it:

   ```
   $ echo 'Blog' > README.md
   ```

7. Add this file to GitHub:

   ```
   $ git add README.md
   ```

8. Add a `commit` so that we have a history of this change of code:

```
$ git commit -m 'Initial Commit'
```

9. Now, to link the local application with the `remote` repository in GitHub, use this command:

```
$ git remote add origin
https://github.com/{github_username}/blog.git
```

10. Finally, we need to `push` this `commit` to GitHub:

```
$ git push -u origin master
```

When it's done, visit the GitHub repository where you will find a history of the commits made to our repository, as follows:

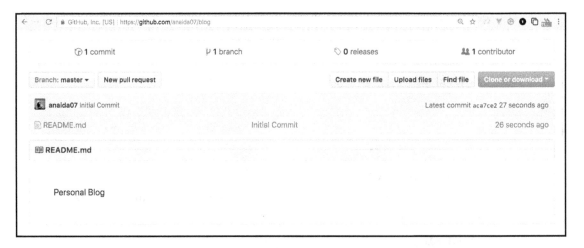

That's it. Now, when we want to write changes, we will first create a branch and push the changes to the branch.

Summary

In this chapter, we learned what an MEVN stack is. We learned what Node.js, npm, and MongoDB, are as well as receiving a brief summary of GitHub and how it helps software engineers for easy access to code history and collaboration.

In the next chapter, we will learn more about Node.js and Node.js modules. We will learn about the MVC architecture and how to implement it by building an application with Express.js.

Building an Express Application

2

Express.js is a Node.js web application framework. Express.js makes it easier to use Node.js and leverages its power. In this chapter, we will be creating an application using solely Express.js. Express.js is also a `node` package. We can use an application generator tool, which lets us create a skeleton of an express app easily, or we can simply create one ourselves from scratch.

In the previous chapter, we learned about what `npm` is, what a package is, and how to install a package. In this chapter, we will cover the following elements:

- What Node.js is and what it can do
- The benefits it adds
- The basic programming of Node.js
- Node.js core and custom modules
- An introduction to Express.js
- Creation of an application using Express.js
- Routes in Express.js
- MVC architecture: what it is and what value it adds when implemented in an application
- File naming conventions for the application
- Folder reorganization to incorporate MVC
- View creation for the Express.js application

There are a lot of `npm` packages out there that can let us create a skeleton for an Express.js application. One such package is `express-generator`. This lets us scaffold the whole application in seconds. It will create all the necessary files and folders in a modular structure. It generates the file structures in such a way that is very easy to understand. The only thing that we need to do is to define the template views and the routes.

We can modify this structure as per our needs and requirements as well. This is very handy when we are on a tight deadline and want to build an application in a day or so. The process is extremely simple.

 `express-generator` is only one of many tools that are available to create a scaffold or a modular structure of an express application. Each generator tool may have its own way of building the file structure as per their standard which can be easily customized.

If you are a beginner and want to understand how the folder structure works, I recommend you build the application from scratch. We will be discussing this further in this chapter.

To get started, first we need to learn more about Node.js before diving into Express.js.

Introduction to Node.js

Node.js is a JavaScript runtime build on a JavaScript engine. It is an open source framework used for server-side management. Node.js is lightweight and efficient and runs on various platforms, such as Windows, Linux, and macOS.

Node.js was created by Ryan Dahl in 2009. JavaScript used to be used mostly for client-side scripting, but Node.js enables JavaScript to be used on the server side as well. The invention of Node.js introduced the use of a single programming language in web applications. Node.js brings with it a lot of benefits, some of which are as follows:

- **Event-driven programming**: It means changing the state of an object from one to another. Node.js uses event-driven programming, which means it uses a user's interactive actions, such as mouse clicks, and key presses, to change the state of objects.
- **Non-blocking I/O**: The non-blocking I/O, or non-synchronous I/O, means an asynchronous I/O. A synchronous process waits until the current running process is completed and, hence, blocks the process. On the other hand, the asynchronous process does not need to wait for that process to finish, which makes it fast and reliable as well.
- **Single threading**: Single threading means that JavaScript runs in only a single event loop. Since an asynchronous process allows us to have multiple processes concurrently, it may seem like all these processes run in their own specific thread. But Node.js handles asynchronous a little differently. The event loop in Node.js triggers the next callback function that is scheduled for execution after the corresponding event has occurred.

Understanding Node.js

Before diving into Node.js programming, let's first look into some fundamentals of Node.js. Node.js runs on the JavaScript V8 engine. The JavaScript V8 engine was built by *The Chromium Project* for Google Chrome and Chromium web browsers. It is an open source project written in C++. This engine is used for both client- and server-side web applications with JavaScript.

Node.js programming

Let's start by running a node process. Open the Terminal and type this command:

```
$ node
```

This will start a new node process. We can write normal JavaScript here.

So, for example, we can write in the new Node shell the following JavaScript command:

```
> var a = 1;
```

It returns 1 when we type a and press enter.

We can also run a file with the .js extension in a node process. Let's create a folder called tutorial in the root directory with the command mkdir tutorial and create a file inside it called tutorial.js.

Now, in the Terminal, let's go into that directory with the following command:

```
$ cd tutorial
$ node tutorial.js
```

We should see something similar to the following:

```
~/P/tutorial git⊳master ››› node tutorial.js
~/P/tutorial git⊳master ››› |
```

This does not return anything because we haven't written anything for tutorial.js yet.

Now, let's add some code to the tutorial.js:

```
console.log('Hello World');
```

Now, run the file with this command:

```
$ node tutorial.js
```

We will see an output that says Hello World. This is how we execute files in Node.js.

Other than running on the V8 engine and executing JavaScript codes in a web browser, Node.js also provides a server running environment. This is the most powerful feature of Node.js. Node.js provides an HTTP module of itself that enables a non-blocking HTTP implementation. Let's build a simple web server to understand this.

On the same file, in tutorial.js, overwrite the file with the following code:

```
const http = require('http');

http.createServer(function (req, res) {
  res.writeHead(200, { 'Content-Type': 'text/plain' });
  res.end('Hello World\n');
}).listen(8080, '127.0.0.1');

console.log('Server running at http://127.0.0.1:8080/');
```

Here, the var http = require('http'); code requires the HTTP module into our application. It means that now we can access the functions defined in the HTTP library via the http variable. Now we need to create a web server. The preceding code tells Node.js to run the web server in the 8080 port. The function parameter in the createServer method takes two arguments, req and res, which are the short form of request and response respectively. The first thing that we need to do inside that function is to set the HTTP header. This is basically defining what type of response we want from that request. Then, we define what we want to get in the response by using res.send. Finally, we ask the web server to listen to port 8080.

When we run this code with $ node tutorial.js, the output looks like this:

```
~/P/tutorial git⊭master ››› node tutorial.js
Server running at http://127.0.0.1:8080/
```

When we type that URL in our browser, we should be able to see this:

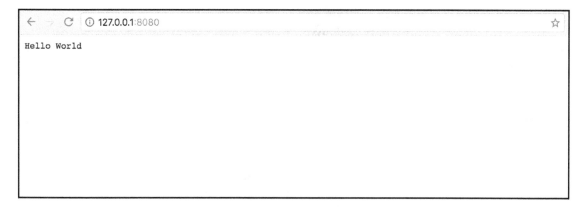

That's how Node.js works as a server program.

To exit the node console, press *Ctrl + C* twice.

Node.js modules

A Node.js module is just a plain JavaScript file that consists of reusable code. Every module has its own specific functionality. We can think of it as a library.

For example, if we want to segregate all our user-related activities in our application, we create a module for it, which will handle all the data libraries about the users.

The way we use a module in Node.js is via `require`. The example we just showed you about creating a web server is also a Node.js module.

Node.js core modules

There are two types of modules in Node.js. The core modules are the modules that are built in Node.js. They come in while we install Node.js. These are also called built-in modules. There are a lot of core modules in Node.js:

- Debugger
- Filesystem
- HTTP
- Path

- Process
- Events

If you want to look into more details about each of the core modules, you can visit the documentation at:
`https://nodejs.org/api/`.

Custom modules

These are the modules we create ourselves on top of Node.js. Since Node.js has a very large ecosystem, there are tons of different modules out there to grab for free according to our needs. We can build one ourselves or just use someone else's module. This is another aspect in which Node.js is powerful. It gives us the flexibility of using the modules from the community or we can build them by ourselves.

We can view the list of all existing available modules at `https://www.npmjs.com/browse/depended`:

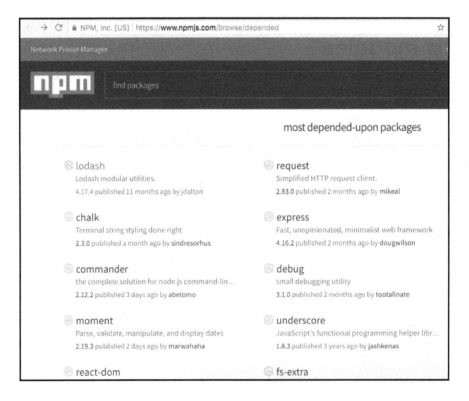

Introducing Express.js

Express.js is a minimalist server-side web framework for Node.js. It is built on top of Node.js to make it easy to manage the Node.js server. The most important strength of Express.js is that it makes the routing very, very easy. The robust API that it provides is very easy to configure. It is easy to receive requests from the frontend and easy to connect to the database. Express.js is also the most popular web framework for Node.js. It uses the **Model View Controller** (**MVC**) design pattern, which we will be discussing later on in this chapter.

Installing Express.js

We have already covered how to install node modules via npm. Similarly, we can install Express.js via NPM using this command:

```
$ npm install express
```

This is an easy way to install node modules. But, while building an application, we're going to need lots of different kinds of modules. We will also want to share these modules across our multiple applications. Hence, to make a module available globally, we will have to install it globally. For that, npm provides the option of adding -g when installing node modules. So, now we can use:

```
$ npm install -g express
```

This will install Express.js globally, which allows us to use the express command across multiple applications.

Creating an Express.js application

Now that we have installed Express.js, let's get started creating an application using Express.js.

We will name our application express_app. Building an outline of an express application is very simple using the express command. We can simply use:

```
$ express express_app
```

The output is as follows:

```
● ● ●                          3. ~/Projects/testproject (zsh)
~/P/testproject git master ››› express express_app                        ■

  warning: the default view engine will not be jade in future releases
  warning: use `--view=jade' or `--help' for additional options


  create : express_app
  create : express_app/package.json
  create : express_app/app.js
  create : express_app/public
  create : express_app/routes
  create : express_app/routes/index.js
  create : express_app/routes/users.js
  create : express_app/views
  create : express_app/views/index.jade
  create : express_app/views/layout.jade
  create : express_app/views/error.jade
  create : express_app/bin
  create : express_app/bin/www
  create : express_app/public/javascripts
  create : express_app/public/images
  create : express_app/public/stylesheets
  create : express_app/public/stylesheets/style.css

  install dependencies:
    $ cd express_app && npm install

  run the app:
    $ DEBUG=express-app:* npm start

~/P/testproject git master ››› |                                          ■
  ✕  .../testproject (zsh)  ⌘1
```

The command creates a lot of files and folders in our application. Let's have a quick look at these:

- `package.json`: This file contains a list of all the `node` packages that we have installed in the application and an introduction to the application.
- `app.js`: This file is the main entry page for an express application. The web server code resides in this file.
- `public`: We can use this folder to insert our assets such as images, stylesheets, or custom JavaScript code.

- `views`: This folder contains all of our view files that are going to be rendered in the browser. It has the main layout file (which contains the basic HTML templating for a view file), an `index.jade` file (which extends the layout file and only has the content that is changeable or dynamic), and an `error.jade` file (which displays when we need to display some sort of error messaging to our frontend).
- `routes`: This folder has a whole list of all the routes that we will be building access different pages of the application. We will discuss more on this in further sections.
- `bin`: This folder contains the executable files for Node.js.

So, these are the basic things that we need to know. Now, use your favorite text editor to work on the application and let's get started. Now, if we look at `package.json`, there are certain packages that we did not install but that are listed in the dependencies:

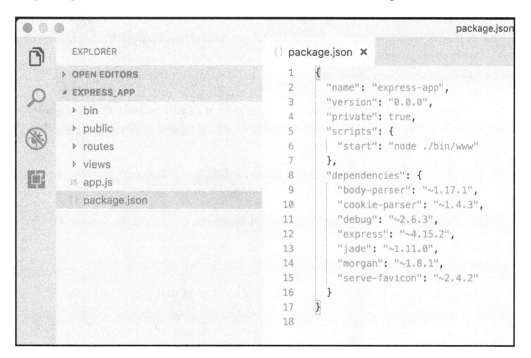

This is because these are the Express.js dependencies for any application. This means, when we create an application using the `express` command, it will automatically install all the dependencies that it needs. For example, the dependencies listed in the preceding `package.json` file do the following things:

- **body-parser**: This is used to parse the parameters of the body that we provide when making an HTTP request
- **debug**: This is a JavaScript utility package that provides pretty formatting to what `console.log` returns

> - We can install or remove packages via the `package.json` file as well. Just add or remove the name of the package in the `package.json` file to install or remove it. Then run `$ npm install`.

- **express**: This is a Node.js JavaScript framework and is used for building scalable web applications on top of Node.js.
- **jade**: As mentioned previously, this is the default templating engine for Node.js. We should have seen a warning while creating the application with the `express` command, saying **The default view engine will not be jade in future releases**. This is because `jade` is going to be replaced by `pug`; `jade` was copyrighted by a company and the name was later changed to `pug`.

The express generator uses the outdated `jade` templating engine. To change the templating engine, run the following steps:

1. In the `package.json` file, remove the `"jade": "~1.11.0"`, line and run:

```
$ cd express_app
$ npm install
```

2. Now, to install the new `pug` templating engine, run:

```
$ npm install pug --save
```

3. If we look into the `package.json` file, we should see a line similar to this: `"pug": "^2.0.0-rc.4"`.

4. Rename the files in the `views` folder:
   - `error.jade` to `error.pug`
   - `index.jade` to `index.pug`
   - `layout.jade` to `layout.pug`

5. Finally, in `app.js`, remove the line which says:

   ```
   app.set('view engine', 'jade');
   ```

6. Add the following line to use `pug` as the view engine:

   ```
   app.set('view engine', 'pug');
   ```

- **morgan**: This is middleware for logging the HTTP requests
- **serve-favicon**: This is for displaying a favicon in the browser to identify our application

 It's not necessary to have all these dependencies for our application. They come from installing Express.js. Just dig around for what you want and then add or remove the packages as per your application needs.

For now, we will leave it as it is. The `express` command just adds the dependencies to our `package.json` file and creates a skeleton for our application. In order to actually install these modules and packages listed in the `package.json` file, we need to run:

```
$ npm install
```

This command will actually install all the dependencies. Now, if we look into the folder structure, we can see a new folder is being added called `node_modules`. This is the place where all of the packages that we installed within that application reside.

Now, the first thing that we want to do is to set up a web server. For that, add the following line in the `app.js` file:

```
// error handler
app.use(function(err, req, res, next) {
  // set locals, only providing error in development
  res.locals.message = err.message;
  res.locals.error = req.app.get('env') === 'development' ? err : {};

  // render the error page
  res.status(err.status || 500);
  res.render('error');
});
```

```
app.listen(3000, function() { console.log('listening on 3000') })
```

```
module.exports = app;
```

Now, run the following command:

```
$ node app.js
```

This will spin up our application server. Now, when we go to the http://localhost:3000/ URL, we should be able to get this:

That's it. We have successfully created an Express application.

Express router

Let's move on to the Express router. As mentioned earlier in the chapter, one of the most important aspects of Express.js is that it provides easy routing for the application. Routing is the definition of the URL for an application. If we look at app.js, we will see a section such as:

```
...
app.use('/', index);
app.use('/users', users);
...
```

This means that when we access a web page, and when a request is made to the home page, the express router redirects it to a router called index. Now, look at routes/index.js, which has the following code:

```
var express = require('express');
var router = express.Router();

/* GET home page. */
router.get('/', function(req, res, next) {
```

```
    res.render('index', { title: 'Express' });
});

module.exports = router;
```

This means that when we access the home page, it renders a page called `index` that resides inside `views/index.pug` and passes a parameter for the `title` to be displayed on the page. Now, look at the `index.pug` file in the views folder, which has the following code:

```
extends layout

block content
  h1= title
  p Welcome to #{title}
```

This means it uses the layout from the `layout.pug` file and displays an `h1` title as well as a paragraph that renders the title that we passed from the route file. Hence, the output is as follows:

Pretty simple and straightforward, right?

Request object

A request object is an object that contains the information about the HTTP request. The properties of the request are:

- **query:** This contains information about the parsed query strings. Accessed via `req.query`.
- **params:** This contains information about the parsed routing parameter. Accessed via `req.params`.
- **body:** This contains information about the parsed request body. Accessed via `req.body`.

Response object

After receiving the `request` on `req` variable, the `res` object is something that we send back as the `response` we want.

The properties of the response are:

- **send:** This is used for sending a response to the views. Accessed via `res.send`. It takes two parameters, the status code, and the response body.
- **status:** If we want to send the success or failure of the application, `res.status` is used. This is the HTTP status code.
- **redirect:** `res.redirect` is used when we want to redirect to a certain page rather than sending responses in other formats.

Introduction to MVC

The MVC model is essential when building applications regardless of any programming languages. The MVC architecture makes it easy to organize our application's structure and separate out logic parts and view parts. We can incorporate this MVC structure at any time, even if we have completed half of our application. The best time to implement it is at the start of any application.

As the name suggests, there are three parts to it:

- **Model:** All of the application's business logic resides under these `models`. These deal with the database. They handle all the logic parts of the application.
- **View:** Everything that the browser renders—what users see—is handled by these view files. It deals with whatever we send to the client.
- **Controller:** `Controllers` basically connect these `models` and views. It is responsible to take the logical calculations done in `models` to the `views` sections:

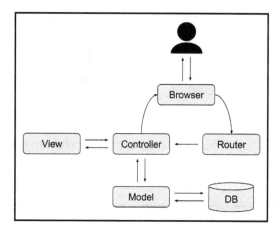

It is not necessary to implement the MVC platform in the application we build. The JavaScript is pattern agnostic, which means we can create our own folder structure. Unlike other programming languages, we can choose whatever structure is easiest for us.

Why MVC?

There are a lot of benefits that are added when we implement an MVC architecture into our application:

- Clear segregation of business logic and views. This separation allows us to reuse the business logic throughout the whole application.
- The development process becomes faster. This is obvious since the parts are clearly separated out. We can just add our views to our views folder and add logic inside the models folder.
- It is easy to modify existing code. This is very handy when multiple developers are working on the same project. Anyone can pick up the application from anywhere and start making changes to it.

Changing the folder structure to incorporate MVC

Now that we know enough about MVC, let's modify the folder structure of the application we created, called express_app. First of all, we need to create these three folders in the root directory. There is already a views folders so we can skip that. Let's go ahead and create models and controllers folders.

After that, in our `app.js`, we need to include our controller files. To do that, we first have to introduce a new package called filesystem. This module makes it easy to perform operations related to files, such as reading/writing to the file.

So, to add this package to our application, run:

```
$ npm install file-system --save
```

This `--save` argument is used when we want a `node` module to only be installed within our application. Also, after installation, this package will be automatically included in our `package.json`.

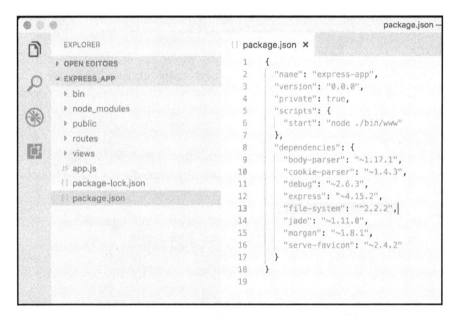

Now, we will need to require this module and use it to include all of our files that reside in the controller. For that, add these lines of code in our `app.js`. Make sure you add these lines before our web server running code:

```
var index = require('./routes/index');
var users = require('./routes/users');

var app = express();

// Require file system module
var fs = require('file-system');
```

```
// Include controllers
fs.readdirSync('controllers').forEach(function (file) {
  if(file.substr(-3) == '.js') {
    const route = require('./controllers/' + file)
    route.controller(app)
  }
})

// view engine setup
app.set('views', path.join(__dirname, 'views'));
app.set('view engine', 'pug');
```

Let's move ahead with adding a route to our controller. Let's create a folder in the root of the application called `controllers` and add an `index.js` file to the `controllers` folder and paste the following code:

```
module.exports.controller = (app) => {
  // get homepage
  app.get('/', (req, res) => {
    res.render('index', { title: 'Express' });
  })
}
```

Now, all of our routes will be handled by the controller files, which means we don't need the codes in `app.js` that control the routing. Hence, we can remove these lines from the file:

```
var index = require('./routes/index');
var users = require('./routes/users');

app.use('/', index);
app.use('/users', users);
```

Actually, we don't need that `routes` folder any longer. Let's also remove the `routes` folder.

Similarly, let's add a new route that controls all the user-related operations. For that, add a new file to the `controllers` folder called `users.js` and paste the following code inside it:

```
module.exports.controller = (app) => {
  // get users page
  app.get('/users', (req, res) => {
    res.render('index', { title: 'Users' });
  })
}
```

```
$ node app.js
```

With this, when we visit `http://localhost:3000/users`, we will be able to see the following:

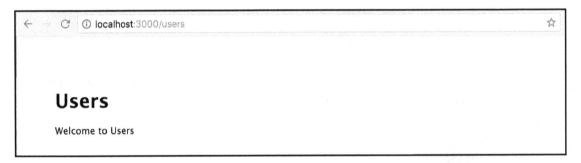

We have successfully set up a `controllers` and `views` part of the MVC architecture. We will cover more on `models` part in further sections.

 In the previous chapter, we talked about GitHub and how to use it for making code history by making small commits. Don't forget to set up a repo and continuously push code to GitHub.

The npm packages are stored in the `node_modules` directory, which we should not push to GitHub. To ignore such files, we can add a file called `.gitignore` and specify the files we do not want to push to GitHub.

Let's create a file within our application as well, called `.gitignore`, and add the following content:

```
node_modules/
```

This way, when we install any packages, it will not show up as the code difference while making commits to GitHub.

We are having to restart our `node` server every time we make some changes to our code which is very time-consuming. To ease this process, `node` provides a package called `nodemon`, which automatically restarts the server every time we make changes to the code.

To install the package, run:

```
$ npm install nodemon --save
```

To run the server, use the following command:

```
$ nodemon app.js
```

File naming conventions

When developing an application, we need to follow a certain convention to name the files. As we go on building the application, we will have a whole lot of files, which can get messy. MVC allows for having parallel naming conventions across different folders, which can lead to the same filenames inside different folders.

We can work on such filenames as well if that is what we find to be easy and maintainable. Otherwise, we can just append the type of filename to each file, as in the following example; for a controller file to handle the user-related activities, we can leave it as `controllers/users.js`, or we can rename it to `controllers/users_controller.js`. We will be using `controllers/users` for our application.

The same goes for `models`, `services`, or any other folders that need to be shared among different areas throughout the application. For this application, we will be using the following naming convention:

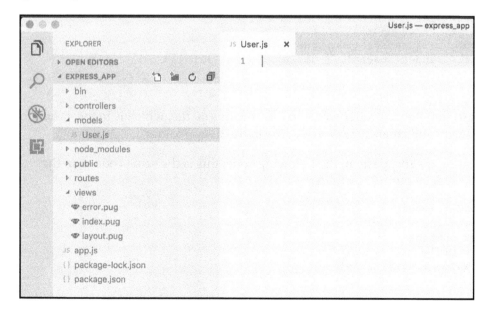

Remember, there is no official naming convention in Node.js. We can definitely customize the way we find simpler. We will discuss more about creating `models` in further chapters. That will require us to create a connection with Mongo, which we will describe in further chapters.

Creating view files for the Express.js application

We learned about how to create `controllers` in the last section. In this section, we will talk about how to add and customize view files. If you remember, we have this code in `controllers/users.js`:

```
module.exports.controller = (app) => {
  // get users page
  app.get('/users', (req, res) => {
    res.render('index', { title: 'Users' });
  })
}
```

Let's change a line that renders the `index` file to this:

```
module.exports.controller = (app) => {
  // get users page
  app.get('/users', (req, res) => {
    res.render('users', { title: 'Users' });
  })
}
```

This means that the controller wants to load the `users` file, which is in the `views` folder. Let's go ahead and create a `users.pug` file in the `views` folder.

After creating the file, paste in the following code; this is the same code as in the `index.pug` file in our `views` folder:

```
extends layout

block content
  h1= title
  p Welcome to #{title}
```

Now, if we used `nodemon`, we don't have to restart our server; just reload the browser with the location `http://localhost:3000/users`. This should render the following:

Now that we know how to connect `controllers` and `views` and how to create view files, let's get a little bit more information on the code of the file.

The first line says:

```
extends layout
```

What this means is that it is asking to extend the views that are already in the `layout.pug` file. Now, look at `layout.pug`:

```
doctype html
html
  head
    title= title
    link(rel='stylesheet', href='/stylesheets/style.css')
  body
    block content
```

This is a simple HTML file with `doctype`, `HTML`, head, and `body` tags. Inside the `body` tag, it says to block content, which means it yields the content from any other files that are written under this `block content` statement. If we look at `users.jade`, we can see that the content is written under the block content statement. Now, this is very useful because we don't have to repeat the entire HTML tags in every view file that we create.

Also, if we look at `users.js` inside the controller, there's a line that says:

```
res.render('users', { title: 'Users' });
```

The render method has two parameters: the view that it wants to load and the variables that it wants to pass to that view. In this example, `Users` is passed to the title variable. And in `users.jade` in the `views` folder, we have:

```
block content
  h1= title
  p Welcome to #{title}
```

This renders that variable inside both the `h1` tag and the `p` tag. This way, we can pass any content that we want from `controllers` to views. Let's add a new variable called `description` to the `render` method in the `users.js` controller:

```
module.exports.controller = (app) => {
  // get homepage
  app.get('/users', (req, res) => {
    res.render('users', { title: 'Users', description: 'This is the
description of all the users' });
  })
}
```

Also, let's make a place where this would be rendered in `users.pug`:

```
extends layout

block content
  h1= title
  p Welcome to #{title}
  p #{description}
```

If we reload the browser, we'll get:

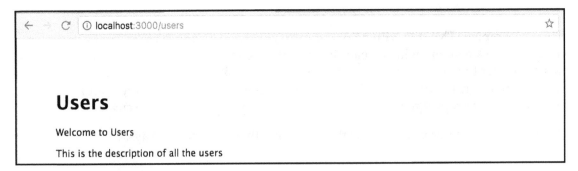

That's how we create the views for an express application. Now, go ahead and add views as you wish for our application.

Always make sure that you commit and push the changes into GitHub. The smaller the commit, the more maintainable the code is.

Summary

In this chapter, we learned what Node.js is and what Express.js is. We learned how to create an application using Express.js and learned about the MVC architecture.

In the next chapter, we will talk about MongoDB and its queries. We will also talk about using Mongoose for fast development and Mongoose queries and validations.

3
Introducing MongoDB

The name MongoDB comes from the phrase huMONGOus data, meaning that it can handle a lot of data. MongoDB is a document-oriented database architecture. It enables us to develop faster and scale better. In relational database designs, we store data by creating tables and rows, but with MongoDB, we can model our data as JSON documents, which is much simpler compared to those relational databases. If we are agile and our requirements keep changing very often, and if we need to do continuous deployment, then MongoDB is our choice. Being a document-based data model, MongoDB is very flexible as well.

The biggest advantage of using MongoDB is that the data is unstructured. We can customize our data in any format we like. In a **relational database management system (RDBMS)**, we have to define exactly the number of fields a table can have, but with MongoDB, each document can have its own number of fields. We can add new data without even having to worry about changing the schema, which is why Mongo has a **schemaless design model** for the database.

If our business is growing fast, we need to scale faster, we need to access data in a more flexible way, and if we need to make changes to our data without having to worry about updating our application's database schemas, then MongoDB is the best choice for us. Adding new columns to tables in RDBMS also creates some performance issues. But, since MongoDB is schemaless, adding new fields is done in an instant without compromising the performance of our application.

In a relational database, the terminologies that we use are **database**, **tables**, and **rows**, whereas in MongoDB, we use **database**, **collections**, and **documents**, respectively.

Here is a brief summary of what we will be covering in this chapter:

- Introducing to MongoDB and the benefits of using MongoDB
- Understanding the MongoDB database, collections, and documents
- Introducing to Mongoose, creating a connection with Mongoose, understanding Mongoose, and CRUD operations with Mongoose
- Adding default and custom validations with Mongoose

Why MongoDB?

MongoDB provides a lot of advantages, some of which are:

- **Flexible documents**: A MongoDB collection holds several documents. Each document under one collection can have variable field names and can have a different size as well, which means we don't have to define the schema.
- **No complex relationships**: The documents in MongoDB are stored as JSON documents, which means we no longer have to scratch our head learning about the relationships between various components of the application.
- **Easy to scale**: MongoDB is easy to scale as it minimizes the database size by using a partitioning method called sharding. Sharding is a database partitioning method that allows us to segregate a large database into smaller pieces.

MongoDB queries

We did quickly review what Mongo queries look like in `Chapter 1`, *Introduction to MEVN*. Here, we will dive deep into these queries.

The first thing we need to do is start the MongoDB server. We can do that with this command:

```
$ mongod
```

Now, let's open the mongo shell by typing `mongo` in our Terminal. When we enter the mongo shell, to display the list of databases, we type `show dbs`.

If you see the database in the list, type `use {database_name}` to start using this database. If we haven't created our database yet, just using `use {database_name}` will create a database for us. It's as simple as that. For this exercise, let's create a database called `mongo_test_queries`. So for that, we need to use:

```
> use mongo_test_queries
```

This should output the following in the Terminal:

```
# switched to db mongo_test_queries
```

Now, once we enter the database, the first thing that we need is a collection. We have a database but there are no collections. The best way to create a collection in MongoDB is by inserting a document. This not only initializes a collection but also adds the document to that collection. Simple as that. Now, let's move on to Mongo queries.

Creating documents

There are different queries to create a document in MongoDB, such as `insertOne()`, `insertMany()`, and `insert()`.

insertOne()

The `insertOne()` command adds a single document to our collection. For example:

```
> db.users.insertOne(
    {
        name: "Brooke",
        email: "brooke@app.com",
        address: 'Kathmandu'
    }
)
```

This command takes only a single parameter, which is an object, and we can pass the field names and values we want for our `users` collection. When we run the preceding code in our Terminal inside the Mongo shell, we should get the following output:

```
                                3. mongo (mongo)
> db.users.insertOne(
...     {
...         name: "Brooke",
...         email: "brooke@app.com",
...         address: 'Kathmandu'
...     }
... )
{
        "acknowledged" : true,
        "insertedId" : ObjectId("5aeb1844599c02966981a563")
}
>
```

It returns the `_id` of the document that just got created. We have successfully created a collection and a document in the `users` collection.

The insertOne() and insertMany() commands only work for Mongo version 3.2 or higher.

insertMany()

This command is used for inserting multiple documents into a collection. In the preceding example, we saw that the insertOne() command takes an argument that is an object. The insertMany() command takes an array as a parameter so that we can pass multiple objects inside it and insert multiple documents in the collection. Let's look at an example:

```
> db.users.insertMany(
    [
        { name: "Jack", email: "jack@mongo.com" },
        { name: "John", email: "john@mongo.com" },
        { name: "Peter", email: "peter@mongo.com" }
    ]
)
```

This snippet creates three documents in the users collection. When we run the command, the output should be:

```
3. mongo (mongo)
> db.users.insertMany(
...     [
...         { name: "Jack", email: "jack@mongo.com" },
...         { name: "John", email: "john@mongo.com" },
...         { name: "Peter", email: "peter@mongo.com" }
...     ]
... )
{
        "acknowledged" : true,
        "insertedIds" : [
                ObjectId("5aeb1888599c02966981a564"),
                ObjectId("5aeb1888599c02966981a565"),
                ObjectId("5aeb1888599c02966981a566")
        ]
}
>
```

insert()

This command inserts single as well as multiple documents into a collection. It does the job of both the `insertOne()` and the `insertMany()` commands. To insert a single document, we can use:

```
> db.users.insert(
    { name: "Mike", email: "mike@mongo.com" }
)
```

If the command is executed successfully, we should see the following output:

```
● ● ●                          3. mongo (mongo)
> db.users.insert(
...        { name: "Mike", email: "mike@mongo.com" }
... )
WriteResult({ "nInserted" : 1 })
> |
```

Now, if we want to insert multiple documents, we can simply use:

```
> db.users.insert(
    [
      { name: "Josh", email: "josh@mongo.com" },
      { name: "Ross", email: "ross@mongo.com" },
    ]
)
```

The output should be as follows:

```
● ● ●                          3. mongo (mongo)
> db.users.insert(
...    [
...        { name: "Josh", email: "josh@mongo.com" },
...        { name: "Ross", email: "ross@mongo.com" },
...    ]
... )
BulkWriteResult({
        "writeErrors" : [ ],
        "writeConcernErrors" : [ ],
        "nInserted" : 2,
        "nUpserted" : 0,
        "nMatched" : 0,
        "nModified" : 0,
        "nRemoved" : 0,
        "upserted" : [ ]
})
> |
```

Retrieving documents

Retrieving documents from collections in MongoDB is done using the `find()` command.
There are many ways to use this command.

Finding all documents

To retrieve all documents from a collection, we can use:

```
> db.users.find()
```

We can also use the following:

```
> db.users.find({})
```

This outputs the following:

```
● ● ●                          3. mongo (mongo)
> db.users.find({})
{ "_id" : ObjectId("5aeb1844599c02966981a563"), "name" : "Brooke", "email" : "brooke@app.com", "addre
ss" : "Kathmandu" }
{ "_id" : ObjectId("5aeb1888599c02966981a564"), "name" : "Jack", "email" : "jack@mongo.com" }
{ "_id" : ObjectId("5aeb1888599c02966981a565"), "name" : "John", "email" : "john@mongo.com" }
{ "_id" : ObjectId("5aeb1888599c02966981a566"), "name" : "Peter", "email" : "peter@mongo.com" }
{ "_id" : ObjectId("5aeb18b5599c02966981a567"), "name" : "Mike", "email" : "mike@mongo.com" }
{ "_id" : ObjectId("5aeb1915599c02966981a568"), "name" : "Josh", "email" : "josh@mongo.com" }
{ "_id" : ObjectId("5aeb1915599c02966981a569"), "name" : "Ross", "email" : "ross@mongo.com" }
>
```

Finding documents via filters

We can add filters to the `find()` command as well. Let's retrieve documents with the name `Mike`. For that, we can use:

```
> db.users.find({ name: 'Mike' })
```

It should return a document with the following:

```
● ● ●                          3. mongo (mongo)
> db.users.find({ name: 'Mike' })
{ "_id" : ObjectId("5aeb18b5599c02966981a567"), "name" : "Mike", "email" : "mike@mongo.co
m" }
>
```

We can also specify multiple conditions with AND or OR queries.

To find a collection with the name `Mike` and the email `mike@mongo.com`, we can simply use:

```
> db.users.find({ name: 'Mike', email: 'mike@mongo.com' })
```

The comma operator means an AND operator. We can specify as many conditions as we like with comma-separated values. The preceding command should output:

```
●  ●  ●                           3. mongo (mongo)
> db.users.find({ name: 'Mike', email: 'mike@mongo.com' })
{ "_id" : ObjectId("5aeb18b5599c02966981a567"), "name" : "Mike", "email" : "mike@mongo.co
m" }
>
```

Now, specifying conditions with AND or comma operators is simple. If we want to use the OR operator, then we should use:

```
> db.users.find(
  {
    $or: [ { email: "josh@mongo.com" }, { name: "Mike" } ]
  }
)
```

Here, we are saying: retrieve those documents for users whose name is Mike, and the email can be josh@mongo.com as well. The output is as follows:

```
> db.users.find(
...  {
...      $or: [ { email: "josh@mongo.com" }, { name: "Mike" } ]
...  }
... )
{ "_id" : ObjectId("5a2d137fc410c53f42ac73cb"), "name" : "Mike", "email" : "mike@mongo.com" }
{ "_id" : ObjectId("5a2d13e2c410c53f42ac73cc"), "name" : "Josh", "email" : "josh@mongo.com" }
>
```

Updating documents

Just like insert(), there are three methods of using the update() command in MongoDB: updateOne(), updateMany(), and update().

updateOne()

This command updates only a single document in the collection. Here, we have inserted a couple of user entries with the incorrect emails. For the user with the name `Peter`, the email is `jack@mongo.com`. Let's update this document using `updateOne()`:

```
> db.users.updateOne(
  { "name": "Peter" },
  {
    $set: { "email": "peter@mongo.com" }
  }
)
```

This command will update Peter's email to `peter@mongo.com`. The output is:

```
> db.users.updateOne(
...     { "name": "Peter" },
...     {
...         $set: { "email": "peter@mongo.com" }
...     }
... )
{ "acknowledged" : true, "matchedCount" : 1, "modifiedCount" : 1 }
>
```

As the output says, the `modifiedCount` is 1 and the `matchedCount` is 1, which means the document with the given condition was found and updated.

updateMany()

This command is used to update multiple documents in a collection. The command for updating documents with `updateOne()` and `updateMany()` is the same. To update the multiple records, we specify the condition and then set the desired values:

```
> db.users.updateOne(
  { "name": "Peter" },
  {
    $set: { "email": "peter@mongo.com" }
  }
)
```

The only difference between updateOne() and updateMany() is that updateOne() updates only the first document that is matched whereas updateMany() updates all the documents that are matched.

update()

Just like insert, the update() command does the job for updateOne() and updateMany(). To remove confusion, we can just use the update() command instead of updateOne() and updateMany():

```
> db.users.update(
  { "name": "John" },
  {
    $set: { "email": "john@mongo.com" }
  }
)
```

The output is as follows:

```
> db.users.update(
...    { "name": "John" },
...    {
...        $set: { "email": "john@mongo.com" }
...    }
... )
WriteResult({ "nMatched" : 1, "nUpserted" : 0, "nModified" : 1 })
>
```

Deleting documents

MongoDB provides multiple commands for deleting and removing documents from collections.

deleteOne()

deleteOne() removes only a single document from a collection:

```
> db.users.deleteOne( { name: "John" } )
```

This removes the entry of a user whose name is John. The output is as follows:

```
> db.users.deleteOne( { name: "John" } )
{ "acknowledged" : true, "deletedCount" : 1 }
>
```

As you can see in the output, the deletedCount is 1, which means the record has been deleted.

deleteMany()

The command for deleteMany() is the same as deleteOne(). The only difference is that deleteOne() removes only a single entry with the matched filter whereas deleteMany() removes all the documents which match the given criteria:

```
> db.users.deleteMany( { name: "Jack" } )
```

The output is as follows:

```
> db.users.deleteMany( { name: "Jack" } )
{ "acknowledged" : true, "deletedCount" : 1 }
>
```

remove()

The remove() command works to remove a single entry, as well as multiple entries, from a collection. If we want to remove only a single document that matched certain criteria, then we can pass the count of entries that we wish to delete. For example, let's first create an entry:

```
> db.users.insertOne({ name: 'Mike', email: 'mike@mike.com' })
```

With this, now we have two entries for Mike. Now, if we want to remove just one entry using remove(), we can do so with:

```
> db.users.remove({ name: 'Mike' }, 1)
```

The output is as follows:

```
> db.users.remove({ name: 'Mike' }, 1)
WriteResult({ "nRemoved" : 1 })
>
```

As you can see, we had two entries with the name Mike, but it only removed one. Similarly, if we want to remove all the documents, we can just use:

```
> db.users.remove({})
```

All documents will be removed.

We talked about the basic ideas on how we can query the documents in Mongo. To find out more details, visit https://docs.mongodb.com/v3.2/tutorial/query-documents/.

Introducing Mongoose

Mongoose is an elegant MongoDB object modeling library for Node.js. As I mentioned earlier, MongoDB is a schemaless database design. While this has its own advantages, sometimes we need to add certain validations as well, and this means defining the schemas for our documents. Mongoose provides an easy way to add such validations and to typecast the fields in a document.

For example, to insert data into a MongoDB document, we can use:

```
> db.posts.insert({ title : 'test title', description : 'test
description'})
```

Now, if we want to add another document and we want an extra field in that document, we can use:

```
> db.posts.insert({ title : 'test title', description : 'test description',
category: 'News'})
```

This is possible in MongoDB because no schemas are defined. These types of documents are also needed when building an application. MongoDB will silently accept any kind of document. However, there are times when we need to have documents look similar in order to behave in certain validations or to have a specific data type. In such situations, Mongoose comes to the rescue. We can also leverage these features with raw MongoDB as well, but writing validations in MongoDB is an extremely painful task. That's why Mongoose was created.

Mongoose is a data modeling technique for Mongo written in Node.js. Every document inside a Mongoose collection requires a fixed amount of fields. We have to explicitly define a `Schema` and adhere to it. An example of a Mongoose schema is:

```
const UserSchema = new Schema({
  name: String,
  bio: String,
  extras: {}
})
```

This means that the name and description fields must be a string, whereas the extras can take a whole JSON object in which we can store nested values as well.

Installing Mongoose

Like any other package, Mongoose can be installed in our project using NPM. Run the following command in our Terminal inside our `express_app` folder which we created in the previous chapter to install Mongoose inside that application:

```
$ npm install mongoose --save
```

If this is successfully installed, we should have a line added to our `package.json` file:

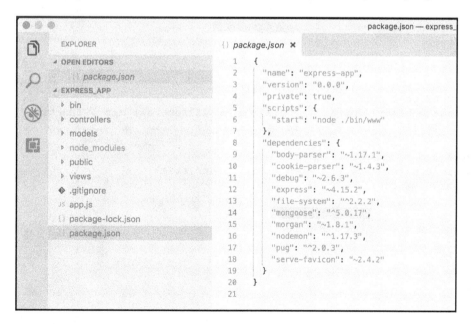

Connecting Mongoose to MongoDB

Once Mongoose is installed, we have to connect it to the MongoDB in order to start working with it. This is pretty straightforward with Mongoose; we just have to add a piece of code to `require` Mongoose in our `app.js` file and use the `mongoose.connect` method to connect it to the database. Let's go ahead and do that. In the `app.js` file, add the following code:

```
var express = require('express');
var path = require('path');
var favicon = require('serve-favicon');
var logger = require('morgan');
var cookieParser = require('cookie-parser');
var bodyParser = require('body-parser');
var mongoose = require('mongoose');
```

This will import the Mongoose module into our codebase.

Now, to connect to the MongoDB database, add the following line of code in our `app.js`:

```
var express = require('express');
var path = require('path');
var favicon = require('serve-favicon');
var logger = require('morgan');
var cookieParser = require('cookie-parser');
var bodyParser = require('body-parser');
var mongoose = require('mongoose');

var app = express();

//connect to mongodb
mongoose.connect('mongodb://localhost:27017/express_app', function() {
  console.log('Connection has been made');
})
.catch(err => {
  console.error('App starting error:', err.stack);
  process.exit(1);
});

// Require file system module
var fs = require('file-system');
```

This creates a connection with our Mongoose database. Now, let's run the app with the following command:

```
$ nodemon app.js
```

and displays a message in our Terminal if it succeeded or failed:

```
~/P/express_app git⊬master >>> nodemon app.js
[nodemon] 1.17.3
[nodemon] to restart at any time, enter `rs`
[nodemon] watching: *.*
[nodemon] starting `node app.js`
listening on 3000
Connection has been made
```

That's it! We have successfully made a connection to our MongoDB database. The URL here is the locally hosted database URL.

Creating records in Mongoose

Let's start by creating a new model in our application's `express_app`. Create a folder called `models` in the root of the project and name it `User.js`.

 We are using a capital letter for the starting letter of the file name. Also, we are using the single form for `models`. Contrary to this, for `controllers`, we use the plural form and lowercase letters, such as `users.js`.

Once we create the file, paste the following code into it:

```
const mongoose = require('mongoose');

const Schema = mongoose.Schema;

const UserSchema = new Schema({
  name: String,
  email: String
})

const User = mongoose.model("User", UserSchema)
module.exports = User
```

The first line here just imports the Mongoose module. This Mongoose package provides us with several properties, one of which is to define the Schema. Now, the original Schema definition here is this highlighted part:

```
const mongoose = require('mongoose');

const Schema = mongoose.Schema;

const UserSchema = new Schema({
  name: String,
  email: String
})

const User = mongoose.model("User", UserSchema)
module.exports = User
```

What this does is it adds a validation to our User data model, where it says there must be two fields in total. It will not accept either one or more than two data fields while creating a document for a Mongoose collection. Also, it adds a validation layer to this Schema as well, which says that the two fields, both name, and email, should be a valid string. It won't accept an integer, Boolean, or anything other than a string for both of these fields. This is how we define the Schema:

```
const mongoose = require("mongoose")
const Schema = mongoose.Schema

const UserSchema = new Schema({
  name: String,
  email: String
})

const User = mongoose.model("User", UserSchema)
module.exports = User
```

The highlighted part of this code represents the way to create a model. The first argument of the method is our model name, which maps to the corresponding plural version of the collection name. So, when we create a User model, this automatically maps to the user collections in our database.

Now, to create a user, the first thing to do is to create a resource:

```
const user_resource = new User({
  name: 'John Doe',
  email: 'john@doe.com'
})
```

Now, finally, the part that actually creates the `user` is:

```
user_resource.save((error) => {
  if (error)
    console.log(error);

  res.send({
    success: true,
    code: 200,
    msg: "User added!"
  })
})
```

The previous code uses a Mongoose function called `save`. The save method has a callback function that is used for error handling. We can do whatever we want when we encounter an error while saving the resource to our database there:

```
user_resource.save((error) => {
  if (error)
    console.log(error);

  res.send({
    success: true,
    code: 200,
    msg: "User added!"
  })
})
```

The `res.send` method allows us to set what we want to send to the client when the resource is successfully saved to the database. The first element of the object is `success: true`, which denotes if the execution was successful or not. The second element is the status code or the response code. A `200` response code denotes successful execution. We will discuss this in further chapters as well.The last element is the message that is sent to the client; the users see this in the frontend.

That's how we create a resource in Mongoose.

Fetching records from Mongoose

Now that we have successfully created a user, we have a record in the `users` collections in the database. There are two ways to fetch this record in our client: fetch all the records of users that we have or fetch a specific user.

Fetching all records

There are lots of methods that come out of the box with a Mongoose model to make our lives easier. Two such methods are `find()` and `findById()`. In MongoDB, we saw how we could retrieve a collection's records data via raw MongoDB queries. This is similar, the only difference being that Mongoose has a very easy way to do it. I recommend you learn MongoDB first instead of Mongoose because MongoDB gives you an overall idea of what a database is and you will learn the fundamentals of the database and about its queries. Mongoose just adds a layer on top of MongoDB to make it look a little bit easier for faster developments.

With that, let's look into the code snippet here:

```
User.find({}, 'name email', function (error, users) {
  if (error) { console.error(error); }
  res.send({
    users: users
  })
})
```

The Mongoose model `User` calls a method called `find()`. The first parameter is our query string, which is left empty: `{}` in the preceding query. So, if we want to retrieve all users who share the same name, say, Peter, then we can replace that empty `{}` with `{ name: 'Peter'}`.

The second parameter denotes which fields we want to retrieve from the database. We can leave it blank if we want to retrieve all fields or we can just specify it here. For this example, we are just retrieving user names and emails.

The third parameter has a callback function attached to it. This function takes two parameters, unlike the `create` method. The first parameter handles the error. If, somehow, the execution is not done successfully, it returns an error and we can customize it the way we want. The second parameter is the important one here; it returns the response when the execution is successfully done. In this case, the `users` parameter is an array of objects that are retrieved from the `users` collection. The output of this call would be:

```
users: [
  {
    name: 'John Doe',
    email: 'john@doe.com'
  }
]
```

Now we have all the records from the `users` collection.

Fetching a specific record

This is also as simple as fetching all records from a collection. We talked about using `find()` in the previous section. To fetch a single record, we have to use `findById()` or `findOne()`, or we can also use the `where` query. The `where` query is the same as we talked about previously when we had to pass a parameter to fetch records that fell under the same category.

Let's move ahead on using the following query:

```
User.findById(1, 'name email', function (error, user) {
  if (error) { console.error(error); }
  res.send(user)
})
```

As you can see, the syntax for both `find()` and `findById()` are similar. Both take the same amount of parameters and behave the same. The only difference between these two is that the preceding `find()` method returned an array of records as a response, whereas `findById()` returns a single object. So, the response to the preceding query would be:

```
{
  name: 'John Doe',
  email 'john@doe.com'
}
```

That's it – simple!

Updating records in Mongoose

Let's move on to updating a record in a collection. There are multiple ways to update the collection records as well, just as in retrieving data from the collections. Updating a document in Mongoose is the combination of `read` and `create`(save) methods. To update a document, we first need to find that document using the read query of Mongoose, alter that document, and then save the changes.

findById() and save()

Let's look at an example as follows:

```
User.findById(1, 'name email', function (error, user) {
  if (error) { console.error(error); }

  user.name = 'Peter'
  user.email = 'peter@gmail.com'
  user.save(function (error) {
    if (error) {
      console.log(error)
    }
    res.send({
      success: true
    })
  })
})
```

So, the first thing we need to do is find the user document, which we are doing by `findById()`. This method returns back the user with the given ID. Now that we have that user, we can alter whatever we like for this user. In the preceding case, we are changing the name and email of that person.

Now the important part. The job of updating this user's document is done by the `save()` method here. We have already altered the name and email of the user by doing:

```
user.name = 'Peter'
user.email = 'peter@gmail.com'
```

We are changing the object that was returned via `findById()` in the first place directly. Now, when we use `user.save()`, this method overwrites whatever value it was before for this user with this new name and email.

There are other methods we can use to update a document in Mongoose.

findOneAndUpdate()

This method can be used when we want to update a single entry. For example:

```
User.findOneAndUpdate({name: 'Peter'}, { $set: { name: "Sara" } },
function(err){
  if(err){
    console.log(err);
  }
});
```

As you can see, the first parameter defines the criteria describing the record we want to update, which, in this case, is the user whose name is Peter. The second parameter is the object in which we define what attributes of `user` do we want to update, which is defined by `{ $set: { name: "Sara" }`. This sets the `name` of `Peter` to `Sara`.

Now, let's make a small alteration to the preceding code:

```
User.findOneAndUpdate({name: 'Peter'}, { $set: { name: "Sara" } },
function(err, user){
  if(err){
    console.log(err);
  }
  res.send(user);
});
```

Here, notice that I have added a second parameter to the callback function called `user`. What this does is that when Mongoose is done updating that document in the database, it returns the object. This is very useful when we want to make some decisions after we update the record and want to play with the newly updated document.

findByIdAndUpdate()

This is somewhat similar to `findOneAndUpdate()`. This method takes an ID as a parameter, unlike `findOneAndUpdate()`, where we can add our own criteria, and updates that document:

```
User.findByIdAndUpdate(1, { $set: { name: "Sara" } },    function(err){
  if(err){
    console.log(err);
  }
});
```

The only difference here is that the first parameter takes a single integer value, which is the ID of the document rather than an object. This method also returns the object that is being updated. So we can use:

```
User.findByIdAndUpdate(1, { $set: { name: "Sara" } }, function(err){
    if(err, user){
        console.log(err);
    }
    res.send(user);
});
```

Deleting records in Mongoose

Just as there are many ways to create, fetch and update records in Mongoose, it also provides several ways to delete records from collections as well, such as `remove()`, `findOneAndRemove()`, and `findByIdAndRemove()`. We can use `remove()` to remove one or many documents. We can also find the documents we want to remove first and then use the `remove()` command to remove only those documents. If we want to find a specific document with some criteria, we can use `findOneAndRemove()`. We can use `findByIdAndRemove()` when we know the ID of the document we wish to remove.

remove()

Let's look at a sample for using this method:

```
User.remove({
    _id: 1
}, function(err){
    if (err)
        res.send(err)
    res.send({
        success: true
    })
})
```

The first argument of the `remove()` method takes the criteria for filtering which user we want to remove. It takes an ID as a parameter. It finds the user with the given ID and removes the document from the collection. The second parameter is the callback function, which we talked about before. If something goes wrong with the above operation, it returns an error, which we can use to better handle the exceptions or the errors that occur in our application. In the case of success, we can define our own logic as to what to return. In the preceding case, we are returning `{ success: true }`.

findOneAndRemove

findOneAndRemove() behaves the same way as remove() does and takes the same amount of parameters:

```
User.findOneAndRemove({
  _id: 1
}, function(err){
  if (err)
    res.send(err)
  res.send({
    success: true
  })
})
```

We just have to define the criteria for which documents we want to delete.

Now, we can also modify the preceding code:

```
User.findOneAndRemove({
  _id: 1
}, function(err, user){
  if (err)
    res.send(err)
  res.send({
    success: true,
    user: user
  })
})
```

Here, I have highlighted the added piece of code. We can also pass on a second parameter to the callback function which returns the user object being deleted. Now, this is helpful if we want to display a certain message to the frontend and also add some user attributes such as name or email of the user. For example, if we want to display a message saying **User with name {x} has been deleted.** on the frontend, then we can pass user or other attributes of user here; in this case, it's the name, to be displayed on the frontend.

The main difference between remove() and findOneAndRemove() is that remove does not return the documents that were deleted but findOneAndRemove() does. Now we know when to use these two methods.

findByIdAndRemove()

This is the same as `findOneAndRemove()`, except that this always needs an `id` to be passed as a parameter:

```
User.findByIdAndRemove(1, function(err){
  if (err)
    res.send(err)
  res.send({
    success: true
  })
})
```

Did you find any difference in the code between `findOneAndRemove()` and the preceding code for `findByIdAndRemove()`? If we look at the first parameter of this method, it only takes a simple integer value, which is the document ID. Now, if we look into the preceding `findOneAndRemove()` code, we will notice that we have passed an object in the first parameter. That's because, for `findOneAndRemove()`, we can pass different arguments other than ID as well. For example, we can also pass { `name: 'Anita'` } in that parameter for `findOneAndRemove()`. But, for `findByIdAndRemove()`, as is obvious from the method name, we don't need to pass an object but just an integer that denotes the document's ID.

It finds a document with the mentioned ID in the parameter and removes that document from the collections. Like `findOneAndRemove()`, this also returns the document that is being deleted.

Adding validation with Mongoose

Validations in Mongoose are defined at the schema level. Validations can be set in both strings and in numbers. Mongoose provides us with built-in validation techniques for strings and numbers. Also, we can customize these according to our need as well. Since validations are defined in the schemas, they are triggered when we hit the `save()` method for any document. If we only want to test these validations, we can do that as well by executing the validation method only via `{doc}.validate()`.

`validate()` is also middleware, which means it has control when we are executing some methods in an asynchronous way.

Default validations

Let's talk about some of the default validations that Mongoose provides us with. These are also called built-in validators.

required()

The `required()` validator checks if the field we added this validation on has some value or not. Previously, in the `User` model, we had this code:

```
var mongoose = require("mongoose");
var Schema = mongoose.Schema;

var UserSchema = new Schema({
  name: String,
  email: String
});

var User = mongoose.model("User", UserSchema);
module.exports = User;
```

This code also has a validation associated with the fields of the user. It requires the name and email of a user to be a string and not numbers, or Boolean, or anything else. But this code doesn't make sure the name and email fields are set for the user.

So, if we want to add a `required()` validation, the code should be modified in this way:

```
var mongoose = require("mongoose");
var Schema = mongoose.Schema;

var UserSchema = new Schema({
  name: {
    required: true
  },
  email: {
    required: true
  }
});

var User = mongoose.model("User", UserSchema);
module.exports = User;
```

As you can see, we have changed the value of the name key to an object instead of just a string. Here, we can add as many validations as we want. So, the added validation `required: true` checks if there is some value set on the name and email of the user before saving that document in the collection. It returns an error if the validation is not met.

We can also pass a message when the validation returns an error. For example:

```
var mongoose = require("mongoose");
var Schema = mongoose.Schema;

var UserSchema = new Schema({
  name: {
    required: [true, 'Let us know you by adding your name!']
  },
  email: {
    required: [true, 'Please add your email as well.']
  }
});

var User = mongoose.model("User", UserSchema);
module.exports = User;
```

This way, we can also customize the messages as per our requirements. Very cool, right?

Type validation

The type validation method defines the types of fields in a document. The different variations of type can be `String`, `boolean`, and `number`.

String

The string itself has several validators under it, such as `enum`, `match`, `maxlength`, and `minlength`.

`maxlength` and `minlength` define the length of a string.

Numbers

Numbers have two validators: `min` and `max`. The `min` and `max` values define the range of values for a field in a collection.

Custom validations

We can also add custom validations in case the default built-in validations are not enough. We can pass a `validate` function and write our custom code into that function. Let's look at an example:

```
var userSchema = new Schema({
  phone: {
    type: String,
    validate: {
      validator: function(v) {
        return /\d{3}-\d{3}-\d{4}/.test(v);
      },
      message: '{VALUE} is not a valid phone number!'
    }
  }
});
```

Here, we have passed a `validate` method to the `Schema`. It takes a validator function where we can add our own code for the validation. The preceding method checks if the phone number field of the user is in the correct format or not. If it does not pass the validation, then it displays the message `{value} is not a valid phone number`.

We can also add nested validations in Mongoose: for example, if the name in our user collection is saved as `{ name: { first_name: 'Anita', last_name: 'Sharma' } }`, we will need to add validations for both `first_name` and `last_name`. To do that, we can use:

```
var nameSchema = new Schema({
  first_name: String,
  last_name: String
});

userSchema = new Schema({
  name: {
    type: nameSchema,
    required: true
  }
});
```

First, we define the `Schema` for a low-level object, which is `first_name` and `last_name`. Then, for the `userSchema`, we pass on the `nameSchema` for the name field.

Remember, we cannot add nested validations in a single `Schema` like this:

```
var nameSchema = new Schema({
  first_name: String,
  last_name: String
});

personSchema = new Schema({
  name: {
    type: {
      first_name: String,
      last_name: String
    },
    required: true
  }
});
```

You can look into Mongoose validations here: `http://mongoosejs.com/docs/validation.html`.

Summary

In this chapter, we covered basic information about MongoDB and its benefits, how to make CRUD operations and queries in MongoDB, and the basic validations with Mongoose.

Going further, in the next chapter, we will talk more about the REST APIs and the RESTful architecture design in our application.

4
Introducing REST APIs

An **Application Programming Interface** (**API**), in general, is used to get data from one application to another. There are different kinds of APIs that are used in different areas, such as hardware and programming, but we will be talking only about web APIs. Web APIs are a form of web service that provides an interface to communicate between multiple applications. Data from one application is sent to another application via an HTTP protocol using such APIs.

In this chapter, we will talk about:

- REST architecture and RESTful APIs
- HTTP verbs and status codes
- Developing and testing APIs using Postman

Web APIs work in a similar way to how the browser interacts with our application server. The client requests some data from the server and the server responds with the formatted data to the client; APIs do something similar. For example, there is a contract set beforehand between the multiple applications. So, if there are two applications that need to share data, then one application will submit a request to another application, saying it needs this data in this format. When another application receives the request, it fetches the data from its server and responds with the structured and formatted data to the client or the requester.

Web APIs are classified into **Simple Object Access Protocol** (**SOAP**), **Remote Procedure Call** (**RPC**), or **Representational State Transfer** (**REST**) categories. The response format for these APIs can be in various forms, such as XML, JSON, HTML, images, and videos.

APIs also have different models, such as Public APIs and Private APIs:

- **Private APIs**: Private or internal APIs are only used in internal applications within an organization
- **Public APIs**: Public or external APIs are designed in a way such that they can be shared with the public parties outside of an organization as well

What is REST?

REST is a web service used for exchanging data between multiple applications via an HTTP protocol. RESTful Web Services are scalable and easily maintainable.

Here is a simple diagram that explains how the REST Web Service works:

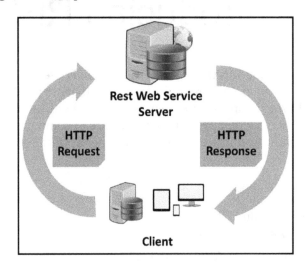

As we can see in the diagram, the client requests some data by making a call to the Rest Web Service Server. Here, when we send an HTTP Request, we also provide some headers, such as what type of data we want as a response. These responses could be JSON, XML, HTML, or any other form. When the server receives the request and pulls data from storage, it does not simply return the database resources as a response. It sends a representation of these resources. That's why it is called **representational**. When the server responds to the client with this formatted data, the state of our application changes. And that's why it's called **state transfer**.

Introducing REST APIs

REST APIs are designed with a RESTful architecture. The APIs built with the principles of RESTful architecture are called RESTful APIs. RESTful architecture is also called a **stateless architecture** because the connection between the client and server is not preserved. The connection is reset after every transaction between the client and the server.

Since there are multiple web services, we have to be able to choose what our requirements and needs are in order to build the perfect API for our application. The SOAP and REST protocols both have some benefits as well as limitations.

The SOAP protocol was designed in 1998 by Dave Winer. It uses **Extensible Markup Language** (**XML**) for data exchange. The choice between whether to use SOAP or REST depends on which programming language we choose when we are developing and the needs of the application.

REST APIs let us communicate between the applications in a JSON/XML data format. JSON/XML is a representation of data that is easy to format and readable for a human. With RESTful APIs, we can perform **Create**, **Read**, **Update**, and **Delete** (**CRUD**) operations from one application to another.

Benefits of REST API

REST API provides a lot of benefits. Here are some of the advantages that we can get by using REST APIs:

- It is easy to make requests and get responses from one application to other.
- Responses can be retrieved in human readable format in the form of JSON or XML.
- Everything is manipulated in the form of URI, which means every request is identified by the URI request.
- The separation between client and server makes it easy to migrate to a different server when needed with minimal change. The segregation between client and server makes it easy to scale as well.
- It is independent of any programming languages. We can implement REST architecture irrespective of whether we are using PHP, JAVA, Rails, Node.js, and so on.
- it is very easy to get started and the learning curve is short.

HTTP verbs

HTTP verbs are the different methods that are used to define the action that we want to execute for the resources. The most used HTTP verbs are GET, POST, PUT, PATCH, and DELETE. HTTP verbs are the request methods that make it possible to communicate between multiple applications. These HTTP verbs make it possible to perform several actions on a resource without needing to alter the URLs entirely. Let's look into each of these in more detail.

GET

GET requests are the idempotent requests. This is used when we want to fetch the information about resources. This does not modify or delete the resource. The equivalent CRUD operation for GET requests is READ, which means it only fetches the information and that's it. An example URL for a GET request is:

- To fetch all records:

    GET http://www.example.com/users

- To fetch information about a single user:

    GET http://www.example.com/users/{user_id}

POST

The equivalent CRUD operation for the POST request is CREATE. This is used with new records to the collection. Since this changes the state of the server, this is not an idempotent request. If we request a POST method twice with the same parameters, that will create two new identical resources in the database. An example URL for a POST request is:

POST http://www.example.com/users/

PUT

The PUT request is used to create or update a record. It creates a new record if the resource does not exist yet and updates the existing record if the resource already exists. The equivalent CRUD operation is update(). It replaces the existing representation of the resource. An example URL for a PUT request is as follows:

```
PUT http://www.example.com/users/
```

DELETE

This is used to remove resources from a collection. The equivalent CRUD operation is delete().

An example URL for a DELETE request is as follows:

```
DELETE http://www.example.com/users/{user_id}
```

HTTP status codes

Status codes are the part of a response made by the server for a request made to that server. It indicates the status of a request, irrespective of whether it got successfully executed or not. The status codes have three digits. The first digit represents the class or the category of that response. The HTTP status codes range from *100-500*. We will be covering some of the major status codes in this section.

2XX codes

The 200 range status code is the success range for any request in the API. Within the 200 range, there is a lot of code that represents different forms of success. Explained here are a few of the many status codes that are available:

- **200 OK:** This response is the standard one. It is just a representation of the request being successful. This status code also returns the resource on which the request was executed.

- **201 Created**: This represents the successful creation of a resource.
- **204 No Content**: This status code executes the request successfully, but does not return anything.

4XX codes

The 400 range status codes appear when there is an error on the client side:

- **400 Bad Request**: When the request parameters are not well formatted, or the syntax is broken, then a 400 status code is returned by the server.
- **401 Unauthorized**: This status code is returned when an unauthorized party tries to send the API request. This basically checks the authentication part.
- **403 Forbidden**: This is somewhat similar to 401. This checks the authorization of the party performing the API request. This is basically done when there are different permission settings for different users performing the API.
- **404 Not Found**: This is returned when the resource that we are trying to perform some action on is not found by the server in the database.

5XX codes

The 500 range status code informs us that there is something wrong with the execution of the action performed in the given resource:

- **500 Internal Server Error**: This status code is displayed when the action is not executed successfully. Like the 200 status code, this is a generic code returned by the server when something goes wrong.
- **503 Service Unavailable**: This status code is displayed when our server is not running.
- **504 Gateway Timeout**: This indicates that the request was sent to the server, but it did not get any response in the given time.

Introducing Postman

Postman is a tool that lets us develop and test our APIs faster. This tool provides a GUI that makes it easy to tweak our APIs faster, which decreases the development time of our APIs. We can also maintain a history by creating a collection of all the APIs that we have developed.

There are different alternatives for Postman as well, such as Runscope and Paw. We will be using Postman for this book.

Installing Postman

There are different ways to use Postman:

1. We can get the Chrome extension as follows: If you visit `https://chrome.google.com/webstore/detail/postman/fhbjgbiflinjbdggehcddcbncdddomop?hl=en`, we will see the following:

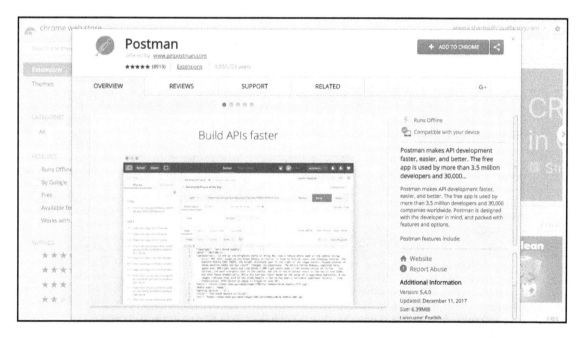

Click on the **Add to Chrome** button and the extension will be installed.

2. We can download the right desktop application for our operating system via `https://www.getpostman.com/`.

We have used the desktop application for this book.

Testing APIs with Postman

First, let's have a quick recap of what we have done so far. In the app that we are building, the `app.js` file should have the following code:

```
var express = require('express');
var path = require('path');
var favicon = require('serve-favicon');
var logger = require('morgan');
var cookieParser = require('cookie-parser');
var bodyParser = require('body-parser');
var fs = require('file-system');
var mongoose = require('mongoose');

var app = express();
var mongoose = require('mongoose');
mongoose.connect('mongodb://localhost:27017/tutorial2', {
  useMongoClient: true
});
var db = mongoose.connection;
db.on("error", console.error.bind(console, "connection error"));
db.once("open", function(callback){
  console.log("Connection Succeeded");
});

// view engine setup
app.set('views', path.join(__dirname, 'views'));
app.set('view engine', 'pug');

// uncomment after placing our favicon in /public
//app.use(favicon(path.join(__dirname, 'public', 'favicon.ico')));
app.use(logger('dev'));
app.use(bodyParser.json());
app.use(bodyParser.urlencoded({ extended: false }));
app.use(cookieParser());
app.use(express.static(path.join(__dirname, 'public')));

// Include controllers
fs.readdirSync("controllers").forEach(function (file) {
  if(file.substr(-3) == ".js") {
```

```
      const route = require("./controllers/" + file)
      route.controller(app)
    }
  })

  // catch 404 and forward to error handler
  app.use(function(req, res, next) {
    var err = new Error('Not Found');
    err.status = 404;
    next(err);
  });

  // error handler
  app.use(function(err, req, res, next) {
    // set locals, only providing error in development
    res.locals.message = err.message;
    res.locals.error = req.app.get('env') === 'development' ? err : {};

    // render the error page
    res.status(err.status || 500);
    res.render('error');
  });

  module.exports = app;

  app.listen(3000, function() {
    console.log('listening on 3000')
  })
```

Since this file is auto-generated when we build the application via command CLI, it uses typescript syntax. If we want to use the ES 6 syntax, we can replace `var` with `const`.

In our `models/User.js`, we have the following:

```
const mongoose = require("mongoose")
const Schema = mongoose.Schema
const UserSchema = new Schema({
 name: String,
 email: String
})

const User = mongoose.model("User", UserSchema)
module.exports = User
```

Also, in `controllers/users.js`, we have the following:

```
module.exports.controller = (app) => {
  // get homepage
  app.get('/users', (req, res) => {
    res.render('index', { title: 'Users' });
  })
}
```

Adding a GET endpoint in the users controller

Let's add a route to our `controllers/users.js` that will fetch all the user's records from the database.

Currently, with the code we have in our `users` controller, when we visit `http://localhost:3000/users`, it only returns a title, `Users`. Let's modify this code to incorporate a `GET` request to fetch all user requests.

Fetching all users

First, start the server with `$ nodemon app.js`. Now, in `controllers/users.js`:

```
var User = require("../models/User");

module.exports.controller = (app) => {
  // get all users
  app.get('/users', (req, res) => {
    User.find({}, 'name email', function (error, users) {
      if (error) { console.log(error); }
      res.send(users);
    })
  })
}
```

Now that we have our code in place, let's test this endpoint using the Postman app. In the Postman app, add the necessary details in the URL. When we hit the **Send** button, we should see the response as follows:

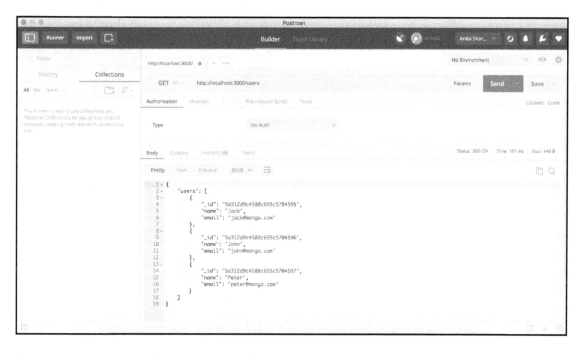

The _id is the Mongo ID of the user, which is sent by Mongoose query by default, and we are fetching the name and email of the user. If we want the names only, we can change our query in the users controller to fetch only the name.

Postman lets us edit the endpoints and requests are easy to develop. If we want to use our own local browser to test, we can do that as well.

I have used a Chrome plugin called JSONview to format the JSON response. You can get the plugin from here:
https://chrome.google.com/webstore/detail/jsonview/
chklaanhfefbnpoihckbnefhakgolnmc.

As I mentioned earlier, if we visit `http://localhost:3000/users`, we should be able to see something similar to the following:

```
←  →  C   ⓘ localhost:3000/users            Q  ☆

{
  - users: [
     - {
           _id: "5a312d9c4588c655c5704597",
           name: "Peter",
           email: "peter@mongo.com"
       },
     - {
           _id: "5a315372ba3a827ecb241777"
       },
     - {
           _id: "5a31537c4588c655c5704598",
           name: "Jack",
           email: "jack@mongo.com"
       },
     - {
           _id: "5a31537c4588c655c5704599",
           name: "John",
           email: "john@mongo.com"
       },
     - {
           _id: "5a31537c4588c655c570459a",
           name: "Peter",
           email: "peter@mongo.com"
       },
     - {
           _id: "5a3153baba3a827ecb241778",
           name: "Dave",
           email: "dave@mongo.com"
       },
     - {
           _id: "5a3153d7ba3a827ecb241779",
           name: "Dave Smith",
           email: "dave@smith.com"
       },
     - {
           _id: "5a31544b2a1df6807b89090f",
           name: "Dave",
           email: "dave@mongo.com"
       },
     - {
           _id: "5a31544b2a1df6807b890910",
           name: "Dave",
           email: "dave@mongo.com"
       },
     - {
           _id: "5a3154532a1df6807b890911",
           name: "Dave",
           email: "dave@mongo.com"
       }
  ]
}
```

We can use the `save` query feature given by Postman to run those queries in future as well. Just click the Save button, which is in the top right-hand corner of the app. And create new queries as we go forward.

Fetching a single user

As mentioned in the HTTP verbs section, to fetch a single record from the collection, we have to pass an `id` of the user in the parameter in order to get the user details. From the preceding Postman response example, let's pick an `id` and use it to fetch the record of a user. First, let's add the endpoint to our controller. In `controllers/users.js`, add the following lines of code:

```
var User = require("../models/User");

module.exports.controller = (app) => {
  // get all users
  app.get('/users', (req, res) => {
    User.find({}, 'name email', function (error, users) {
      if (error) { console.log(error); }
      res.send({
        users: users
      })
    })
  })

  //get a single user details
  app.get('/users/:id', (req, res) => {
    User.findById(req.params.id, 'name email', function (error, user) {
      if (error) { console.log(error); }
      res.send(user)
    })
  })
}
```

Now create a new query in Postman with the following parameters. We will create a GET request with the URL `http://localhost:3000/users/:user_id` where `user_id` is the id of any user that you have created in your database. With this setting, we should be able to view something like this:

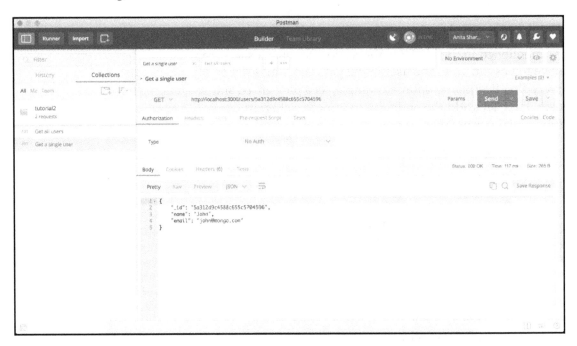

The query should return the details of the user with the given ID in the URL.

Adding a POST endpoint in the users controller

Let's look at an example. Let's create an API that will use the MongoDB `insert()` command to save user resources in the database. In the users controller, add a new endpoint:

```
// add a new user
  app.post('/users', (req, res) => {
    const user = new User({
      name: req.body.name,
      email: req.body.email
    })

    user.save(function (error, user) {
```

```
        if (error) { console.log(error); }
        res.send(user)
    })
})
```

In Postman, set the method as POST, the URL as `http://localhost:3000/users`, set the parameters to raw JSON, and provide the following input:

```
{
    "name": "Dave",
    "email": "dave@mongo.com"
}
```

Unlike the GET request, we have to pass the name and email of the user we want to add in the body parameter. Now, if we run a GET all users query, we should be able to see this new user. If we run the POST request twice with the same parameters, then it creates two different resources.

Adding a PUT endpoint in the users controller

Let's update a user with ID `5a3153d7ba3a827ecb241779` (change this ID to the ID of your document), which we just created. Let's rename the email: to do that, first let's add the endpoint in our users controller, in other words, `controllers/user.js`:

```
// update a user
app.put('/users/:id', (req, res) => {
  User.findById(req.params.id, 'name email', function (error, user) {
    if (error) { console.error(error); }

    user.name = req.body.name
    user.email = req.body.email
    user.save(function (error, user) {
      if (error) { console.log(error); }
      res.send(user)
    })
  })
})
```

What we did here is, we added an endpoint for a `PUT` request, which takes the name and email as parameters and saves it to the database. The corresponding Postman would look as follows:

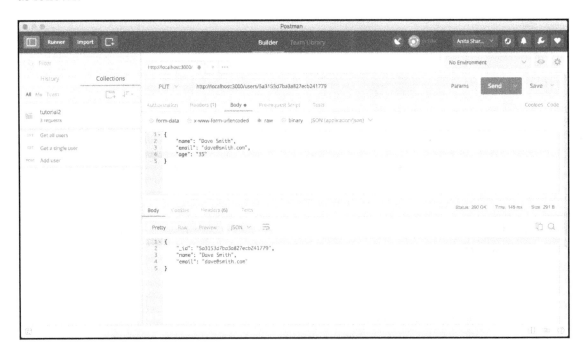

Here, we can see that the user's name has been updated. And, if we look at the request parameters, we have also added an `age` parameter. But since we haven't added `age` to our Schema while defining the User model, it discards the age value but updates the rest.

 We can also use the `PATCH` method to update a resource. The difference between the `PUT` and `PATCH` methods is: the `PUT` method updates the whole resource, whereas `PATCH` is used for a partial update on resources.

Adding a DELETE endpoint in the users controller

Similarly, for delete, let's add an endpoint in `controllers/users.js`:

```
// delete a user
app.delete('/users/:id', (req, res) => {
  User.remove({
    _id: req.params.id
  }, function(error, user){
    if (error) { console.error(error); }
    res.send({ success: true })
  })
})
```

The preceding code takes the ID of the user and removes the user with the given ID from the database. In Postman, the endpoint would look as follows:

Summary

In this chapter, we learned about what a RESTful API is, the different HTTP verbs and the status codes, and how to develop RESTful APIs and test them using Postman.

In the next chapter, we will be jumping into the Vue.js introduction and will be building an application using Vue.js.

Building the Real Application

5

We have covered the basic components that we need to have knowledge of in order to build a full-stack JavaScript application. From this point on, we will work on building a whole web application using all of these technologies.

We will be building a movie rating application that will have the following features throughout this book:

- A home page that lists all the movies with other attributes
- There will be an admin section where the administrator will be able to add movies
- The user will be able to log in and sign up
- The user will be able to rate a movie
- There will be a movie profile section where the logged-in user can rate the movie

So, let's get started.

Introducing Vue.js

Vue.js is an open source, progressive JavaScript framework for building user interfaces. The rise of new JavaScript frameworks has been tremendous. With such growth, you might get confused about where to get started and how. There are hundreds of JavaScript frameworks today; among them, there are dozens of frameworks that stood out. But still, to choose from those dozens might be a daunting task.

There are quite a few popular frameworks today, such as React, Ember, and Angular. While these frameworks have their own advantages, there are some limitations to them as well. While building an application with React or Angular is good in itself, Vue.js helps eliminate some of the limitations associated with these frameworks.

Vue.js is **progressive.** With Vue.js, you can start with small and then progress gradually toward building bigger applications. This means that if you are just starting out, you might want to start with a very small application and scale slowly. Vue.js is perfect for such applications. It is lightweight and flexible as well. The learning curve is also very easy and super easy to get started.

Vue.js was invented by Evan You. It was first released in February 2014 and gained huge popularity around 2016. He used to work for Google and in Angular projects. The motivation for this invention was mainly because he didn't want to use Angular for small projects, since Angular provides a lot of packages out of the box and, hence, is not lightweight and not suitable for small applications. Having said that, Vue.js does not only target the smaller applications. It definitely does not provide all the packages with it, but you can add them as you progress with your application. That is the beauty of Vue.js.

Installing Vue.js

Let's get started with the installation of Vue.js. There are three ways to install and use Vue.js.

Including it in a script tag

The easiest way to use Vue.js is to download it and include it in your `script` tag. You can download it from `https://cdn.jsdelivr.net/npm/vue`:

```
<script type="text/javascript" src="vue.js"></script>
```

Using Content Delivery Network (CDN) links directly

CDN is a network of distributed servers. It stores the cached version of contents in different geographical locations so that the content loads faster when fetched. We can use the CDN link directly in our `script` tag:

```
<script type="text/javascript"
src="https://cdn.jsdelivr.net/npm/vue.js"></script>
```

Using Vue.js as an npm package

npm also has a package for vue, which can be installed as follows:

```
$ npm install vue
```

Introducing vue-cli

CLI stands for Command Line Interface. A cli runs one or multiple commands successively in a command line interface. Vue.js also has a cli which, when installed, makes it super easy to spin up a project. We will be using a vue-cli in this book to create the Vue.js application. Let's install vue-cli with the following command. You can execute this command in your root folder:

```
$ npm install -g vue-cli
```

Initializing projects with vue-cli

Let's go ahead with creating a new project folder for our movie rating application. We will call it movie_rating_app. Go to the directory where you want to create your application in the Terminal and run the following:

```
$ vue init webpack movie_rating_app
```

The preceding command initializes an application with all the dependencies that a Vue.js project requires. It will ask you a few questions about the project setup, to which you can answer either *y*, as in *yes*, or *n*, as in *no*:

- **Vue build**: You will find two options to build the Vue.js app: runtime + compiler, or runtime Only. This has to do with the template compiler:
    - **Runtime only**: The runtime option is used to create the vue instances. This option does not include the template compiler.
    - **Runtime + compiler**: This option includes the template compiler, which means the vue templates are compiled to the plain JavaScript render functions.

- **Vue-router**: Vue-router is the official router for Vue.js applications. This option is specially used when we want to make our application a **Single Page Application (SPA)**. When using this option, the application makes all the necessary requests one time when the page initially loads and sends requests to the server when new data is needed. We will be talking more about Single Page and Multi-Page applications in future chapters as well. For now, we will be using the Vue-router.
- **ESLint**: ESLint is a JavaScript linter tool. It is a static code analysis tool used to find the errors or the mistakes in the code. It basically makes sure that the code follows the standard guidelines. There are two options for choosing the ESLint from as well: standard linting or the Airbnb linting. We will be going with Airbnb for this project.
- **Setup test**: By setting up tests, the project creates a wrapper for the tests that we will be writing for our application. It creates the necessary structure and configuration for the tests codes to be able to be run. We will be using this option as well. For the test runner, we will be using Mocha and Karma, and for the end to end testing, we will be using Nightwatch, which we will learn about in further chapters.
- **Dependency management**: Lastly, to manage the packages and the dependencies, here we have two options: npm and Yarn. We mostly talked about npm in previous chapters. Yarn is also a dependency management tool just like npm. Both Yarn and npm have their own benefits, but for this application, we are going to use npm. You can learn more about Yarn here (https://yarnpkg.com/en/).

This will take some time as it will install all the dependencies. Here are the options that we selected for our application:

```
●●●                          1. vue (node)
~/Projects git»master »»» vue init webpack movie_rating_app              ■

? Project name movie_rating_app
? Project description A Vue.js project
? Author Aneeta Sharma <get.aneeta@gmail.com>
? Vue build standalone
? Install vue-router? Yes
? Use ESLint to lint your code? Yes
? Pick an ESLint preset Airbnb
? Set up unit tests Yes
? Pick a test runner karma
? Setup e2e tests with Nightwatch? Yes
? Should we run `npm install` for you after the project has been created? (recommended) npm


   vue-cli   Generated "movie_rating_app".



# Installing project dependencies ...
# ═══════════════════════════
```

When the command is successfully executed, you should be able to see the further steps on your Terminal:

```
# Project initialization finished!
# ═══════════════════════════

To get started:

  cd movie_rating_app
  npm run dev

Documentation can be found at https://vuejs-templates.github.io/webpack

~/Projects git»master »»» ▊                                               ■
```

If the build is successful, we will be able to see the preceding output. Now, let's do as it says in the Terminal:

```
$ cd movie_rating_app
$ npm run dev
```

This will start your application. The default port of the Vue.js application is 8080. As you can see in your Terminal, it should say:

Go to the browser and open the URL `http://localhost:8080/#/`, and we should be able to see our application:

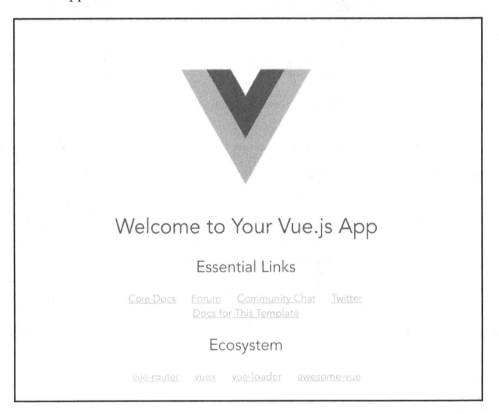

Great job! That was super easy. You have successfully created and run a Vue.js application.

Project folder structure

Now, if you have noticed, `vue-cli` commands add a bunch of dependencies to your application, which is listed in the `package.json` file. The `cli` command also sets up a folder structure that you can customize to your needs as well. Let's review and understand the structure that the `cli` has made for us:

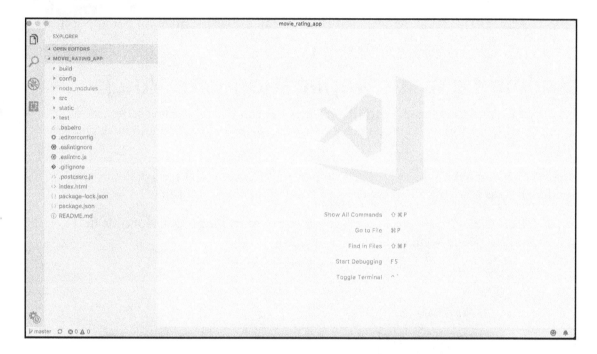

- `build` folder: This folder contains the `webpack` configuration files for different environments: development, test, and production
- `config` folder: All the configurations of the application would go here
- `node_modules`: All the `npm` packages that we install reside in this folder
- `src`: This folder contains all the files related to rendering the components in the browser:
    - `assets`: You can add your CSS and images for your application inside this folder.
    - `components`: This folder will house all the frontend rendering files that will have a `.vue` extension.
    - `router`: This folder will take care of all the URL routes for different pages throughout the application.

- App.vue: You can think of App.vue as the main component for rendering the view files. Other files will extend the layout defined on this file to create different views.
  - main.js: This is the main entry point for any Vue.js application.
- Static: You can use this folder as well to keep your static files, such as CSS and images.
- Test: This folder will be used to handle all the tests written for our application.

Building a static application with Vue.js

Now that we have initialized a project, let's move ahead with creating a static web application. Don't forget to make a repository on GitHub and commit and push changes regularly.

When you visit the URL http://localhost:8080/#/, you will see a default page rendered. This piece of code is written in src/components/HelloWorld.vue.

If you look into build/webpack.base.conf.js, you will see this line of code in the module.exports section:

```
module.exports = {
  context: path.resolve(__dirname, '../'),
  entry: {
    app: './src/main.js'
  },
  output: {
```

This means, when you run the app, this main.js will be the entry point for the app. Everything will start from there. Let's have a quick look at that main.js file inside src:

```
// The Vue build version to load with the `import` command
// (runtime-only or standalone) has been set in webpack.base.conf with an
alias.
import Vue from 'vue';
import App from './App';
import router from './router';

Vue.config.productionTip = false;

/* eslint-disable no-new */
new Vue({
  el: '#app',
```

```
  router,
  template: '<App/>',
  components: { App },
});
```

The first three lines import the necessary packages required for this app to run. App.vue is
the main template layout for this app. All other .vue files will extend this layout.

The bottom block defines which component to render when you run the app. In this
case, this is telling our app to take the template <App> and render it inside
the #app element. Now, if we look into App.vue:

```
<template>
  <div id="app">
    <img src="./assets/logo.png">
    <router-view/>
  </div>
</template>

<script>
export default {
  name: 'app',
};
</script>

<style>
#app {
  font-family: 'Avenir', Helvetica, Arial, sans-serif;
  -webkit-font-smoothing: antialiased;
  -moz-osx-font-smoothing: grayscale;
  text-align: center;
  color: #2c3e50;
  margin-top: 60px;
}
</style>
```

Here we have the template that has a div element with an ID #app. It means that the vue
templates that we create will get rendered in this.

Redefining the home page

Let's make our own view page for the home. For this, we can just modify the `HelloWorld.vue` component. The `.vue` file should always start with a template. Hence, a basic template for this file is:

```
<template>
  <div>
  </div>
</template>
```

You can also include your style sheets and JavaScript codes definitions in this page, but it will be much cleaner if we separate these out somewhere else.

Let's remove everything from `HelloWorld.vue` and add these lines of code:

```
<template>
  <div>
    Hello World
  </div>
</template>
```

We also don't need a Vue.js logo, so let's delete that as well from `src/assets` and the line of code in `App.vue`:

```
<img src="./assets/logo.png">
```

Now, if you revisit the URL `http://localhost:8080/#/`, you will see `Hello World` rendered:

Segregating CSS

Time for segregating CSS. Let's create a folder inside the `src/assets` folder called `stylesheets` and add a `main.css` file. Add the following line of code in `main.css`:

```
@import './home.css';
```

The `main.css` will be our main CSS file that includes all other CSS components. We can directly add all our style code here as well. But to maintain readability, we will be creating separate style sheets for different sections in our applications and importing them here.

Since we will be importing all the style sheets here, now we need to include only the `main.css` file in the main application so that it gets loaded. To do that, let's add the following line of code in `src/App.vue`:

```
<template>
  <div id="app">
    <router-view/>
  </div>
</template>

<script>
import './assets/stylesheets/main.css';

export default {
  name: 'App',
};
</script>
```

We have imported a style sheet called `home.css` in `main.css` that does not yet exist. So let's go ahead and create that in the same directory, which is `src/assets`. Also, let's remove the following piece of code from `App.vue` and paste it into the `home.css` file: so that our component is clean:

```
#app {
  font-family: 'Avenir', Helvetica, Arial, sans-serif;
  -webkit-font-smoothing: antialiased;
  -moz-osx-font-smoothing: grayscale;
  text-align: center;
  color: #2c3e50;
  margin-top: 60px;
  width: 100%;
}
```

Introduction to Vuetify

Vuetify is a module that can be used to build materialistic web page designs for Vue.js applications. It provides several features that can be used as building blocks for our application. It is a UI framework like Bootstrap, but it mostly has the material components. For more details, you can go to this link `https://vuetifyjs.com`.

We will be using both Vuetify and Bootstrap combined when building the application. The first step is to install the packages:

```
$ npm install bootstrap bootstrap-vue vuetify --save
```

After these get installed, the next thing we need to do is require these packages in our main file. So, in the `src/main.js` file, add the following lines:

```
// The Vue build version to load with the `import` command
// (runtime-only or standalone) has been set in webpack.base.conf with an
alias.
import 'bootstrap/dist/css/bootstrap.min.css';
import 'bootstrap-vue/dist/bootstrap-vue.css';
import BootstrapVue from 'bootstrap-vue';

import Vue from 'vue';
import Vuetify from 'vuetify';
import App from './App';
import router from './router';

Vue.use(BootstrapVue);
Vue.use(Vuetify);

Vue.config.productionTip = false;

/* eslint-disable no-new */
new Vue({
  el: '#app',
  router,
  components: { App },
  template: '<App/>',
});
```

We also need to use `vuetify.css`, which holds all the style sheets related to its design. We will need this as well. We can just simply link a style sheet for this. In the `index.html` file, add the following lines of code in your `head` section:

```
...
<head>
    <meta charset="utf-8">
    <meta name="viewport" content="width=device-width,initial-scale=1.0">
    <link href="https://unpkg.com/vuetify/dist/vuetify.min.css"
rel="stylesheet">
    <title>movie_rating_app</title>
  </head>
...
```

Vuetify uses material icons well, so also import the fonts. Add the following line of code in `index.html` as well:

```html
<head>
    <meta charset="utf-8">
    <meta name="viewport" content="width=device-width,initial-scale=1.0">
    <link href="https://unpkg.com/vuetify/dist/vuetify.min.css"
rel="stylesheet">
    <link
href="https://fonts.googleapis.com/css?family=Roboto:300,400,500,700|Materi
al+Icons" rel="stylesheet">
    <title>movie_rating_app</title>
  </head>
```

Redesigning pages with Vuetify

Now that we have Vuetify, let's move on to creating the pages for the application. provides us with some predefined themes as well. We will use a very simple and minimalistic theme for the app. Of course, we can also customize these according to our needs.

The outcome of this section will look as follows:

Redesigning the home page

In our `App.vue`, replace the file content with the following code:

```
<template>
  <v-app id="inspire">
    <v-navigation-drawer
      fixed
      v-model="drawer"
      app
    >
      <v-list dense>
        <router-link v-bind:to="{ name: 'Home' }" class="side_bar_link">
          <v-list-tile>
            <v-list-tile-action>
              <v-icon>home</v-icon>
            </v-list-tile-action>
            <v-list-tile-content>Home</v-list-tile-content>
          </v-list-tile>
        </router-link>
        <router-link v-bind:to="{ name: 'Contact' }" class="side_bar_link">
          <v-list-tile>
            <v-list-tile-action>
              <v-icon>contact_mail</v-icon>
            </v-list-tile-action>
            <v-list-tile-content>Contact</v-list-tile-content>
          </v-list-tile>
        </router-link>
      </v-list>
    </v-navigation-drawer>
    <v-toolbar color="indigo" dark fixed app>
      <v-toolbar-side-icon @click.stop="drawer = !drawer"></v-toolbar-side-icon>
      <v-toolbar-title>Home</v-toolbar-title>
    </v-toolbar>
    <v-content>
      <v-container fluid>
        <div id="app">
          <router-view/>
        </div>
      </v-container>
    </v-content>
    <v-footer color="indigo" app>
      <span class="white--text">&copy; 2018</span>
    </v-footer>
  </v-app>
</template>
```

```
<script>
import './assets/stylesheets/main.css';

export default {
  data: () => ({
    drawer: null,
  }),
  props: {
    source: String,
  },
};
</script>
```

This contains several tags that mostly start with v-. These are the tags given by Vuetify to define our blocks in UI. We have attached a `stylesheet` file with the preceding file called `main.css`. Let's add some styling to our `App.vue` page.

Add the following code to `src/assets/stylesheets/home.css`:

```css
#app {
  font-family: 'Avenir', Helvetica, Arial, sans-serif;
  -webkit-font-smoothing: antialiased;
  -moz-osx-font-smoothing: grayscale;
  text-align: center;
  color: #2c3e50;
}

#inspire {
  font-family: 'Avenir', Helvetica, Arial, sans-serif;
}

.container.fill-height {
  align-items: normal;
}

a.side_bar_link {
  text-decoration: none;
}
```

We still have a `div` section with an ID app in it. This is the section where all our other `.vue` files will get rendered.

Now, in `HelloWorld.vue`, replace the content with this:

```
<template>
  <v-layout>
    this is home
```

```
    </v-layout>
  </template>
```

Now, if you visit `http://localhost:8080/#/`, you should be able to view the home page.

Redesigning the contact page

Let's go ahead with adding a new contact page. The first thing to do is add a route to our routes file. In `router/index.js`, add the following code:

```
import Vue from 'vue';
import Router from 'vue-router';
import HelloWorld from '@/components/HelloWorld';
import Contact from '@/components/Contact';

Vue.use(Router);

export default new Router({
  routes: [
    {
      path: '/',
      name: 'HelloWorld',
      component: HelloWorld,
    },
    {
      path: '/contact',
      name: 'Contact',
      component: Contact,
    },
  ],
});
```

What we did here is add a path for the contact page, the name of the component, which we did in our export module in the `.vue` file, and the actual name of the component. Now we need to build a view file. So let's create a `Contact.vue` file in `src/components/` and add the following content to it:

```
<template>
  <v-layout>
    this is contact
  </v-layout>
</template>
```

Now, visit `http://localhost:8080/#/contact` and you should be able to view both pages.

To make it usable and easily readable for our app, let's rename the `HelloWorld` component to the `Home` component. Rename the file `HelloWorld.vue` to `Home.vue`

Also, change the binding route from `HelloWorld` to `Home` in `App.vue`:

```
<template>
  <v-app id="inspire">
    <v-navigation-drawer
      fixed
      v-model="drawer"
      app
    >
      <v-list dense>
        <router-link v-bind:to="{ name: 'Home' }" class="side_bar_link">
          <v-list-tile @click="">
            <v-list-tile-action>
              <v-icon>home</v-icon>
```

In the `routes/index.js` as well, change the component name and the route to `Home` from `HelloWorld`:

```
import Vue from 'vue';
import Router from 'vue-router';
import Home from '@/components/Home';
import Contact from '@/components/Contact';

Vue.use(Router);

export default new Router({
  routes: [
    {
      path: '/',
      name: 'Home',
      component: Home,
    },
    {
      path: '/contact',
      name: 'Contact',
      component: Contact,
    },
  ],
});
```

We should be able to see something like this when we visit the URL `http://localhost:8080/#/`:

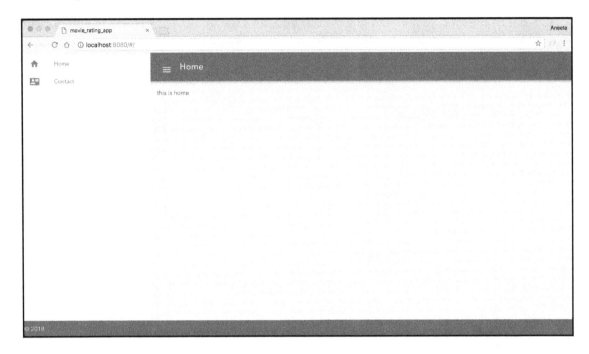

That's it. You have successfully created a basic static two-page web application!

Understanding Vue.js components

The `vue` components are equivalent to the HTML files that you write in an application. You can write the plain HTML syntax in `.vue` files. The only thing that needs to be taken care of is to wrap all the content with `<template></template>`.

Vue.js directives

Directives are used with a markup language to perform some functions on the DOM elements. For example, in HTML markup language, when we write:

```
<div class='app'></div>
```

The `class` used here is a directive for HTML language. Similarly, Vue.js also provides a lot of such directives to make application development easier, such as:

- v-text
- v-on
- v-ref
- v-show
- v-pre
- v-transition
- v-for

v-text

You can use `v-text` when you want to display some variables that you have to define dynamically. Let's see with an example. In `src/components/Home.vue`, let's add the following:

```
<template>
  <v-layout>
    <div v-text="message"></div>
  </v-layout>
</template>
<script type="text/javascript">
export default {
  data() {
    return {
      message: 'Hello there, how are you this morning?',
    };
  },
};
</script>
```

The code inside the script tag is a data variable, which binds the data defined inside it to this component. When you change the value of that variable message, the `div` element with that directive also gets updated.

If we visit the URL (http://localhost:8080/#/), we can see the following:

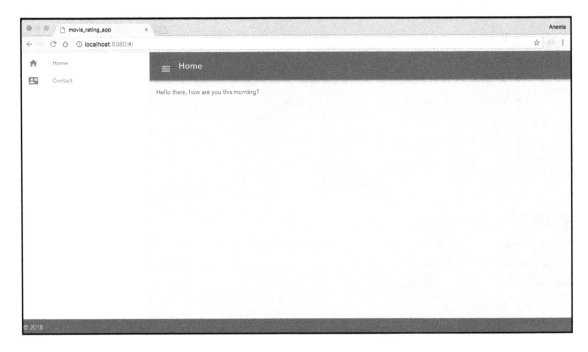

v-on

This directive is used for event handling. We can use this to trigger some logic in your application. For example, let's say we want to reply to a question that we did in the last example, for that we can do the following. Change the code in src/components/Home.vue to the following:

```
<template>
  <v-layout row wrap>
    <v-flex xs12>
      <div v-text="message"></div>
    </v-flex>
    <v-flex xs12>
      <v-btn color="primary" v-on:click="reply">Reply</v-btn>
    </v-flex>
  </v-layout>
</template>
<script type="text/javascript">
export default {
  data() {
```

```
      return {
        message: 'Hello there, how are you this morning?',
      };
    },
  methods: {
    reply() {
      this.message = "I'm doing great. Thank You!";
    },
  },
};
</script>
```

The first screen will be as follows:

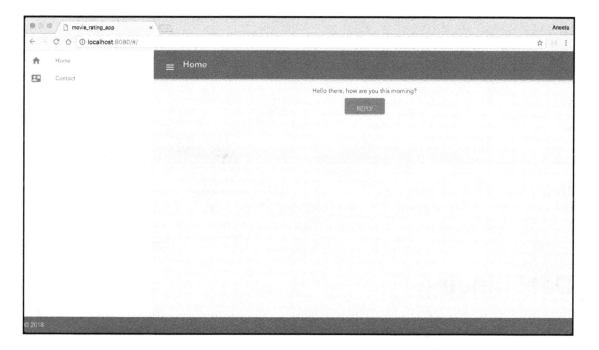

When you click **REPLY**, you will see the following:

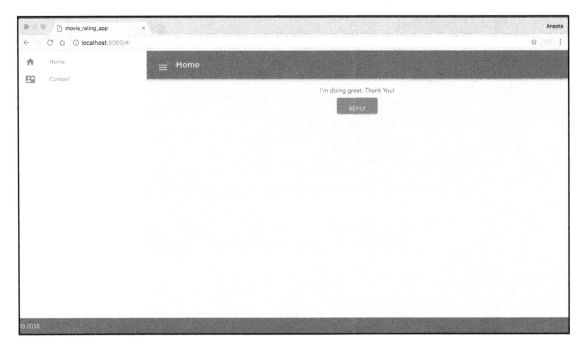

These are the directives that we will be using mostly in our app. There are a lot more other directives as well that we will explore on the way. If you want to learn more about each of these, you can visit https://012.vuejs.org/api/directives.html.

Data binding

Data binding is the process of synchronizing data. For example, for the same example for what we did on v-text, we can do it with data binding with the mustaches, in other words using the {{}} operators.

For example, we can use the {{message}} instead of using the Vue.js directive for the message. Let's change the code in src/components/Home.vue to the following:

```
<template>
  <v-layout row wrap>
    <v-flex xs12>
      <div>{{message}}</div>
    </v-flex>
    <v-flex xs12>
```

```
      <v-btn color="primary" v-on:click="reply">Reply</v-btn>
    </v-flex>
  </v-layout>
</template>
<script type="text/javascript">
  export default {
    data () {
      return {
        message: 'Hello there, how are you?',
      }
    },
    methods: {
      reply () {
        this.message = "I'm doing great. Thank You!"
      }
    }
  }
</script>
```

This will behave the same way as what we did with v-text.

Handling forms with Vue.js

Now that we have a basic idea of how Vue.js works, let's roll ahead with our first form, where we will be adding the details of movies and displaying those movies in the home page so that users can view them.

Creating a movies listing page

First of all, let's start with creating static movie cards for our home page and we will make this data dynamic in the next step. In Home.vue, replace the content inside template with the following code:

```
<template>
  <v-layout row wrap>
    <v-flex xs4>
      <v-card>
        <v-card-title primary-title>
          <div>
            <div class="headline">Batman vs Superman</div>
            <span class="grey--text">2016 · Science fiction film/Action
fiction · 3h 3m</span>
          </div>
```

```
        </v-card-title>
        <v-card-text>
            It's been nearly two years since Superman's (Henry Cavill)
colossal battle with Zod (Michael Shannon) devastated the city of
Metropolis. The loss of life and collateral damage left many feeling angry
and helpless, including crime-fighting billionaire Bruce Wayne (Ben
Affleck). Convinced that Superman is now a threat to humanity, Batman
embarks on a personal vendetta to end his reign on Earth, while the
conniving Lex Luthor (Jesse Eisenberg) launches his own crusade against the
Man of Steel.
        </v-card-text>
        <v-card-actions>
            <v-btn flat color="purple">Rate this movie</v-btn>
            <v-spacer></v-spacer>
        </v-card-actions>
    </v-card>
  </v-flex>
  <v-flex xs4>
    <v-card>
      <v-card-title primary-title>
        <div>
          <div class="headline">Logan</div>
          <span class="grey--text">2017 · Drama/Science fiction film · 2h
21m</span>
        </div>
      </v-card-title>
      <v-card-text>
          In the near future, a weary Logan (Hugh Jackman) cares for an
ailing Professor X (Patrick Stewart) at a remote outpost on the Mexican
border. His plan to hide from the outside world gets upended when he meets
a young mutant (Dafne Keen) who is very much like him. Logan must now
protect the girl and battle the dark forces that want to capture her.
      </v-card-text>
      <v-card-actions>
          <v-btn flat color="purple">Rate this movie</v-btn>
          <v-spacer></v-spacer>
      </v-card-actions>
    </v-card>
  </v-flex>
  <v-flex xs4>
    <v-card>
      <v-card-title primary-title>
        <div>
          <div class="headline">Star Wars: The Last Jedi</div>
          <span class="grey--text">2017 · Fantasy/Science fiction film ·
2h 35m</span>
        </div>
      </v-card-title>
```

```
      <v-card-text>
        Luke Skywalker's peaceful and solitary existence gets upended
when he encounters Rey, a young woman who shows strong signs of the Force.
Her desire to learn the ways of the Jedi forces Luke to make a decision
that changes their lives forever. Meanwhile, Kylo Ren and General Hux lead
the First Order in an all-out assault against Leia and the Resistance for
supremacy of the galaxy.
      </v-card-text>
      <v-card-actions>
        <v-btn flat color="purple">Rate this movie</v-btn>
        <v-spacer></v-spacer>
      </v-card-actions>
    </v-card>
  </v-flex>
  <v-flex xs4>
    <v-card>
      <v-card-title primary-title>
        <div>
          <div class="headline">Wonder Woman</div>
          <span class="grey--text">2017 · Fantasy/Science fiction film ·
2h 21m</span>
        </div>
      </v-card-title>
      <v-card-text>
        Before she was Wonder Woman (Gal Gadot), she was Diana, princess
of the Amazons, trained to be an unconquerable warrior. Raised on a
sheltered island paradise, Diana meets an American pilot (Chris Pine) who
tells her about the massive conflict that's raging in the outside world.
Convinced that she can stop the threat, Diana leaves her home for the first
time. Fighting alongside men in a war to end all wars, she finally
discovers her full powers and true destiny.
      </v-card-text>
      <v-card-actions>
        <v-btn flat color="purple">Rate this movie</v-btn>
        <v-spacer></v-spacer>
      </v-card-actions>
    </v-card>
  </v-flex>
  <v-flex xs4>
    <v-card>
      <v-card-title primary-title>
        <div>
          <div class="headline">Dunkirk</div>
          <span class="grey--text">2017 · Drama/Thriller · 2 hours</span>
        </div>
      </v-card-title>
      <v-card-text>
        In May 1940, Germany advanced into France, trapping Allied troops
```

on the beaches of Dunkirk. Under air and ground cover from British and French forces, troops were slowly and methodically evacuated from the beach using every serviceable naval and civilian vessel that could be found. At the end of this heroic mission, 330,000 French, British, Belgian and Dutch soldiers were safely evacuated.

```
        </v-card-text>
        <v-card-actions>
          <v-btn flat color="purple">Rate this movie</v-btn>
          <v-spacer></v-spacer>
        </v-card-actions>
      </v-card>
    </v-flex>
    <v-flex xs4>
      <v-card>
        <v-card-title primary-title>
          <div>
            <div class="headline">The Revenant</div>
            <span class="grey--text">2015 · Drama/Thriller · 2h 36m</span>
          </div>
        </v-card-title>
        <v-card-text>
```

While exploring the uncharted wilderness in 1823, frontiersman Hugh Glass (Leonardo DiCaprio) sustains life-threatening injuries from a brutal bear attack. When a member (Tom Hardy) of his hunting team kills his young son (Forrest Goodluck) and leaves him for dead, Glass must utilize his survival skills to find a way back to civilization. Grief-stricken and fueled by vengeance, the legendary fur trapper treks through the snowy terrain to track down the man who betrayed him.

```
        </v-card-text>
        <v-card-actions>
          <v-btn flat color="purple">Rate this movie</v-btn>
          <v-spacer></v-spacer>
        </v-card-actions>
      </v-card>
    </v-flex>
  </v-layout>
</template>
```

Also, replace the content in home.css as follows:

```
#app {
  font-family: 'Avenir', Helvetica, Arial, sans-serif;
  -webkit-font-smoothing: antialiased;
  -moz-osx-font-smoothing: grayscale;
  text-align: center;
  color: #2c3e50;
  width: 100%;
}
```

```css
#inspire {
  font-family: 'Avenir', Helvetica, Arial, sans-serif;
}

.container.fill-height {
  align-items: normal;
}

a.side_bar_link {
  text-decoration: none;
}

.card__title--primary, .card__text {
  text-align: left;
}

.card {
  height: 100% !important;
}
```

Also, in `App.vue`, replace the content with the following:

```html
<template>
  <v-app id="inspire">
    <v-navigation-drawer
      fixed
      v-model="drawer"
      app
    >
      <v-list dense>
        <router-link v-bind:to="{ name: 'Home' }" class="side_bar_link">
          <v-list-tile>
            <v-list-tile-action>
              <v-icon>home</v-icon>
            </v-list-tile-action>
            <v-list-tile-content>Home</v-list-tile-content>
          </v-list-tile>
        </router-link>
        <router-link v-bind:to="{ name: 'Contact' }" class="side_bar_link">
          <v-list-tile>
            <v-list-tile-action>
              <v-icon>contact_mail</v-icon>
            </v-list-tile-action>
            <v-list-tile-content>Contact</v-list-tile-content>
          </v-list-tile>
        </router-link>
      </v-list>
    </v-navigation-drawer>
```

```
<v-toolbar color="indigo" dark fixed app>
    <v-toolbar-side-icon @click.stop="drawer = !drawer"></v-toolbar-side-
icon>
    <v-toolbar-title>Home</v-toolbar-title>
    <v-spacer></v-spacer>
    <v-toolbar-items class="hidden-sm-and-down">
      <v-btn flat v-bind:to="{ name: 'AddMovie' }">Add Movie</v-btn>
    </v-toolbar-items>
  </v-toolbar>
  <v-content>
    <v-container fluid>
      <div id="app">
        <router-view/>
      </div>
    </v-container>
  </v-content>
  <v-footer color="indigo" app>
    <span class="white--text">&copy; 2018</span>
  </v-footer>
  </v-app>
</template>

<script>
import './assets/stylesheets/main.css';

export default {
  data: () => ({
    drawer: null,
  }),
  props: {
    source: String,
  },
};
</script>
```

Finally, replace the content in `src/main.js`:

```
// The Vue build version to load with the `import` command
// (runtime-only or standalone) has been set in webpack.base.conf with an
alias.
import 'bootstrap/dist/css/bootstrap.min.css';
import 'bootstrap-vue/dist/bootstrap-vue.css';

import BootstrapVue from 'bootstrap-vue';
import Vue from 'vue';
import Vuetify from 'vuetify';
import App from './App';
import router from './router';
```

```
Vue.use(BootstrapVue);
Vue.use(Vuetify);

Vue.config.productionTip = false;

/* eslint-disable no-new */
new Vue({
  el: '#app',
  router,
  components: { App },
  template: '<App/>',
});
```

With this, we should have a page like this on the home page:

We will be making these pages dynamic as we go.

Creating an Add movie form

First, we need to add a link that takes us to a form to add the movies. For that, we need to change the toolbar in `App.vue`. So, let's add a link to the toolbar in `App.vue`:

```
<v-toolbar color="indigo" dark fixed app>
  <v-toolbar-side-icon @click.stop="drawer = !drawer"></v-toolbar-side-icon>
  <v-toolbar-title>Home</v-toolbar-title>
  <v-spacer></v-spacer>
  <v-toolbar-items class="hidden-sm-and-down">
    <v-btn flat v-bind:to="{ name: 'AddMovie' }">Add Movie</v-btn>
  </v-toolbar-items>
</v-toolbar>
```

Now that we have the link, we need to add a route to link it to the page. Just like we did for our `Contact` page, let's add a route that will be used to add movies to our application. So, in `routes/index.js`:

```
import Vue from 'vue';
import Router from 'vue-router';
import Home from '@/components/Home';
import Contact from '@/components/Contact';
import AddMovie from '@/components/AddMovie';

Vue.use(Router);

export default new Router({
  routes: [
    {
      path: '/',
      name: 'Home',
      component: Home,
    },
    {
      path: '/contact',
      name: 'Contact',
      component: Contact,
    },
    {
      path: '/movies/add',
      name: 'AddMovie',
      component: AddMovie,
    },
  ],
});
```

Here, we added a route for `AddMovie`, which now means that we can access the add movie page at `http://localhost:8080/#/movies/add`.

The next thing we need to do now is to create the `vue` component file. For that, let's add a new `AddMovie.vue` file in `src/components`. Vuetify provides a very simple way to create forms and add validations as well. You can look for more information at `https://vuetifyjs.com/components/forms`.

Let's add the following content to `src/components/AddMovie.vue`:

```
<template>
  <v-form v-model="valid" ref="form" lazy-validation>
    <v-text-field
      label="Movie Name"
      v-model="name"
      :rules="nameRules"
      required
    ></v-text-field>
    <v-text-field
      name="input-7-1"
      label="Movie Description"
      v-model="description"
      multi-line
    ></v-text-field>
    <v-select
      label="Movie Release Year"
      v-model="release_year"
      :items="years"
    ></v-select>
    <v-text-field
      label="Movie Genre"
      v-model="genre"
    ></v-text-field>
    <v-btn
      @click="submit"
      :disabled="!valid"
    >
      submit
    </v-btn>
    <v-btn @click="clear">clear</v-btn>
  </v-form>
</template>
```

Vuetify also provides some basic validations to the form. Let's add some validation to it as well.

Add the following code to `AddMovie.vue` inside the `script` tag:

```
<template>
...
</template>
<script>
export default {
  data: () => ({
    valid: true,
    name: '',
    description: '',
    genre: '',
    release_year: '',
    nameRules: [
      v => !!v || 'Movie name is required',
    ],
    select: null,
    years: [
      '2018',
      '2017',
      '2016',
      '2015',
    ],
  }),
  methods: {
    submit() {
      if (this.$refs.form.validate()) {
        // Perform next action
      }
    },
    clear() {
      this.$refs.form.reset();
    },
  },
};
</script>
```

If we look into the form element in `AddMovie.vue`, the line that says:

```
<v-form v-model="valid" ref="form" lazy-validation>
```

What `v-model="valid"` part does here is, it makes sure the form does not get submitted until it is true, which again ties back to the script that we have added in the bottom. Also, let's look into the validations that we have added to the form.

The first basic validation is the `required` validation:

```
<v-text-field
  label="Movie Name"
  v-model="name"
  :rules="nameRules"
  required
></v-text-field>
```

This adds a `required` validation in the `name` field.

Also, for the `release_year` field, we want it to be a dropdown of years, so, for that, we have added the following:

```
<script>
export default {
  data: () => ({
    valid: true,
    name: '',
    description: '',
    genre: '',
    release_year: '',
    nameRules: [
      v => !!v || 'Movie name is required',
    ],
    select: null,
    years: [
      '2018',
      '2017',
      '2016',
      '2015',
    ],
  }),
  methods: {
    submit() {
      if (this.$refs.form.validate()) {
        // Perform next action
      }
    },
    clear() {
      this.$refs.form.reset();
    },
  },
};
</script>
```

This adds items to the select list dynamically through the script.

As regards the last part, we have two buttons `Submit` and `Clear`, which call the methods `submit()` and `clear()`, respectively.

Now, you should have a form like this when you visit the URL (`http://localhost:8080/#/movies/add`):

The * in the **Movie Name** denotes that it is a required field.

If you have noticed, we have been adding a # to all the routes that we have added. That is because it is the default setting for the Vue.js router. We can remove that by adding `mode:
'history'` in `routes/index.js`:

```
import Vue from 'vue';
import Router from 'vue-router';
import Home from '@/components/Home';
import Contact from '@/components/Contact';
import AddMovie from '@/components/AddMovie';

Vue.use(Router);

export default new Router({
```

```
  mode: 'history',
  routes: [
    {
      path: '/',
      name: 'Home',
      component: Home,
    },
    {
      path: '/contact',
      name: 'Contact',
      component: Contact,
    },
    {
      path: '/movies/add',
      name: 'AddMovie',
      component: AddMovie,
    },
  ],
});
```

Now, we can all route without adding the # in the URL as follows:

- `http://localhost:8080/`
- `http://localhost:8080/contact`
- `http://localhost:8080/movies/add`

Communicating with servers

We now have a movie listing page, we have an add movie page, so the next thing we have to do is save the data into the MongoDB when we submit the form.

Adding express to our application

Now that we have all the components in place, it's time to add the server layer to our application.

Let's start by adding the express package with the following:

```
npm install express --save
```

The next part is to create the necessary endpoints and models so that we can add the movies to the database.

To do that, we first need to install the required packages:

- `body-parser`: To parse the incoming requests
- `cors`: To handle cross-origin requests between frontend and backend
- `morgan`: HTTP request logger
- `mongoose`: Object modeling for MongoDB

Let's install all of these packages by running the following command in the Terminal:

```
$ npm install morgan body-parser cors mongoose --save
```

Adding a server file

Now, we need to set up the server for our application. Let's add a file called `server.js` in the root of the application and add the following content:

```js
const express = require('express');
const bodyParser = require('body-parser');
const mongoose = require('mongoose');
const cors = require('cors');
const morgan = require('morgan');
const fs = require('fs');

const app = express();
const router = express.Router();
app.use(morgan('combined'));
app.use(bodyParser.json());
app.use(cors());

//connect to mongodb
mongoose.connect('mongodb://localhost/movie_rating_app', function() {
  console.log('Connection has been made');
})
.catch(err => {
  console.error('App starting error:', err.stack);
  process.exit(1);
});

router.get('/', function(req, res) {
  res.json({ message: 'API Initialized!'});
});
```

```
const port = process.env.API_PORT || 8081;
app.use('/', router);
app.listen(port, function() {
  console.log(`api running on port ${port}`);
});
```

Here, we have set up a server that tells the express server to run on the 8081 port. We will be using this server to handle all the API requests via express.

Also, we have required and used all the packages that we need in this `server.js` file.

Also, for the mongoose connection, we have added a connection to our local database called `movie_rating_app` with the following code block:

```
//connect to mongodb
mongoose.connect('mongodb://localhost/movie_rating_app', function() {
  console.log('Connection has been made');
})
.catch(err => {
  console.error('App starting error:', err.stack);
  process.exit(1);
});
```

As I mentioned earlier, if the database does not exist yet, it will automatically get created when we add our very first Mongoose document to the DB.

The next thing is to run our MongoDB server. Let's do that by running the following command in the Terminal:

```
$ mongod
```

Once the Mongo server is up, let's spin up our `node` server for this application using the following command:

```
$ node server.js
```

Now, when we open `http://localhost:8081/`, you should be able to see the following message:

```
←  →  C  ⓘ localhost:8081                                    ☆
{
    message: "API Initialized!"
}
```

Until now, we have our frontend server up and running on port 8080 with the following:

```
$ npm run dev
```

The backend server running on port 8081 with the following:

```
$ node server.js
```

One important thing to remember is that whenever we change the code in server.js, we have to restart the server by running the following command:

```
$ node server.js
```

This is a very tedious task. However, there is one good way to get rid of that. There is a package called nodemon, which, when installed, restarts the server automatically whenever the code gets updated and we don't have to do it manually every time. So, let's go ahead and install the package:

```
$ npm install nodemon --save
```

With the package installed, now we can start our server with the following command:

```
$ nodemon server.js
```

Adding a Movie model

The next thing is to add the movies to the database when we submit the form. Let's go ahead and create a folder called models in the root directory and add a Movie.js file in the models directory:

 We will be using singular capitalized names for Models, and all lowercase plural names for Controllers files.

The following code into the Movie.js:

```
const mongoose = require('mongoose');

const Schema = mongoose.Schema;
const MovieSchema = new Schema({
  name: String,
  description: String,
  release_year: Number,
  genre: String,
```

```
});

const Movie = mongoose.model('Movie', MovieSchema)
module.exports = Movie;
```

Here, we have created a Movie model that would take all the four attributes that we have added to our `AddMovie.vue` form earlier.

Adding movies controller

Now, the last thing we need to set up is an endpoint to save the movie to the database. Let's create a folder called `controllers` in the root directory and add a file called `movies.js` inside the directory and add the following code:

```
const MovieSchema = require('../models/Movie.js');

module.exports.controller = (app) => {
  // add a new movie
  app.post('/movies', (req, res) => {
    const newMovie = new MovieSchema({
      name: req.body.name,
      description: req.body.description,
      release_year: req.body.release_year,
      genre: req.body.genre,
    });

    newMovie.save((error, movie) => {
      if (error) { console.log(error); }
      res.send(movie);
    });
  });
};
```

Here we have added an endpoint that takes the post requests with the given params and creates a Mongoose document in the database that we have configured.

Since these controllers have the routes, we need to include these files in our main entry point as well. For our backend, the main entry file is `server.js`. So, let's add the following highlighted code block in `server.js`:

```
...
//connect to mongodb
mongoose.connect('mongodb://localhost/movie_rating_app', function() {
  console.log('Connection has been made');
})
.catch(err => {
  console.error('App starting error:', err.stack);
  process.exit(1);
});

// Include controllers
fs.readdirSync("controllers").forEach(function (file) {
  if(file.substr(-3) == ".js") {
    const route = require("./controllers/" + file)
    route.controller(app)
  }
})

router.get('/', function(req, res) {
  res.json({ message: 'API Initialized!'});
});
...
```

This code block will include all our controllers' files and we don't have to add each of them manually.

Connecting frontend and backend

Now, we have the model and an endpoint. The next thing to do is to call this endpoint when we hit the **Submit** button in `AddMovie.vue`.

This is the part where we need to communicate the frontend and the backend. For this, we need to use a separate package called axios.

The axios package helps us to make the HTTP requests from the Node.js. It helps to make the Ajax calls from the frontend. There are several alternatives for axios as well, such as fetch, and superagent. But axios has been successful enough to become the most popular among these. So we will be using the same as well.

Installing axios

Now, in order to communicate between the client and the server, we will be using the `axios` library. So, let's install the library first:

```
npm install axios --save
```

Connecting all the pieces

Now, we have all the things in place (movie model, movies controller, and axios) to communicate between the client and server. The last thing to do now is to connect these pieces when we click the **submit** button in the Movie Add form. If you remember, we added a placeholder before while submitting the button in `AddMovie.vue`:

```
<v-select
      label="Movie Release Year"
      v-model="select"
      :items="years"
></v-select>
<v-text-field
      label="Movie Genre"
      v-model="genre"
></v-text-field>
<v-btn
    @click="submit"
    :disabled="!valid"
>
      submit
</v-btn>
<v-btn @click="clear">clear</v-btn>
```

This code tells us to execute the `submit()` method when the button is clicked. We also have it in the `script` section:

```
...
methods: {
    submit() {
      if (this.$refs.form.validate()) {
        // Perform next action
      }
    },
    clear() {
      this.$refs.form.reset();
    },
```

```
    },
    ...
```

All the methods that we will have will be added in this section. Now that we have our placeholder for `submit`, let's modify this piece of code to incorporate the Movie Add form:

```
<script>
import axios from 'axios';

export default {
  data: () => ({
    valid: true,
    name: '',
    description: '',
    genre: '',
    release_year: '',
    nameRules: [
      v => !!v || 'Movie name is required',
    ],
    select: null,
    years: [
      '2018',
      '2017',
      '2016',
      '2015',
    ],
  }),
  methods: {
    submit() {
      if (this.$refs.form.validate()) {
        return axios({
          method: 'post',
          data: {
            name: this.name,
            description: this.description,
            release_year: this.release_year,
            genre: this.genre,
          },
          url: 'http://localhost:8081/movies',
          headers: {
            'Content-Type': 'application/json',
          },
        })
          .then(() => {
            this.$router.push({ name: 'Home' });
            this.$refs.form.reset();
          })
```

```
            .catch(() => {
            });
        }
        return true;
    },
    clear() {
      this.$refs.form.reset();
    },
  },
};
</script>
```

This should suffice. Now, let's go ahead and add a movie from the UI itself from the `http://localhost:8080/movies/add` endpoint. We should be able to save a movie's record in the MongoDB. Let me explain what we did here a little bit.

When we hit the `Submit` button, we made an AJAX request via axios to hit the post endpoint in the movies controller. The `post` method in movies controller, in turn, saves the record with the parameters that we gave according to the model schema we designed for the movies. And, when the process is complete, redirect the page back to the homepage.

To check whether the record was actually created or not, let's look into MongoDB:

```
$ mongo
$ use movie_rating_app
$ db.movies.find()
```

We can see the record being created with the parameters we provided in the form:

```
> db.movies.find()
{ "_id" : ObjectId("5a62ef429f46cfb300f39f83"), "name" : "Wonder wonder", "description" : "again I wonder", "genre"
: "Fiction", "__v" : 0 }
>
```

Adding form validations

We covered how to add the validations in the previous section as well. Let's go ahead and add a few validations to our movie add form. We will add the following validations:

- `Movie Name` cannot be empty
- `Movie Description` is optional
- `Movie Release Year` cannot be blank
- The genre of the movie will be required and will be maxed to 80 characters

In `AddMovie.vue`, let's add the rules in input fields and bind the rules from the script:

```
<template>
  <v-form v-model="valid" ref="form" lazy-validation>
    <v-text-field
      label="Movie Name"
      v-model="name"
      :rules="nameRules"
      required
    ></v-text-field>
    <v-text-field
      name="input-7-1"
      label="Movie Description"
      v-model="description"
      multi-line
    ></v-text-field>
    <v-select
      label="Movie Release Year"
      v-model="release_year"
      required
      :rules="releaseRules"
      :items="years"
    ></v-select>
    <v-text-field
      label="Movie Genre"
      v-model="genre"
      required
      :rules="genreRules"
    ></v-text-field>
    <v-btn
      @click="submit"
      :disabled="!valid"
    >
      submit
    </v-btn>
    <v-btn @click="clear">clear</v-btn>
  </v-form>
</template>
<script>
  import axios from 'axios';

  export default {
    data: () => ({
      valid: true,
      name: '',
      description: '',
      genre: '',
```

```
        release_year: '',
        nameRules: [
          (v) => !!v || 'Movie name is required'
        ],
        genreRules: [
          v => !!v || 'Movie genre year is required',
          v => (v && v.length <= 80) || 'Genre must be less than equal to 80
characters.',
        ],
        releaseRules: [
          v => !!v || 'Movie release year is required',
        ],
        select: null,
        years: [
          '2018',
          '2017',
          '2016',
          '2015'
        ],
        checkbox: false
      }),
      methods: {
        submit () {
          if (this.$refs.form.validate()) {
            return axios({
              method: 'post',
              data: {
                name: this.name,
                description: this.description,
                release_year: this.release_year,
                genre: this.genre
              },
              url: 'http://localhost:8081/movies',
              headers: {
                'Content-Type': 'application/json'
              }
            })
            .then((response) => {
              this.$router.push({ name: 'Home' });
              this.$refs.form.reset();
            })
            .catch((error) => {
            });
```

```
      }
    },
    clear () {
      this.$refs.form.reset()
    }
  }
}
</script>
```

Now, if we try to submit the form with all the fields blank, and the field `Movie Genre` with more than 80 characters, we should not be able to submit the form. The form will display these error messages:

Adding a flash message

We have covered the basics of app building. Now that we can add a movie, what would be really nice is to have a certain message when the movie is saved successfully in the DB or notify if something goes wrong. There are several npm packages to do just that. We can also build our own as well. For this application, we will be using a package called: vue-swal (https://www.npmjs.com/package/vue-swal). Let's add the package first:

```
$ npm install vue-swal --save
```

Now, let's include the package in our main.js file:

```
// The Vue build version to load with the `import` command
// (runtime-only or standalone) has been set in webpack.base.conf with an
alias.
import 'bootstrap/dist/css/bootstrap.min.css';
import 'bootstrap-vue/dist/bootstrap-vue.css';

import BootstrapVue from 'bootstrap-vue';
import Vue from 'vue';
import Vuetify from 'vuetify';
import VueSwal from 'vue-swal';
import App from './App';
import router from './router';

Vue.use(BootstrapVue);
Vue.use(Vuetify);
Vue.use(VueSwal);

Vue.config.productionTip = false;

/* eslint-disable no-new */
new Vue({
  el: '#app',
  router,
  components: { App },
  template: '<App/>',
});
```

Now, let's modify our `AddMovie.vue` to display the flash message when the action is performed successfully or when it fails:

```
...
methods: {
  submit() {
    if (this.$refs.form.validate()) {
      return axios({
        method: 'post',
        data: {
          name: this.name,
          description: this.description,
          release_year: this.release_year,
          genre: this.genre,
        },
        url: 'http://localhost:8081/movies',
        headers: {
          'Content-Type': 'application/json',
        },
      })
        .then(() => {
          this.$swal(
            'Great!',
            'Movie added successfully!',
            'success',
          );
          this.$router.push({ name: 'Home' });
          this.$refs.form.reset();
        })
        .catch(() => {
          this.$swal(
            'Oh oo!',
            'Could not add the movie!',
            'error',
          );
        });
    }
    return true;
  },
  clear() {
    this.$refs.form.reset();
  },
},
...
```

Now, with this, when we submit a movie, we should be able to see a success message before redirecting to the homepage:

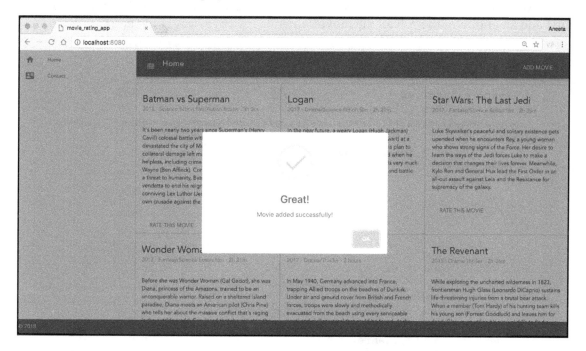

There are also several other packages for the message alerting, such as `vue-flash`, `vuex-flash`, and `sweet-alert`.

Loading dynamic content on the homepage

Currently, our homepage has all the static movies in the content. Let's fill the data with the data that we have added to the movies in our database. For that, the first thing to do is to add a few movies to the database, which we can do via the `http://localhost:8080/movies/add` endpoint from the UI.

API endpoint to fetch all movies

First, we need to add an endpoint to fetch all the movies from the Mongo database. So, let's first add an endpoint to fetch all the movies in `controllers/movies.js`:

```
const MovieSchema = require('../models/Movie.js');

module.exports.controller = (app) => {
  // fetch all movies
  app.get('/movies', (req, res) => {
    MovieSchema.find({}, 'name description release_year genre', (error,
movies) => {
      if (error) { console.log(error); }
      res.send({
        movies,
      });
    });
  });

  // add a new movie
  app.post('/movies', (req, res) => {
    const newMovie = new MovieSchema({
      name: req.body.name,
      description: req.body.description,
      release_year: req.body.release_year,
      genre: req.body.genre,
    });

    newMovie.save((error, movie) => {
      if (error) { console.log(error); }
      res.send(movie);
    });
  });
};
```

Now, if you hit the URL `http://localhost:8081/movies`, we should be able to see the entire movie list that we have added via UI or the mongo shell itself. Here is what I have:

Modifying Home.vue to display dynamic content

Now, let's update our `Home.vue`, which will fetch the movies from our Mongo database and display the dynamic content. Replace the code in `Home.vue` with the following content:

```
<template>
  <v-layout row wrap>
    <v-flex xs4>
      <v-card>
        <v-card-title primary-title>
          <div>
            <div class="headline">Batman vs Superman</div>
            <span class="grey--text">2016 · Science fiction film/Action
            fiction · 3h 3m</span>
          </div>
        </v-card-title>
        <v-card-text>
            It's been nearly two years since Superman's (Henry Cavill)
colossal battle with Zod (Michael Shannon) devastated the city of
Metropolis. The loss of life and collateral damage left many feeling angry
and helpless, including crime-fighting billionaire Bruce Wayne (Ben
Affleck). Convinced that Superman is now a threat to humanity, Batman
embarks on a personal vendetta to end his reign on Earth, while the
```

conniving Lex Luthor (Jesse Eisenberg) launches his own crusade against the Man of Steel.

```
    </v-card-text>
    <v-card-actions>
      <v-btn flat color="purple">Rate this movie</v-btn>
      <v-spacer></v-spacer>
    </v-card-actions>
  </v-card>
</v-flex>
<v-flex xs4>
  <v-card>
    <v-card-title primary-title>
      <div>
        <div class="headline">Logan</div>
        <span class="grey--text">2017 · Drama/Science fiction film ·
        2h 21m</span>
      </div>
    </v-card-title>
    <v-card-text>
```

In the near future, a weary Logan (Hugh Jackman) cares for an ailing Professor X (Patrick Stewart) at a remote outpost on the Mexican border. His plan to hide from the outside world gets upended when he meets a young mutant (Dafne Keen) who is very much like him. Logan must now protect the girl and battle the dark forces that want to capture her.

```
    </v-card-text>
    <v-card-actions>
      <v-btn flat color="purple">Rate this movie</v-btn>
      <v-spacer></v-spacer>
    </v-card-actions>
  </v-card>
</v-flex>
<v-flex xs4>
  <v-card>
    <v-card-title primary-title>
      <div>
        <div class="headline">Star Wars: The Last Jedi</div>
        <span class="grey--text">2017 · Fantasy/Science fiction film
        · 2h 35m</span>
      </div>
    </v-card-title>
    <v-card-text>
```

Luke Skywalker's peaceful and solitary existence gets upended when he encounters Rey, a young woman who shows strong signs of the Force. Her desire to learn the ways of the Jedi forces Luke to make a decision that changes their lives forever. Meanwhile, Kylo Ren and General Hux lead the First Order in an all-out assault against Leia and the Resistance for supremacy of the galaxy.

```
    </v-card-text>
```

```
        <v-card-actions>
          <v-btn flat color="purple">Rate this movie</v-btn>
          <v-spacer></v-spacer>
        </v-card-actions>
      </v-card>
    </v-flex>
    <v-flex xs4>
      <v-card>
        <v-card-title primary-title>
          <div>
            <div class="headline">Wonder Woman</div>
            <span class="grey--text">2017 · Fantasy/Science fiction film
            · 2h 21m</span>
          </div>
        </v-card-title>
        <v-card-text>
```
Before she was Wonder Woman (Gal Gadot), she was Diana, princess
of the Amazons, trained to be an unconquerable warrior. Raised on a
sheltered island paradise, Diana meets an American pilot (Chris Pine) who
tells her about the massive conflict that's raging in the outside world.
Convinced that she can stop the threat, Diana leaves her home for the first
time. Fighting alongside men in a war to end all wars, she finally
discovers her full powers and true destiny.
```
        </v-card-text>
        <v-card-actions>
          <v-btn flat color="purple">Rate this movie</v-btn>
          <v-spacer></v-spacer>
        </v-card-actions>
      </v-card>
    </v-flex>
    <v-flex xs4>
      <v-card>
        <v-card-title primary-title>
          <div>
            <div class="headline">Dunkirk</div>
            <span class="grey--text">2017 · Drama/Thriller · 2
            hours</span>
          </div>
        </v-card-title>
        <v-card-text>
```
In May 1940, Germany advanced into France, trapping Allied troops
on the beaches of Dunkirk. Under air and ground cover from British and
French forces, troops were slowly and methodically evacuated from the beach
using every serviceable naval and civilian vessel that could be found. At
the end of this heroic mission, 330,000 French, British, Belgian and Dutch
soldiers were safely evacuated.
```
        </v-card-text>
        <v-card-actions>
```

```
            <v-btn flat color="purple">Rate this movie</v-btn>
            <v-spacer></v-spacer>
          </v-card-actions>
        </v-card>
      </v-flex>
      <v-flex xs4>
        <v-card>
          <v-card-title primary-title>
            <div>
              <div class="headline">The Revenant</div>
              <span class="grey--text">2015 · Drama/Thriller · 2h
              36m</span>
            </div>
          </v-card-title>
          <v-card-text>
```
While exploring the uncharted wilderness in 1823, frontiersman
Hugh Glass (Leonardo DiCaprio) sustains life-threatening injuries from a
brutal bear attack. When a member (Tom Hardy) of his hunting team kills his
young son (Forrest Goodluck) and leaves him for dead, Glass must utilize
his survival skills to find a way back to civilization. Grief-stricken and
fueled by vengeance, the legendary fur trapper treks through the snowy
terrain to track down the man who betrayed him.
```
          </v-card-text>
          <v-card-actions>
            <v-btn flat color="purple">Rate this movie</v-btn>
            <v-spacer></v-spacer>
          </v-card-actions>
        </v-card>
      </v-flex>
    </v-layout>
</template>
<script>
import axios from 'axios';

export default {
  name: 'Movies',
  data() {
    return {
      movies: [],
    };
  },
  mounted() {
    this.fetchMovies();
  },
  methods: {
    async fetchMovies() {
      return axios({
        method: 'get',
```

```
        url: 'http://localhost:8081/movies',
      })
        .then((response) => {
          this.movies = response.data.movies;
        })
        .catch(() => {
        });
    },
   },
  };
  </script>
```

This code calls a method when the page loads, which is defined in the `mounted` method. The method fetches the movies using an axios request. Now we have pulled the data from the server to the client. Now, we will use the `vue` directive to loop through these movies and render in the home page. Replace the content of the `<template>` tag with the following code in `Home.vue`:

```
<template>
  <v-layout row wrap>
    <v-flex xs4 v-for="movie in movies" :key="movie._id">
      <v-card>
        <v-card-title primary-title>
          <div>
            <div class="headline">{{ movie.name }}</div>
            <span class="grey--text">{{ movie.release_year }} · {{
movie.genre }}</span>
          </div>
        </v-card-title>
        <v-card-text>
          {{ movie.description }}
        </v-card-text>
      </v-card>
    </v-flex>
  </v-layout>
</template>
. . .
```

As you can see, we have used the `vue` directive `for`. The key is used to assign a unique identity to each record. Now, when you visit `http://localhost:8080/`, you will see the following:

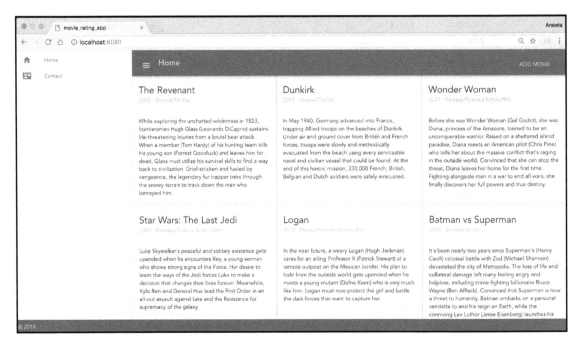

We have successfully built an application where we can add the movies to the MongoDB and display the DB records on the home page.

Adding a movie profile page

Now, we need a page where a logged-in user can go and rate the movie. To do that, let's add a link to the title of the movie on the home page. In `Home.vue`, replace the template part with the following content:

```
<template>
  <v-layout row wrap>
    <v-flex xs4 v-for="movie in movies" :key="movie._id">
      <v-card>
        <v-card-title primary-title>
          <div>
            <div class="headline">
              <v-btn flat v-bind:to="`/movies/${movie._id}`">
```

```
                      {{ movie.name }}
                  </v-btn>
              </div>
              <span class="grey--text">{{ movie.release_year }} · {{
movie.genre }}</span>
            </div>
          </v-card-title>
          <v-card-text>
            {{ movie.description }}
          </v-card-text>
        </v-card>
      </v-flex>
    </v-layout>
</template>
```

Here, we added a link to the title that will take the user to its corresponding detail page.

Let's add a page for the detailed view of the movie page where a logged-in user can go and rate the movie. Create a file called Movie.vue inside the src/components directory and add the following content:

```
<template>
  <v-layout row wrap>
    <v-flex xs4>
      <v-card>
        <v-card-title primary-title>
          <div>
            <div class="headline">{{ movie.name }}</div>
            <span class="grey--text">{{ movie.release_year }} · {{
movie.genre }}</span>
          </div>
        </v-card-title>
        <h6 class="card-title">Rate this movie</h6>
        <v-card-text>
          {{ movie.description }}
        </v-card-text>
      </v-card>
    </v-flex>
  </v-layout>
</template>
<script>
import axios from 'axios';

export default {
  name: 'Movie',
  data() {
    return {
```

```
        movie: [],
      };
    },
    mounted() {
      this.fetchMovie();
    },
    methods: {
      async fetchMovie() {
        return axios({
          method: 'get',
          url: `http://localhost:8081/api/movies/${this.$route.params.id}`,
        })
          .then((response) => {
            this.movie = response.data;
          })
          .catch(() => {
          });
      },
    },
  };
</script>
```

We have added an axios request here to fetch the movie when a user clicks on the title of the movie.

Now, we also need to define the routes to the page. So, in `routes/index.js`, replace the content with the following:

```
import Vue from 'vue';
import Router from 'vue-router';
import Home from '@/components/Home';
import Contact from '@/components/Contact';
import AddMovie from '@/components/AddMovie';
import Register from '@/components/Register';
import Login from '@/components/Login';
import Movie from '@/components/Movie';

Vue.use(Router);

export default new Router({
  mode: 'history',
  routes: [
    {
      path: '/',
      name: 'Home',
      component: Home,
    },
```

```
    {
      path: '/contact',
      name: 'Contact',
      component: Contact,
    },
    {
      path: '/movies/add',
      name: 'AddMovie',
      component: AddMovie,
    },
    {
      path: '/movies/:id',
      name: 'Movie',
      component: Movie,
    },
  ],
});
```

Now, we need to add an endpoint for a GET request to fetch the movie with the specified ID.

Replace the content in `controllers/movies.js` with the following:

```
const MovieSchema = require('../models/Movie.js');

module.exports.controller = (app) => {
  // fetch all movies
  app.get('/movies', (req, res) => {
    MovieSchema.find({}, 'name description release_year genre', (error,
movies) => {
      if (error) { console.log(error); }
      res.send({
        movies,
      });
    });
  });

  // fetch a single movie
  app.get('/api/movies/:id', (req, res) => {
    MovieSchema.findById(req.params.id, 'name description release_year
genre', (error, movie) => {
      if (error) { console.error(error); }
      res.send(movie);
    });
  });

  // add a new movie
```

```
app.post('/movies', (req, res) => {
  const newMovie = new MovieSchema({
    name: req.body.name,
    description: req.body.description,
    release_year: req.body.release_year,
    genre: req.body.genre,
  });

  newMovie.save((error, movie) => {
    if (error) { console.log(error); }
    res.send(movie);
  });
});
};
```

Now, when we click the link on the title of the movie, we should be able to see the following page:

Here, we have also added an area where a user can click on to **Rate this Movie**. Let's move ahead to add the functionality to rate the movie. For this, we will be using a package called `vue-star-rating`, which makes it easy to add the rating component. You can find this example on this link as well at https://jsfiddle.net/anteriovieira/8nawdjs7/.

Let's first add the package:

```
$ npm install vue-star-rating --save
```

In `Movie.vue`, replace the content with the following:

```
<template>
  <v-layout row wrap>
    <v-flex xs4>
      <v-card>
        <v-card-title primary-title>
          <div>
            <div class="headline">{{ movie.name }}</div>
            <span class="grey--text">{{ movie.release_year }} · {{
movie.genre }}</span>
          </div>
        </v-card-title>
        <h6 class="card-title" v-if="current_user">Rate this movie</h6>
        <v-card-text>
          {{ movie.description }}
        </v-card-text>
      </v-card>
    </v-flex>
  </v-layout>
</template>
<script>
import axios from 'axios';
import Vue from 'vue';
import StarRating from 'vue-star-rating';

const wrapper = document.createElement('div');
// shared state
const state = {
  note: 0,
};
// crate component to content
const RatingComponent = Vue.extend({
  data() {
    return { rating: 0 };
  },
  watch: {
```

```
      rating(newVal) { state.note = newVal; },
    },
    template: `
      <div class="rating">
        How was your experience getting help with this issues?
        <star-rating v-model="rating" :show-rating="false"></star-rating>
      </div>`,
    components: { 'star-rating': StarRating },
});

const component = new RatingComponent().$mount(wrapper);

export default {
  name: 'Movie',
  data() {
    return {
      movie: [],
    };
  },
  mounted() {
    this.fetchMovie();
  },
  methods: {
    async rate() {
      this.$swal({
        content: component.$el,
        buttons: {
          confirm: {
            value: 0,
          },
        },
      }).then(() => {
        const movieId = this.$route.params.id;
        return axios({
          method: 'post',
          data: {
            rate: state.note,
          },
          url: `http://localhost:8081/movies/rate/${movieId}`,
          headers: {
            'Content-Type': 'application/json',
          },
        })
          .then(() => {
            this.$swal(`Thank you for rating! ${state.note}`, 'success');
          })
          .catch((error) => {
            const message = error.response.data.message;
```

```
            this.$swal('Oh oo!', `${message}`, 'error');
        });
      });
    },
    async fetchMovie() {
      return axios({
        method: 'get',
        url: `http://localhost:8081/api/movies/${this.$route.params.id}`,
      })
        .then((response) => {
          this.movie = response.data;
        })
        .catch(() => {
        });
    },
  },
};
</script>
```

Let's also update the code to call the `rate` method when **Rate this Movie** is clicked. In `Movie.vue`, update the following line of code:

```
...
<h6 class="card-title" v-if="current_user" @click="rate">Rate this
movie</h6>
...
```

Now, the last thing we need to do is add the `rate` endpoint in `movies.js`:

```
var Movie = require("../models/Movie");

module.exports.controller = (app) => {
  // fetch all movies
  app.get("/movies", function(req, res) {
    Movie.find({}, 'name description release_year genre', function (error,
movies) {
      if (error) { console.log(error); }
      res.send({
        movies: movies
      })
    })
  })

  // fetch a single movie
  app.get("/api/movies/:id", function(req, res) {
    Movie.findById(req.params.id, 'name description release_year
    genre', function (error, movie) {
```

```
        if (error) { console.error(error); }
        res.send(movie)
      })
    })

    // rate a movie
    app.post('/movies/rate/:id', (req, res) => {
      const rating = new Rating({
        movie_id: req.params.id,
        user_id: req.body.user_id,
        rate: req.body.rate,
      })

      rating.save(function (error, rating) {
        if (error) { console.log(error); }
        res.send({
          movie_id: rating.movie_id,
          user_id: rating.user_id,
          rate: rating.rate
        })
      })
    })

    // add a new movie
    app.post('/movies', (req, res) => {
      const movie = new Movie({
        name: req.body.name,
        description: req.body.description,
        release_year: req.body.release_year,
        genre: req.body.genre
      })

      movie.save(function (error, movie) {
        if (error) { console.log(error); }
        res.send(movie)
      })
    })
  }
```

The endpoint saves the user ratings in a separate collection called Rating, which we haven't created yet. Let's go ahead and do that as well. Create a file called Rating.js inside the models directory and add the following content:

```
const mongoose = require('mongoose')
const Schema = mongoose.Schema
const RatingSchema = new Schema({
  movie_id: String,
```

```
    user_id: String,
    rate: Number
})

const Rating = mongoose.model("Rating", RatingSchema)
module.exports = Rating
```

Include the same model in `movies.js` as well:

```
const Movie = require("../models/Movie");
const Rating = require("../models/Rating");
```

That's it! Now a user should be able to rate a movie when logged-in. The user should get a popup when **Rate this movie** is clicked and display the rated score upon successful rating with a thank you message:

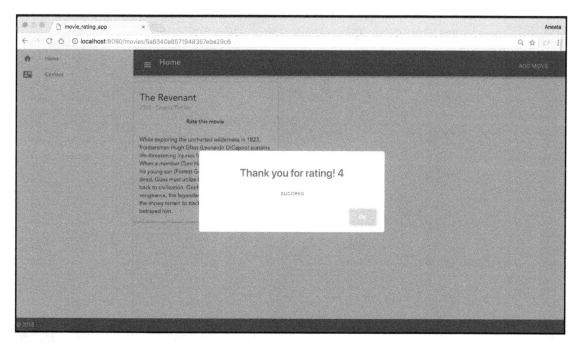

Summary

In this chapter, we covered what Vue.js is! We built a static application that lists the movies followed by adding the dynamic functionality to a movies listing via a form that stores the movies in the MongoDB. We also learned about Vue.js components, Data Binding, and Vue.js Directives.

We also added the functionality for users to be able to rate the movies.

In the next chapter, we will add the users and sign in/sign up functionality in the same application.

6
Building Authentication with passport.js

Authentication is a vital part of any application. Authentication is a way to secure the applications we build. Every application needs some kind of mechanism for authentication. It helps us to identify the users making requests to the application server.

In this chapter, we will discuss the following topics:

- Creating a login and a register page
- Installing and configuring `passport.js`
- Learning more about the `passport.js` strategy, that is, the **JSON Web Token (JWT)** strategy
- Learn more about `passport.js` Local Strategy
- Creating necessary endpoints in the application server to handle register and login requests

We can build the user authentication by ourselves. However, it adds a lot of configuration and lot of headaches. `passport.js` is a package that allows us to configure authentication efficiently, taking a very small amount of time. If you want to learn and develop all by yourself, I encourage you to do so. That will give you more insights into how everything works. However, for this book, we will use this awesome tool called `passport.js`, which is very easy to integrate and learn.

Up until this chapter, we have created a dynamic web application that displays all the movies that we have added via the Movie Add form and the API on the home page. We have a way of adding these movies to the database via the frontend as well. Now, since this will be a public web application, we cannot allow everyone to add movies by themselves without logging in. Only a user who logs in will have access and be able to add movies. Also, in order to rate a movie, a user should log in first and then rate the movie.

Introduction to passport.js

`passport.js` is a middleware provided by Node.js for authentication. The functionality of `passport.js` is to authenticate the requests that are made to the server. It provides several strategies for authentication. `passport.js` provides strategies to such as local strategy, Facebook strategy, Google strategy, Twitter strategy, and JWT strategy. In this chapter, we will focus on using the JWT strategy.

JWT

JWT is a way of authenticating the requests using a token-based approach. There are two methods of authenticating requests: cookie-based authentication, and token-based authentication. The cookie-based authentication mechanism saves the user's session ID in the browser's cookie, whereas the token-based mechanism uses a signed token that will look like this:

```
eyJhbGciOiJIUzI1NiIsInR5cCI6IkpXVCJ9.eyJpZCI6IjVhNjhhNDMzMDJkMWN1ZDU5YjExND
g3MCIsImlhdCI6MTUxNzI0MjM1M30.5xY59iTIjpt9ukDmxseNAGbOdz6weWL1drJkeQzoO3M
```

This token is then validated on every request that we make to the `controllers`.

For our application, we will use a combination of both. When a user requests to log in to the app, we will create a signed token for them and then add that token to the browser's cookie. The next time when the user logs in, we will read that token from the cookie and validate that token using the `passport-jwt` module in the server, and then decide whether or not to log that user in.

If you look at the preceding token carefully, you will see that the token has three parts separated by a period (`.`); each part has its own meaning:

- The first part represents the header
- The second part represents the payload
- The third part represents the signature

To be able to use this JWT, we will need to add a package. To do that, we can just run the following command:

```
$ npm install jsonwebtoken --save
```

To start using this package, let's define it in `server.js` as well:

```
...
const morgan = require('morgan')
const fs = require('fs')
const jwt = require('jsonwebtoken');
...
```

Installing passport.js

Just like any other npm package, we can install `passport.js` by running the following command:

```
$ npm install passport --save
```

On successful installation, you should have those package listed on your `package.json` as well:

```
...
"nodemon": "^1.14.10",
"passport": "^0.4.0",
"sass-loader": "^6.0.6",
...
```

You can also do this by first adding the package to your `package.json` file and then running the following command:

```
$ npm install
```

Configuring passport

Just like any other `node` package, we will need to configure the package for `passport.js`. In our `server.js` file, add the following lines of code:

```
...
const mongoose = require('mongoose');
const cors = require('cors');
const morgan = require('morgan');
const fs = require('fs');
const jwt = require('jsonwebtoken');
const passport = require('passport');

const app = express();
const router = express.Router();
```

```
app.use(morgan('combined'));
app.use(bodyParser.json());
app.use(cors());
app.use(passport.initialize());
...
```

The preceding code just initialized `passport.js` in our application. We still need to configure a couple of things to start using the JWT authentication mechanism.

passport.js strategies

As mentioned previously, `passport.js` provides a lot of strategies for easy integration. One of the strategies that we will be working on with is the JWT strategy. We have already added `passport.js` and initialized it. Now, let's add this strategy as well.

Installing the passport-jwt strategy

Just installing passport module is not sufficient for our needs. `passport.js` provides its strategies in separate npm packages. For `jwt` authentication, we have to install the `passport-jwt` module, as follows:

```
$ npm install passport-jwt --save
```

On successful installation, you should have these packages listed in the `package.json` file of the application:

```
...
"nodemon": "^1.14.10",
"passport": "^0.4.0",
"passport-jwt": "^3.0.1",
"sass-loader": "^6.0.6",
...
```

Configuring the passport-jwt strategy

Now that we have all the things we need, let's jump into the configuration setting for the JWT strategy. Add the following lines of code in `server.js`:

```
...
const morgan = require('morgan');
const fs = require('fs');
```

```
const jwt = require('jsonwebtoken');
const passport = require('passport');
const passportJWT = require('passport-jwt');
const ExtractJwt = passportJWT.ExtractJwt;
const JwtStrategy = passportJWT.Strategy;
const jwtOptions = {}
jwtOptions.jwtFromRequest = ExtractJwt.fromAuthHeaderWithScheme('jwt');
jwtOptions.secretOrKey = 'movieratingapplicationsecretkey';

const app = express();
const router = express.Router();
...
```

The preceding code is enough to get us started. We will need
JwtStrategy from passport.js, and ExtractJwT will be used to extract the payload
data in the jwt token.

We have also defined a variable to set the JWT auth settings, which has a secret key
configured. This secret key will be used to sign the payloads of any requests.

You can also create a separate file to store your important keys.

Using the JWT strategy

Now we are all set up to use the services provided by passport.js. Let's quickly recap
what we have done so far:

1. Installed passport, passport-jwt, and jsonwebtoken
2. Configured all settings for these three packages

The next steps are as follows:

1. Creating our user model
2. Creating API endpoints for the user entity, that is, sign in and sign up
3. Building our authentication views, that is, the login page and register page
4. Using the JWT strategy to finally authenticate the requests

Setting up user registration

Let's start with adding the functionality to sign up users to our app.

Creating a User model

We don't have a collection yet to manage the users. We will have three parameters in our User model: name, email, and password. Let's go ahead and create our User model called User.js in the models directory:

```
const mongoose = require('mongoose');

const Schema = mongoose.Schema;
const UserSchema = new Schema({
  name: String,
  email: String,
  password: String,
});

const User = mongoose.model('User', UserSchema);
module.exports = User;
```

As you can see, the following are the three attributes for the user: name, email, and password.

Installing bcryptjs

Now, we cannot save these user's passwords in plain text, so we will need a mechanism to encrypt them. Fortunately, we already have a package designed to encrypt passwords, which is bcryptjs. Let's first add this package to our application:

```
$ npm install bcryptjs --save
```

When the package is installed, let's add the initialization block in the User.js model:

```
const mongoose = require('mongoose');
const bcryptjs = require('bcryptjs');

const Schema = mongoose.Schema;
const UserSchema = new Schema({
  name: String,
  email: String,
  password: String,
});

const User = mongoose.model('User', UserSchema);
module.exports = User;
```

Now, when we save a user, we should create our own method to add users to the database, as we want to encrypt their passwords. So, let's add the following code to `models/User.js`:

```
...
const User = mongoose.model('User', UserSchema);
module.exports = User;

module.exports.createUser = (newUser, callback) => {
  bcryptjs.genSalt(10, (err, salt) => {
    bcryptjs.hash(newUser.password, salt, (error, hash) => {
      // store the hashed password
      const newUserResource = newUser;
      newUserResource.password = hash;
      newUserResource.save(callback);
    });
  });
};
...
```

In the preceding code, we have used the `bcrypt` library, which uses a `genSalt` mechanism to convert a password into an encrypted string. The preceding method—`createUser`—in the `User` model takes the `user` object, converts the user-provided password into a bcrypted password, and then saves it to the database.

Adding API endpoint to register a user

Now that we have our model ready, let's move on to creating an endpoint to create a user. For that, let's first create a controller called `users.js` in the `controllers` folder to manage all user related requests. Since we have added a code block to initialize all the files inside the `controllers` directory in `server.js`, we do not need to require those files here.

In `users.js`, replace the file's contents with the following code:

```
const User = require('../models/User.js');

module.exports.controller = (app) => {
  // register a user
  app.post('/users/register', (req, res) => {
    const name = req.body.name;
    const email = req.body.email;
    const password = req.body.password;
    const newUser = new User({
```

```
        name,
        email,
        password,
    });
    User.createUser(newUser, (error, user) => {
        if (error) { console.log(error); }
        res.send({ user });
    });
  });
};
```

In the preceding code, we have added an endpoint, that makes a POST request to the `http://localhost:8081/users/register` URL, takes the `name`, `email`, and `password` of the user, and saves them to our database. In the response, it returns the user that was just created. It's quite simple.

Now, let's test this endpoint in Postman. You should be able to see the user returned in the response:

Creating a register view page

Let's add a view page for the users to sign up. For that, we will need to create a form that takes the `name`, `email`, and `password` parameters. Create a file called `Register.vue` inside `src/components`:

```
<template>
  <v-form v-model="valid" ref="form" lazy-validation>
    <v-text-field
      label="Name"
      v-model="name"
      required
    ></v-text-field>
    <v-text-field
      label="Email"
      v-model="email"
      :rules="emailRules"
      required
    ></v-text-field>
    <v-text-field
      label="Password"
      v-model="password"
      required
    ></v-text-field>
    <v-text-field
      name="input-7-1"
      label="Confirm Password"
      v-model="confirm_password"
    ></v-text-field>
    <v-btn
      @click="submit"
      :disabled="!valid"
    >
      submit
    </v-btn>
    <v-btn @click="clear">clear</v-btn>
  </v-form>
</template>
```

The `vue` file is a simple template file that contains the form components. The next step is to add a route for that file.

In `src/router/index.js`, add the following lines of code:

```
import Vue from 'vue';
import Router from 'vue-router';
import Home from '@/components/Home';
import Contact from '@/components/Contact';
import AddMovie from '@/components/AddMovie';
import Movie from '@/components/Movie';
import Register from '@/components/Register';

Vue.use(Router);

export default new Router({
  mode: 'history',
  routes: [
    {
      path: '/',
      name: 'Home',
      component: Home,
    },
    {
      path: '/contact',
      name: 'Contact',
      component: Contact,
    },
    {
      path: '/movies/add',
      name: 'AddMovie',
      component: AddMovie,
    },
    {
      path: '/movies/:id',
      name: 'Movie',
      component: Movie,
    },
    {
      path: '/users/register',
      name: 'Register',
      component: Register,
    },
  ],
});
```

That's it! Now, let's navigate to `http://localhost.com:8080/users/register`:

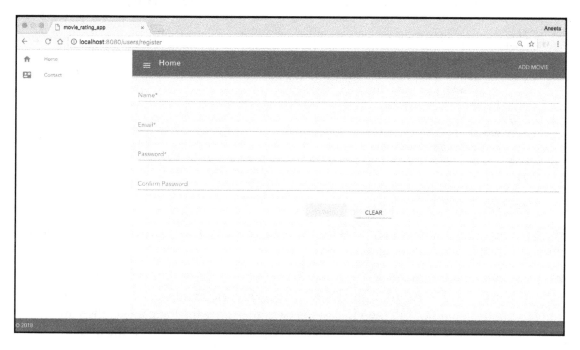

Adding submit and clear methods in the register form

The next step is to add functionality to the `submit` and `clear` methods. Let's add some methods to `Register.vue`:

```
...
    <v-btn @click="clear">clear</v-btn>
  </v-form>
</template>
<script>
export default {
  data: () => ({
    valid: true,
    name: '',
    email: '',
    password: '',
    confirm_password: '',
    emailRules: [
```

```
          v => !!v || 'E-mail is required',
          v => /\S+@\S+\.\S+/.test(v) || 'E-mail must be valid',
      ],
    }),
    methods: {
      async submit() {
        if (this.$refs.form.validate()) {
          // add process here
        }
      },
      clear() {
        this.$refs.form.reset();
      },
    },
  };
</script>
```

We have also added some validations for the registration form here. It validates the email provided by the user according to the given regex.

We have added two methods, submit and clear. The clear method resets the form values; pretty straightforward, right? Now, when we click on the submit button, the validations are run first. If all the validations pass, then only the logic inside the submit method is processed. Here, we need to make a request to the server with the user parameters where axios comes into play.

Introducing axios

The axios is a mechanism to send request data to the server. You can think of it as an AJAX request in JavaScript. With axios, we can handle success and error responses from the server effectively.

To install axios, run the following command:

```
$ npm install axios --save
```

Using axios

Now, let's modify our Register.vue file to implement axios—replace the content inside the script tag as follows:

```
...
</v-form>
```

```
</template>
<script>
import axios from 'axios';

export default {
  data: () => ({
    valid: true,
    name: '',
    email: '',
    password: '',
    confirm_password: '',
    emailRules: [
      v => !!v || 'E-mail is required',
      v => /\S+@\S+\.\S+/.test(v) || 'E-mail must be valid',
    ],
  }),
  methods: {
    async submit() {
      if (this.$refs.form.validate()) {
        return axios({
          method: 'post',
          data: {
            name: this.name,
            email: this.email,
            password: this.password,
          },
          url: 'http://localhost:8081/users/register',
          headers: {
            'Content-Type': 'application/json',
          },
        })
          .then(() => {
            this.$swal(
              'Great!',
              'You have been successfully registered!',
              'success',
            );
            this.$router.push({ name: 'Login' });
          })
          .catch((error) => {
            const message = error.response.data.message;
            this.$swal('Oh oo!', `${message}`, 'error');
          });
      }
      return true;
    },
    clear() {
      this.$refs.form.reset();
```

```
      },
    },
  };
  </script>
```

If you are familiar with `ajax`, you should be able to quickly understand the code. If not, don't worry, it's actually quite simple. The `axios` method takes important parameters, such as the `request` method (in preceding case, `post`), the data parameters or the payloads, and a URL endpoint to hit. It takes these parameters and routes them to either the `then()` method or `catch()` method depending on the server's response.

If the request is successful, it goes to the `then()` method; if not, it goes to the `catch()` method. Now, the success and failure of the requests are also customizable according to our needs. For the preceding scenario, we will simply pass an error response if the `user` is not saved to the database. We can also do it for the validations.

So, let's also modify `users.js` inside the `controller` method to accommodate these changes:

```
const User = require('../models/User.js');

module.exports.controller = (app) => {
  // register a user
  app.post('/users/register', (req, res) => {
    const name = req.body.name;
    const email = req.body.email;
    const password = req.body.password;
    const newUser = new User({
      name,
      email,
      password,
    });
    User.createUser(newUser, (error, user) => {
      if (error) {
        res.status(422).json({
          message: 'Something went wrong. Please try again after some
time!',
        });
      }
      res.send({ user });
    });
  });
};
```

As you can see in the preceding code, if there is a failure in the request, we will send a message saying `Something went wrong`. We can also display different types of message depending on the server's response.

Setting up the user login

Now that we have successfully implemented the login process for a user, let's start building the functionality to log users in to our app.

Modifying the User model

To log in users to the app, we will take the following two parameters: the user's email and their password. We will need to query the database to find the record with their given email; so, let's add a method that will extract the user according to the username:

```
...
const User = mongoose.model('User', UserSchema);
module.exports = User;

module.exports.createUser = (newUser, callback) => {
  bcryptjs.genSalt(10, (err, salt) => {
    bcryptjs.hash(newUser.password, salt, (error, hash) => {
      // store the hashed password
      const newUserResource = newUser;
      newUserResource.password = hash;
      newUserResource.save(callback);
    });
  });
};

module.exports.getUserByEmail = (email, callback) => {
  const query = { email };
  User.findOne(query, callback);
};
```

The preceding method will return the user that has the given email.

As I mentioned, another thing that we will need to check is the password. Let's add method that compares the password provided by the user while logging in to the password that is saved in our database:

```
...
module.exports.getUserByEmail = (email, callback) => {
  const query = { email };
  User.findOne(query, callback);
};

module.exports.comparePassword = (candidatePassword, hash, callback) => {
  bcryptjs.compare(candidatePassword, hash, (err, isMatch) => {
    if (err) throw err;
    callback(null, isMatch);
  });
};
```

The preceding method takes both user-provided password and the saved password and returns `true` or `false` depending on whether the passwords match or not.

Now we are all set to jump into the controller part.

Adding an API endpoint to log a user in

We have added the methods required for a user to be able to log in. Now, the most important part of this chapter lies here. We need to set up the JWT `auth` mechanism to enable a user to log in.

In `users.js`, add the following lines of code:

```
const User = require('../models/User.js');

const passportJWT = require('passport-jwt');
const jwt = require('jsonwebtoken');

const ExtractJwt = passportJWT.ExtractJwt;
const jwtOptions = {};
jwtOptions.jwtFromRequest = ExtractJwt.fromAuthHeaderWithScheme('jwt');
jwtOptions.secretOrKey = 'thisisthesecretkey';

module.exports.controller = (app) => {
  // register a user
  app.post('/users/register', (req, res) => {
    const name = req.body.name;
    const email = req.body.email;
```

```
      const password = req.body.password;
      const newUser = new User({
        name,
        email,
        password,
      });
      User.createUser(newUser, (error, user) => {
        if (error) {
          res.status(422).json({
            message: 'Something went wrong. Please try again after some
time!',
          });
        }
        res.send({ user });
      });
    });

  // login a user
  app.post('/users/login', (req, res) => {
    if (req.body.email && req.body.password) {
      const email = req.body.email;
      const password = req.body.password;
      User.getUserByEmail(email, (err, user) => {
        if (!user) {
          res.status(404).json({ message: 'The user does not exist!' });
        } else {
          User.comparePassword(password, user.password, (error, isMatch) =>
{
            if (error) throw error;
            if (isMatch) {
              const payload = { id: user.id };
              const token = jwt.sign(payload, jwtOptions.secretOrKey);
              res.json({ message: 'ok', token });
            } else {
              res.status(401).json({ message: 'The password is incorrect!'
});
            }
          });
        }
      });
    }
  });
};
```

Since the JWT strategy is a part of `passport.js`, we will need to initialize that as well. We also need to add some configurations for JWT options to extract the data from the payload, and unencrypt it and then encrypt it again when a request is made to the server.

The secret key is something that you can configure. It basically represents the token of your app. Ensure that it is not easily guessable.

Also, we have added an endpoint, which makes a POST request to `localhost:8081/users/login` and takes the user's email and password. The following are a couple of things that this method does:

- Checks whether the user with the given email exists. If it does not exist, it sends a status code of 404, stating that the user does not exist in our app.
- Compares the provided password with our user's password in the app. If there is no match, it sends an error response stating that passwords do not match.
- If everything goes fine, it signs the user's payload with the JWT signature, generates a token, and responds with that token.

Now, let's test this endpoint in Postman. You should be able to see the token returned in the response, as follows:

In the preceding screenshot, note that JWT takes the payload, signs it, and generates a random token.

Creating a register view page

Let's add a view page for the users to log in now. For that, like we did on the register page, we will need to create a form that takes the email and password parameters. Create a file called `Login.vue` inside `src/components`, as follows:

```
<template>
  <v-form v-model="valid" ref="form" lazy-validation>
    <v-text-field
      label="Email"
      v-model="email"
      :rules="emailRules"
      required
    ></v-text-field>
    <v-text-field
      label="Password"
      v-model="password"
      required
    ></v-text-field>
    <v-btn
      @click="submit"
      :disabled="!valid"
    >
      submit
    </v-btn>
    <v-btn @click="clear">clear</v-btn>
  </v-form>
</template>
```

The `vue` file is a simple template file that contains the form components. The next thing to do is to add a route for that file.

In `src/router/index.js`, add the following code:

```
import Vue from 'vue';
import Router from 'vue-router';
import Home from '@/components/Home';
import Contact from '@/components/Contact';
import AddMovie from '@/components/AddMovie';
import Movie from '@/components/Movie';
import Register from '@/components/Register';
import Login from '@/components/Login';
```

```
Vue.use(Router);

export default new Router({
  mode: 'history',
  routes: [
    {
      path: '/',
      name: 'Home',
      component: Home,
    },
    {
      path: '/contact',
      name: 'Contact',
      component: Contact,
    },
    {
      path: '/movies/add',
      name: 'AddMovie',
      component: AddMovie,
    },
    {
      path: '/movies/:id',
      name: 'Movie',
      component: Movie,
    },
    {
      path: '/users/register',
      name: 'Register',
      component: Register,
    },
    {
      path: '/users/login',
      name: 'Login',
      component: Login,
    },
  ],
});
```

That's it. Now, let's navigate to `http://localhost.com:8080/users/login`:

Adding submit and clear methods to the login form

The next step is to add functionality in the `submit` and `clear` methods. Let's add some methods to `Login.vue`. The `clear` method is the same as on the register page. For the `submit` method, we will use the `axios` method here. We have already categorized our success and error messages in the controller. Now we just need to make sure that they are displayed in the UI:

```
    ...
    </v-form>
    </template>
    <script>
    import axios from 'axios';

    export default {
      data: () => ({
        valid: true,
```

```
          email: '',
          password: '',
          emailRules: [
            v => !!v || 'E-mail is required',
            v => /\S+@\S+\.\S+/.test(v) || 'E-mail must be valid',
          ],
        }),
      methods: {
        async submit() {
          return axios({
            method: 'post',
            data: {
              email: this.email,
              password: this.password,
            },
            url: 'http://localhost:8081/users/login',
            headers: {
              'Content-Type': 'application/json',
            },
          })
            .then((response) => {
              window.localStorage.setItem('auth', response.data.token);
              this.$swal('Great!', 'You are ready to start!', 'success');
              this.$router.push({ name: 'Home' });
            })
            .catch((error) => {
              const message = error.response.data.message;
              this.$swal('Oh oo!', `${message}`, 'error');
              this.$router.push({ name: 'Login' });
            });
        },
        clear() {
          this.$refs.form.reset();
        },
      },
    };
</script>
```

The validations are the same as on the register page. We have added two methods, submit and clear. The clear method resets the form values, and the submit method simply hits the API endpoint, taking the parameter from the form, and responds with the correct message, which is then displayed in the UI. Upon successful completion, the user will be redirected to the home page.

The important part here is that since we are interacting on the client side, we will need the previously generated JWT token to be saved somewhere. The best way to access the token is by saving it to the browser's session. So, we have set a key called `auth`, which saves the JWT token in the local storage. Whenever any other requests are made, the request will first check whether it is a valid token or not and perform the action accordingly.

The following is what we have done so far:

- Added `getUserByEmail()` and `comparePassword()` to the Users model
- Created a login view page
- Added methods to be able to submit and clear the form
- Generated a JWT signed token and saved it to the session for reuse later
- Displayed success and error messages

Authenticating our user in Home.vue

The last thing we need to do is check whether the current logged in user is authorized to view the movie listing page or not. Although it makes sense to make the home page (movie listing page) accessible to all users, for learning purpose, let's add JWT authorization when a user goes to the home page. Let's make the home page not accessible to the outside users who are not in our app.

In `movies.js`, add the following piece of code:

```
const MovieSchema = require('../models/Movie.js');
const Rating = require('../models/Rating.js');
const passport = require('passport');

module.exports.controller = (app) => {
  // fetch all movies
  app.get('/movies', passport.authenticate('jwt', { session: false }),
(req, res) => {
    MovieSchema.find({}, 'name description release_year genre', (error,
movies) => {
      if (error) { console.log(error); }
      res.send({
        movies,
      });
    });
  });
...
```

Yup, that's it! We will need to initialize passport and just add `passport.authenticate('jwt', { session: false })`. We have to pass the JWT token and the passport JWT strategy automatically authenticates the current user.

Now, let's also send the JWT token while making a request to the movie listing page. In `Home.vue`, add the following code:

```
...
<script>
import axios from 'axios';

export default {
  name: 'Movies',
  data() {
    return {
      movies: [],
    };
  },
  mounted() {
    this.fetchMovies();
  },
  methods: {
    async fetchMovies() {
      const token = window.localStorage.getItem('auth');
      return axios({
        method: 'get',
        url: 'http://localhost:8081/movies',
        headers: {
          Authorization: `JWT ${token}`,
          'Content-Type': 'application/json',
        },
      })
        .then((response) => {
          this.movies = response.data.movies;
          this.current_user = response.data.current_user;
        })
        .catch(() => {
        });
    },
  },
};
</script>
```

While making the `axios` call, we will have to pass one extra parameter in the headers. We need to read the token from the local storage and pass it to the movies API through the headers.

With this, any user who is not logged in to the app will not be able to view the movie listing page.

Serving static files for Vue components

Before jumping into the Local Strategy, let's learn a little bit about how we can make our Vue.js components to be served statically. Since we are using a separate frontend and backend, it can be a daunting task to keep maintaining these two versions, and especially while deploying the app, it can take a lot longer to configure everything. So, to manage our app better, we will build the Vue.js app, which will be a production build, and use the Node.js server only to serve the files. For that, we will be using a separate package called serve-static. So, let's go ahead and install the package:

```
$ npm install serve-static --save
```

Now, let's add the following contents to our `server.js` file:

```
const express = require('express');
const bodyParser = require('body-parser');
const mongoose = require('mongoose');
const cors = require('cors');
const morgan = require('morgan');
const fs = require('fs');
const session = require('express-session');
const config = require('./config/Config');
const passport = require('passport');
const app = express();
const router = express.Router();
const serveStatic = require('serve-static');

app.use(morgan('combined'));
app.use(bodyParser.json());
app.use(cors());

...

// Include controllers
fs.readdirSync("controllers").forEach(function (file) {
  if(file.substr(-3) == ".js") {
    const route = require("./controllers/" + file)
```

```
        route.controller(app)
    }
})
app.use(serveStatic(__dirname + "/dist"));
...
```

With this, let's now build our application with the following command:

```
$ npm run build
```

The preceding command will create the necessary static files inside the dist folder in the application that will be served by the Node.js server, which is in the 8081 port. After the build, we now do not need to run the following command:

```
$ npm run dev
```

Also, now since we will be running our node server only, the application should be available at the URL http://localhost:8081.

The preceding command starts our frontend server. We only need to run the Node.js server with the following command:

```
$ nodemon server.js
```

Since we now only have one port, 8081, we do not need to add the prefix /api in every backend API like we did earlier, we can get rid of those as well. So, let's update the controllers and vue files as well:

Replace the contents in controllers/movies.js, as follows:

```
var Movie = require("../models/Movie");

module.exports.controller = (app) => {
  // fetch all movies
  app.get("/movies", function(req, res) {
    Movie.find({}, 'name description release_year genre', function
    (error, movies) {
      if (error) { console.log(error); }
      res.send({
        movies: movies
      })
    })
  })

  // add a new movie
  app.post('/movies', (req, res) => {
    const movie = new Movie({
```

```
      name: req.body.name,
      description: req.body.description,
      release_year: req.body.release_year,
      genre: req.body.genre
    })

    movie.save(function (error, movie) {
      if (error) { console.log(error); }
      res.send(movie)
    })
  })
}
```

Replace the contents in `controllers/users.js`, as follows:

```
const User = require("../models/User");
const config = require('./../config/Config');
const passport = require('passport');

module.exports.controller = (app) => {
  // local strategy
  const LocalStrategy = require('passport-local').Strategy;
  passport.use(new LocalStrategy({
      usernameField: 'email',
      passwordField: 'password'
    },
    function(email, password, done) {
      User.getUserByEmail(email, function(err, user){
        if (err) { return done(err); }
        if (!user) { return done(null, false); }
        User.comparePassword(password, user.password, function(err,
        isMatch){
          if(isMatch) {
            return done(null, user);
          } else {
            return done(null, false);
          }
        })
      });
    }
  ));

  app.post('/users/login',
    passport.authenticate('local', { failureRedirect: '/users/login' }),
    function(req, res) {
      res.redirect('/');
    });
```

```
passport.serializeUser(function(user, done) {
  done(null, user.id);
});

passport.deserializeUser(function(id, done) {
  User.findById(id, function(err, user){
    done(err, user)
  })
});

// register a user
app.post('/users/register', (req, res) => {
  const email = req.body.email;
  const fullname = req.body.fullname;
  const password = req.body.password;
  const role = req.body.role || 'user';
  const newUser = new User({
    email: email,
    fullname: fullname,
    role: role,
    password: password
  })
  User.createUser(newUser, function(error, user) {
    if (error) {
      res.status(422).json({
        message: "Something went wrong. Please try again after some
        time!"
      });
    }
    res.send({ user: user })
  })
})
}
```

Replace the contents of the script tag of AddMovie.vue with the following code:

```
<script>
import axios from 'axios';

export default {
  data: () => ({
    valid: true,
    name: '',
    description: '',
    genre: '',
    release_year: '',
    nameRules: [
      v => !!v || 'Movie name is required',
```

```
      ],
      genreRules: [
        v => !!v || 'Movie genre year is required',
        v => (v && v.length <= 80) || 'Genre must be less than equal to
        80 characters.',
      ],
      releaseRules: [
        v => !!v || 'Movie release year is required',
      ],
      select: null,
      years: [
        '2018',
        '2017',
        '2016',
        '2015',
      ],
    }),
    methods: {
      submit() {
        if (this.$refs.form.validate()) {
          return axios({
            method: 'post',
            data: {
              name: this.name,
              description: this.description,
              release_year: this.release_year,
              genre: this.genre,
            },
            url: '/movies',
            headers: {
              'Content-Type': 'application/json',
            },
          })
            .then(() => {
              this.$swal(
                'Great!',
                'Movie added successfully!',
                'success',
              );
              this.$router.push({ name: 'Home' });
              this.$refs.form.reset();
            })
            .catch(() => {
              this.$swal(
                'Oh oo!',
                'Could not add the movie!',
                'error',
              );
```

```
        });
      }
      return true;
    },
    clear() {
      this.$refs.form.reset();
    },
  },
};
</script>
```

Replace the contents of the `script` tag of `Home.vue` with the following code:

```
<script>
import axios from 'axios';

export default {
  name: 'Movies',
  data() {
    return {
      movies: [],
    };
  },
  mounted() {
    this.fetchMovies();
  },
  methods: {
    async fetchMovies() {
      return axios({
        method: 'get',
        url: '/movies',
      })
        .then((response) => {
          this.movies = response.data.movies;
        })
        .catch(() => {
        });
    },
  },
};
</script>
```

Replace the contents of the `script` tag of `Login.vue` with the following code:

```
<script>
  import axios from 'axios';
  import bus from "./../bus.js";

  export default {
    data: () => ({
      valid: true,
      email: '',
      password: '',
      emailRules: [
        (v) => !!v || 'E-mail is required',
        (v) => /^\w+([\.-]?\w+)*@\w+([\.-]?\w+)*(\.\w{2,3})+$/.test(v)
        || 'E-mail must be valid'
      ],
      passwordRules: [
        (v) => !!v || 'Password is required',
      ]
    }),
    methods: {
      async submit () {
        if (this.$refs.form.validate()) {
          return axios({
            method: 'post',
            data: {
              email: this.email,
              password: this.password
            },
            url: '/users/login',
            headers: {
              'Content-Type': 'application/json'
            }
          })
          .then((response) => {
            localStorage.setItem('jwtToken', response.data.token)
            this.$swal("Good job!", "You are ready to start!",
            "success");
            bus.$emit("refreshUser");
            this.$router.push({ name: 'Home' });
          })
          .catch((error) => {
            const message = error.response.data.message;
            this.$swal("Oh oo!", `${message}`, "error")
          });
        }
      },
    },
```

```
        clear () {
          this.$refs.form.reset ()
        }
      }
    }
  }
</script>
```

Replace the contents of the script tag of Register.vue with the following code:

```
<script>
  import axios from 'axios';
  export default {
    data: () => ({
      e1: false,
      valid: true,
      fullname: '',
      email: '',
      password: '',
      confirm_password: '',
      fullnameRules: [
        (v) => !!v || 'Fullname is required'
      ],
      emailRules: [
        (v) => !!v || 'E-mail is required',
        (v) => /^\w+([\.-]?\w+)*@\w+([\.-]?\w+)*(\.\w{2,3})+$/.test(v)
        || 'E-mail must be valid'
      ],
      passwordRules: [
        (v) => !!v || 'Password is required'
      ]
    }),
    methods: {
      async submit () {
        if (this.$refs.form.validate()) {
          return axios({
            method: 'post',
            data: {
              fullname: this.fullname,
              email: this.email,
              password: this.password
            },
            url: '/users/register',
            headers: {
              'Content-Type': 'application/json'
            }
          })
          .then((response) => {
            this.$swal(
```

```
                'Great!',
                `You have been successfully registered!`,
                'success'
              )
              this.$router.push({ name: 'Home' })
            })
            .catch((error) => {
              const message = error.response.data.message;
              this.$swal("Oh oo!", `${message}`, "error")
            });
        }
      },
      clear () {
        this.$refs.form.reset()
      }
    }
  }
</script>
```

Finally, we don't need to use the proxy anymore, so we can remove the proxy we set up earlier from `webpack.dev.conf.js`.

Replace the contents inside `devServer` with the following code:

```
devServer: {
    clientLogLevel: 'warning',
    historyApiFallback: {
      rewrites: [
        { from: /.*/, to: path.posix.join(config.dev.assetsPublicPath,
        'index.html') },
      ],
    },
    hot: true,
    contentBase: false, // since we use CopyWebpackPlugin.
    compress: true,
    host: HOST || config.dev.host,
    port: PORT || config.dev.port,
    open: config.dev.autoOpenBrowser,
    overlay: config.dev.errorOverlay
      ? { warnings: false, errors: true }
      : false,
    publicPath: config.dev.assetsPublicPath,
    quiet: true, // necessary for FriendlyErrorsPlugin
    watchOptions: {
      poll: config.dev.poll,
    }
  },
```

With these updated, let's build our application once more with the following command:

```
$ npm run build
```

Our application should work as expected.

Since our application is a **Single Page Application (SPA)**, when we browse through the nested routes and reload the page, we will get an error. For example, if we browse the http://localhost:8081/contact page by clicking the link in the home page, it will work. However, if we try to navigate to the http://localhost:8081/contact page directly, we will get an error because this is an SPA, which means that the browser only renders the static index.html file. When we try to access the /contact page, it will look for the page called contact, which does not exist.

For this, we will need to add a middleware, which acts as a fallback and renders the same index.html file when we try to reload the page directly or try to access the pages with dynamic IDs.

There is a middleware provided by npm to serve our purpose. Let's go ahead and install the following package:

```
$ npm install connect-history-api-fallback --save
```

After the installation, let's modify our server.js file to use the middleware:

```
...
const passport = require('passport');
const serveStatic = require('serve-static');
const history = require('connect-history-api-fallback');
const app = express();
const router = express.Router();

...

// Include controllers
fs.readdirSync("controllers").forEach(function (file) {
  if(file.substr(-3) == ".js") {
    const route = require("./controllers/" + file)
    route.controller(app)
  }
})
app.use(history());
app.use(serveStatic(__dirname + "/dist"));
...
```

With these in place, we should now be able to access all the routes directly. We can also reload the pages now.

 Since we are building our Vue.js components and running our app solely on the Node.js server, whenever we make a change to the Vue.js components, we will need to build the application again with the `npm run build` command.

Passport's Local Strategy

Passport's Local Strategy is easy to integrate. As always, let's start with the installation of this strategy as follows.

Installing Passport's Local Strategy

We can install passport's Local Strategy by running the following command:

```
$ npm install passport-local --save
```

The following code should add the package to your package.json file:

```
...
"node-sass": "^4.7.2",
"nodemon": "^1.14.10",
"passport": "^0.4.0",
"passport-local": "^1.0.0",
...
```

Configuring Passport's Local Strategy

There are a few steps to configure the Passport's Local Strategy. We will discuss each step in detail:

1. Add necessary routes for Local authentication.
2. Add a middleware method to check whether authentication is successful.

Let's dive into the details for each of the preceding steps.

Adding necessary routes for Local Authentication

Let's go ahead and add the necessary routes when we click on the login button. Replace the contents of `controllers/users.js` with the following code:

```js
const User = require('../models/User.js');
const passport = require('passport');
const LocalStrategy = require('passport-local').Strategy;

module.exports.controller = (app) => {
// local strategy
  passport.use(new LocalStrategy({
    usernameField: 'email',
    passwordField: 'password',
  }, (email, password, done) => {
    User.getUserByEmail(email, (err, user) => {
      if (err) { return done(err); }
      if (!user) { return done(null, false); }
      User.comparePassword(password, user.password, (error, isMatch) => {
        if (isMatch) {
          return done(null, user);
        }
        return done(null, false);
      });
      return true;
    });
  }));

// user login
  app.post('/users/login',
    passport.authenticate('local', { failureRedirect: '/users/login' }),
    (req, res) => {
      res.redirect('/');
    });

  passport.serializeUser((user, done) => {
    done(null, user.id);
  });

  passport.deserializeUser((id, done) => {
    User.findById(id, (err, user) => {
      done(err, user);
    });
  });
```

```
    // register a user
    app.post('/users/register', (req, res) => {
      const name = req.body.name;
      const email = req.body.email;
      const password = req.body.password;
      const newUser = new User({
        name,
        email,
        password,
      });
      User.createUser(newUser, (error, user) => {
        if (error) {
          res.status(422).json({
            message: 'Something went wrong. Please try again after some
    time!',
          });
        }
        res.send({ user });
      });
    });
  };
```

Here, we have added a route for users login as `/users/login` which then uses `passport.js` local authentication mechanism to log in the user to the app.

Also, we configured `passport.js` to use LocalStrategy when user logs in which takes the `username` and `password` of the user.

Installing express-session

The next thing we need to do is setup a `session` so that when a user successfully logs in, the `user` data can be stored in the `session` and can be retrieved easily when we make other requests. For this, we need to add a package called `express-session`. Let's go ahead and install the package with the following command:

```
$ npm install express-session --save
```

Configuring express-session

Now, that we have the package, let's configure this package to fulfill our needs to save the user in the `session`. Add the following lines of code in it.

If `username` and `password` matches, the user object is saved in the session in the server and can be access via `req.user` in every request.

Also, let's updated our vue files as well since we do not need the passport JWT strategy now.

Update the contents in `server.js` with the following code:

```
const express = require('express');
const bodyParser = require('body-parser');
const mongoose = require('mongoose');
const cors = require('cors');
const morgan = require('morgan');
const fs = require('fs');
const session = require('express-session');
const config = require('./config/Config');
const passport = require('passport');
const serveStatic = require('serve-static');
const history = require('connect-history-api-fallback');

const app = express();
const router = express.Router();
app.use(morgan('combined'));
app.use(bodyParser.json());
app.use(cors());

app.use(session({
  secret: config.SECRET,
  resave: true,
  saveUninitialized: true,
  cookie: { httpOnly: false }
}))
app.use(passport.initialize());
app.use(passport.session());

//connect to mongodb
mongoose.connect(config.DB, function() {
  console.log('Connection has been made');
})
.catch(err => {
  console.error('App starting error:', err.stack);
  process.exit(1);
});

// Include controllers
fs.readdirSync("controllers").forEach(function (file) {
  if(file.substr(-3) == '.js') {
```

```
        const route = require('./controllers/' + file);
        route.controller(app);
    }
})
app.use(history());
app.use(serveStatic(__dirname + "/dist"));

router.get('/api/current_user', isLoggedIn, function(req, res) {
    if(req.user) {
        res.send({ current_user: req.user })
    } else {
        res.status(403).send({ success: false, msg: 'Unauthorized.' });
    }
})

function isLoggedIn(req, res, next) {
    if (req.isAuthenticated())
        return next();

    res.redirect('/');
    console.log('error! auth failed')
}

router.get('/api/logout', function(req, res){
    req.logout();
    res.send();
});

router.get('/', function(req, res) {
    res.json({ message: 'API Initialized!'});
});

const port = process.env.API_PORT || 8081;
app.use('/', router);
var server = app.listen(port, function() {
    console.log(`api running on port ${port}`);
});

module.exports = server
```

Here, we added the configuration for express-session with the following code block:

```
app.use(session({
    secret: config.SECRET,
    resave: true,
    saveUninitialized: true,
    cookie: { httpOnly: false }
}))
```

```
app.use(passport.initialize());
app.use(passport.session());
```

The above code blocks uses a secret token required to save the user details. We will be defining the token in a separate file so that all of our configuration token reside in a single place.

So, let's go ahead and create a file called `Config.js` inside the `config` directory and the following lines of code:

```
module.exports = {
  DB: 'mongodb://localhost/movie_rating_app',
  SECRET: 'movieratingappsecretkey'
}
```

We also added a GET route called `/api/current_user` to fetch the current logged in user details. This api uses a middleware method called `isLoggedIn` which checks if the user's data is on the session or not. And if the user's data exists in the session, the current user details is sent back as the response.

Another endpoint which we added is the `/logout` which simply logs out the user and destroys the session.

Hence, with this configuration, now we should be able to log in successfully using the `passport.js` Local Strategy.

The only problem that we have now is there is no way to know if the user successfully logged in or not. For that we need to display some user's information such as `email` to indicate the logged in user.

For this, we need to pass the user's information from `Login.vue` to `App.vue` so that we can display the user's email in the top bar. We can use a method called `emit` provided by `Vue` which is used to pass the information between the `Vue` components. Let's go ahead and configure that.

Configuring emit method

Let's first create a transmitter which can communicate between the different Vue components. Create a file called `bus.js` inside `src` directory and add the following contents:

```
import Vue from 'vue';
```

```
const bus = new Vue();

export default bus;
```

Now, replace the contents inside `script` tag of `Login.vue` with the following code:

```
...
<script>
import axios from 'axios';
import bus from './../bus';

export default {
  data: () => ({
    valid: true,
    email: '',
    password: '',
    emailRules: [
      v => !!v || 'E-mail is required',
      v => /\S+@\S+\.\S+/.test(v) || 'E-mail must be valid',
    ],
  }),
  methods: {
    async submit() {
      return axios({
        method: 'post',
        data: {
          email: this.email,
          password: this.password,
        },
        url: 'http://localhost:8081/users/login',
        headers: {
          'Content-Type': 'application/json',
        },
      })
        .then(() => {
          this.$swal('Great!', 'You are ready to start!', 'success');
          bus.$emit('refreshUser');
          this.$router.push({ name: 'Home' });
        })
        .catch((error) => {
          const message = error.response.data.message;
          this.$swal('Oh oo!', `${message}`, 'error');
          this.$router.push({ name: 'Login' });
        });
    },
    clear() {
      this.$refs.form.reset();
    },
```

```
    },
  };
</script>
```

Here we are emitting a method called `refreshUser` which will be defined in the App.vue. Replace the contents inside `App.vue` with the following code:

```
<template>
  <v-app id="inspire">
    <v-navigation-drawer
      fixed
      v-model="drawer"
      app
    >
      <v-list dense>
        <router-link v-bind:to="{ name: 'Home' }" class="side_bar_link">
          <v-list-tile>
            <v-list-tile-action>
              <v-icon>home</v-icon>
            </v-list-tile-action>
            <v-list-tile-content>Home</v-list-tile-content>
          </v-list-tile>
        </router-link>
        <router-link v-bind:to="{ name: 'Contact' }" class="side_bar_link">
          <v-list-tile>
            <v-list-tile-action>
              <v-icon>contact_mail</v-icon>
            </v-list-tile-action>
            <v-list-tile-content>Contact</v-list-tile-content>
          </v-list-tile>
        </router-link>
      </v-list>
    </v-navigation-drawer>
    <v-toolbar color="indigo" dark fixed app>
      <v-toolbar-side-icon @click.stop="drawer = !drawer"></v-toolbar-side-icon>
      <v-toolbar-title>Home</v-toolbar-title>
      <v-spacer></v-spacer>
      <v-toolbar-items class="hidden-sm-and-down">
        <v-btn id="add_movie_link" flat v-bind:to="{ name: 'AddMovie' }"
          v-if="current_user">
          Add Movie
        </v-btn>
        <v-btn id="user_email" flat v-if="current_user">{{
current_user.email }}</v-btn>
        <v-btn flat v-bind:to="{ name: 'Register' }" v-if="!current_user"
id="register_btn">
```

```
          Register
        </v-btn>
        <v-btn flat v-bind:to="{ name: 'Login' }" v-if="!current_user"
id="login_btn">Login</v-btn>
        <v-btn id="logout_btn" flat v-if="current_user"
@click="logout">Logout</v-btn>
      </v-toolbar-items>
    </v-toolbar>
    <v-content>
      <v-container fluid>
        <div id="app">
          <router-view/>
        </div>
      </v-container>
    </v-content>
    <v-footer color="indigo" app>
      <span class="white--text">&copy; 2018</span>
    </v-footer>
  </v-app>
</template>

<script>
import axios from 'axios';

import './assets/stylesheets/main.css';
import bus from './bus';

export default {
  data: () => ({
    drawer: null,
    current_user: null,
  }),
  props: {
    source: String,
  },
  mounted() {
    this.fetchUser();
    this.listenToEvents();
  },
  methods: {
    listenToEvents() {
      bus.$on('refreshUser', () => {
        this.fetchUser();
      });
    },
    async fetchUser() {
      return axios({
        method: 'get',
```

```
        url: '/api/current_user',
    })
      .then((response) => {
        this.current_user = response.data.current_user;
      })
      .catch(() => {
      });
  },
  logout() {
    return axios({
      method: 'get',
      url: '/api/logout',
    })
      .then(() => {
        bus.$emit('refreshUser');
        this.$router.push({ name: 'Home' });
      })
      .catch(() => {
      });
  },
  },
};
</script>
```

Here we have added the method called refreshUser which is being listened by App.vue in the mounted method. Whenever a user logs in to the app, the method called refreshUser in App.vue gets called and fetches the logged in user's information.

Also, we are displaying the user's email in the top bar so that we can know if the user is logged in or not.

Also, let's remove the JWT authentication from movies controller as well. Replace the contents in controllers/movies.js with the following code:

```
const MovieSchema = require('../models/Movie.js');
const Rating = require('../models/Rating.js');

module.exports.controller = (app) => {
  // fetch all movies
  app.get('/movies', (req, res) => {
    MovieSchema.find({}, 'name description release_year genre', (error,
movies) => {
        if (error) { console.log(error); }
        res.send({
          movies,
        });
    });
```

```
  });

  // fetch a single movie
  app.get('/api/movies/:id', (req, res) => {
    MovieSchema.findById(req.params.id, 'name description release_year
genre', (error, movie) => {
      if (error) { console.error(error); }
      res.send(movie);
    });
  });

  // rate a movie
  app.post('/movies/rate/:id', (req, res) => {
    const newRating = new Rating({
      movie_id: req.params.id,
      user_id: req.body.user_id,
      rate: req.body.rate,
    });

    newRating.save((error, rating) => {
      if (error) { console.log(error); }
      res.send({
        movie_id: rating.movie_id,
        user_id: rating.user_id,
        rate: rating.rate,
      });
    });
  });

  // add a new movie
  app.post('/movies', (req, res) => {
    const newMovie = new MovieSchema({
      name: req.body.name,
      description: req.body.description,
      release_year: req.body.release_year,
      genre: req.body.genre,
    });

    newMovie.save((error, movie) => {
      if (error) { console.log(error); }
      res.send(movie);
    });
  });
};
```

With this, we should be able to view the following screen when a user logs in to the app:

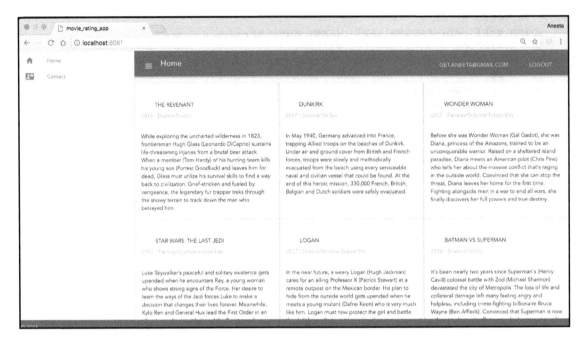

Summary

In this chapter, we covered `passport.js` and how it works. We also covered how to use a simple JWT strategy with a MEVN application and handle register and login for users.

In the next chapter, we will dig into different `passport.js` strategies, such as the Facebook strategy, the Google strategy, and the Twitter strategy.

7
Building OAuth Strategies with passport.js

In the preceding chapter, we discussed the passport-JWT strategy. We discussed how to leverage the JWT package to build a robust user on-boarding process. We covered how to implement the signup and sign-in process for a user. In this chapter, we will dive into the following parts:

- `passport.js` Facebook Strategy
- `passport.js` Twitter Strategy
- `passport.js` Google Strategy
- `passport.js` LinkedIn Strategy

All these parts individually consume a lot of time if we set out to do them from scratch. `passport.js` provides a simpler way to integrate all these strategies in a very flexible way, and also makes them easier to implement.

OAuth is an authentication protocol that lets users log in via different external services. For example, logging in to an application via Facebook or Twitter does not require a user to provide their username and password if the user is already logged in to Facebook or Twitter. It saves the user from setting up a new account in an application, which makes the login process smooth. This makes logging in to an app easier; otherwise, a user first needs to register to our application and then log in using those credentials. Passport's OAuth strategies allow users to log in to our application with a single click if the browser remembers the account. Everything else is done automatically and is handled by the strategy itself.

Passport's Facebook Strategy

Passport's Facebook Strategy is easy to integrate. As always, let's start with the installation of this strategy.

Installing Passport's Facebook Strategy

We can install passport's Facebook Strategy by running the following command:

```
$ npm install passport-facebook --save
```

The following code should add the package to your `package.json` file:

```
...
"node-sass": "^4.7.2",
"nodemon": "^1.14.10",
"passport": "^0.4.0",
"passport-facebook": "^2.1.1",
...
```

Configuring Passport's Facebook Strategy

There are a few steps to configure the Passport's Facebook Strategy. We will discuss each step in detail:

1. Create and set up a Facebook app. This will provide us with an `App ID` and an `App Secret`.
2. Add a button to our login page that allows our users to log in via Facebook.
3. Add the necessary routes for Facebook authentication.
4. Add a middleware method to check whether authentication is successful.

Let's dive into the details for each of the preceding steps.

Creating and setting up a Facebook app

To be able to use the Facebook Strategy, you have to build a Facebook application first. The developers, portal for Facebook is at `https://developers.facebook.com/`.

After logging in, click on the **Get Started** button and then click on **Next**.

Then, you will see a drop-down menu in the top-right corner of the screen called **My Apps**, where you can find the option to create a new application.

Choose a display name that you want to name your application. In this case, we will name it `movie_rating_app`:

Click on **Create App ID**. If you go the settings page, you will see the **App ID** and **App Secret** for your application:

You will be needing the values mentioned in the preceding screenshot.

Adding a button to our login page that allows users to log in via Facebook

The next step is to add a **LOGIN WITH FACEBOOK** button in your login page, which you will be linking to your Facebook application. Replace the contents of `Login.vue`, with the following:

```
<template>
  <div>
    <div class="login">
      <a class="btn facebook" href="/login/facebook"> LOGIN WITH
FACEBOOK</a>
    </div>
    <v-form v-model="valid" ref="form" lazy-validation>
      <v-text-field
        label="Email"
        v-model="email"
        :rules="emailRules"
        required
      ></v-text-field>
      <v-text-field
        label="Password"
        v-model="password"
        :rules="passwordRules"
        required
      ></v-text-field>
      <v-btn
        @click="submit"
        :disabled="!valid"
      >
        submit
      </v-btn>
      <v-btn @click="clear">clear</v-btn><br/>
    </v-form>
  </div>
</template>
...
```

Let's also add some styling to these buttons. In `src/assets/stylesheets/home.css`, add the following code:

```
#app {
  font-family: 'Avenir', Helvetica, Arial, sans-serif;
  -webkit-font-smoothing: antialiased;
  -moz-osx-font-smoothing: grayscale;
  text-align: center;
```

```
  color: #2c3e50;
  width: 100%;
}

#inspire {
  font-family: 'Avenir', Helvetica, Arial, sans-serif;
}

.container.fill-height {
  align-items: normal;
}

a.side_bar_link {
  text-decoration: none;
}

.card__title--primary, .card__text {
  text-align: left;
}

.card {
  height: 100% !important;
}

.btn.facebook {
  background-color: #3b5998 !important;
  border-color: #2196f3;
  color: #fff !important;
}

.btn.twitter {
  background-color: #2196f3 !important;
  border-color: #2196f3;
  color: #fff !important;
}

.btn.google {
  background-color: #dd4b39 !important;
  border-color: #dd4b39;
  color: #fff !important;
}

.btn.linkedin {
  background-color: #4875B4 !important;
  border-color: #4875B4;
  color: #fff !important;
}
```

The preceding code will add a **LOGIN WITH FACEBOOK** button:

Adding configurations for Facebook app

Let's configure the Facebook Strategy just as we did for the local strategy. We will create a separate file to handle Facebook login so that the code is simpler. Let's create a file called `facebook.js` inside the `controllers` folder and add the following contents to it:

```
const User = require('../models/User.js');
const passport = require('passport');
const config = require('./../config/Config');
const Strategy = require('passport-facebook').Strategy;

module.exports.controller = (app) => {
  // facebook strategy
  passport.use(new Strategy({
    clientID: config.FACEBOOK_APP_ID,
    clientSecret: config.FACEBOOK_APP_SECRET,
    callbackURL: '/login/facebook/return',
    profileFields: ['id', 'displayName', 'email']
  },
  (accessToken, refreshToken, profile, cb) => {
```

```
    // Handle facebook login
  }));
};
```

In the preceding code, the first line inside the `exports` method imports the Facebook Strategy. The configuration takes three parameters: `clientID`, `clientSecret`, and callback URL. `clientID` and `clientSecret` are the `App ID` and `App Secret` for your Facebook app, respectively.

Let's add those secrets into our config file. In `config/Config.js`, let's add our Facebook keys, the `facebook_client_id` and `facebook_client_secret`:

```
module.exports = {
  DB: 'mongodb://localhost/movie_rating_app',
  SECRET: 'movieratingappsecretkey',
  FACEBOOK_APP_ID: <facebook_client_id>,
  FACEBOOK_APP_SECRET: <facebook_client_secret>
}
```

The callback URL is the URL that you want to route your application to after the successful transaction with Facebook.

The callback we have defined here is `http://127.0.0.1:8081/login/facebook/return`, which we have to define. The configuration is followed by a function that takes the following four parameters:

- `accessToken`
- `refreshToken`
- `profile`
- `cb` (callback)

Upon successful request, our application will get redirected to the home page.

Adding necessary routes for Facebook login

Now, let's go ahead and add the necessary routes for when we click on the login button and when we receive the callback from Facebook. In the same file, `facebook.js`, add the following routes:

```
const User = require("../models/User");
const passport = require('passport');
const config = require('./../config/Config');
```

```
module.exports.controller = (app) => {
  // facebook strategy
  const Strategy = require('passport-facebook').Strategy;

  passport.use(new Strategy({
    clientID: config.FACEBOOK_APP_ID,
    clientSecret: config.FACEBOOK_APP_SECRET,
    callbackURL: '/api/login/facebook/return',
    profileFields: ['id', 'displayName', 'email']
  },
  function(accessToken, refreshToken, profile, cb) {
  }));

  app.get('/login/facebook',
    passport.authenticate('facebook', { scope: ['email'] }));

  app.get('/login/facebook/return',
    passport.authenticate('facebook', { failureRedirect: '/login' }),
    (req, res) => {
      res.redirect('/');
    });
}
```

In the preceding code, we have added two routes. If you remember, in Login.vue, we have added a link to http://127.0.0.1:8081/login/facebook, which will be served by the first route that we defined here.

Also, if you recall, in the configuration setting, we have added a callback function that will be served by the second route, which we have defined here as well.

Now, the final thing to do is to actually log in the user using the strategy. Replace the contents of facebook.js with the following:

```
const User = require('../models/User.js');
const passport = require('passport');
const config = require('./../config/Config');
const Strategy = require('passport-facebook').Strategy;

module.exports.controller = (app) => {
  // facebook strategy
  passport.use(new Strategy({
    clientID: config.FACEBOOK_APP_ID,
    clientSecret: config.FACEBOOK_APP_SECRET,
    callbackURL: '/login/facebook/return',
    profileFields: ['id', 'displayName', 'email'],
  },
  (accessToken, refreshToken, profile, cb) => {
```

```
      const email = profile.emails[0].value;
      User.getUserByEmail(email, (err, user) => {
        if (!user) {
          const newUser = new User({
            fullname: profile.displayName,
            email,
            facebookId: profile.id,
          });
          User.createUser(newUser, (error) => {
            if (error) {
              // Handle error
            }
            return cb(null, user);
          });
        } else {
          return cb(null, user);
        }
        return true;
      });
    }));

  app.get('/login/facebook',
    passport.authenticate('facebook', { scope: ['email'] }));

  app.get('/login/facebook/return',
    passport.authenticate('facebook', { failureRedirect: '/login' }),
    (req, res) => {
      res.redirect('/');
    });
};
```

While logging in with the Facebook login, if the user already exists in our database, the user simply gets logged in and saved in the session. The session data is not stored in the browser cookies but on the server-side itself. If the user doesn't exist in our database, then we create a new user with the provided email from Facebook.

The last thing to configure here is to add the return URLs or the redirect URL from Facebook to our application. For this, we can add the URLs in the **App Settings** page in Facebook. In the app Settings page, under the Valid OAuth Redirect URIs, add the redirect URLs to our application from Facebook.

Now, we should be able to log in via Facebook. When the `login` function is successful, it will redirect the user to the home page. If you notice, Facebook redirects us to `http://localhost:8081/#=` instead of just `http://localhost:8081`. This is because of a security vulnerability. We can remove the # from the URL by adding the following piece of code in the main file, which is `index.html`:

```html
<!DOCTYPE html>
<html>
  <head>
    <meta charset="utf-8">
    <meta name="viewport" content="width=device-width,initial-scale=1.0">
    <link
href="https://fonts.googleapis.com/css?family=Roboto:300,400,500,700|Materi
al+Icons" rel="stylesheet">
    <link href="https://unpkg.com/vuetify/dist/vuetify.min.css"
rel="stylesheet">
    <title>movie_rating_app</title>
  </head>
  <body>
    <div id="app"></div>
    <!-- built files will be auto injected -->
  </body>
  <script type="text/javascript">
    if (window.location.hash == '#_=_'){
      history.replaceState
          ? history.replaceState(null, null,
window.location.href.split('#')[0])
          : window.location.hash = '';
    }
  </script>
</html>
```

This will remove the # symbol from the preceding URL. When you are successfully logged in, we should see your email in the top bar view similar to this:

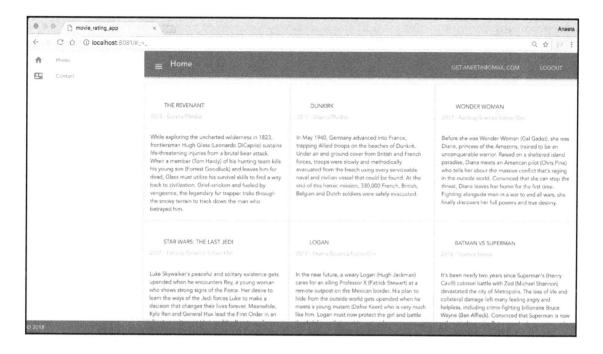

Passport's Twitter Strategy

The next strategy is Passport's Twitter Strategy. Let's start with the installation of this strategy.

Installing Passport's Twitter Strategy

Run the following command to install the Twitter Strategy:

```
$ npm install passport-twitter --save
```

The preceding command should add the package to your `package.json` file:

```
...
"node-sass": "^4.7.2",
"nodemon": "^1.14.10",
"passport": "^0.4.0",
"passport-twitter": "^2.1.1",
...
```

Configuring Passport's Twitter Strategy

Just like Facebook Strategy, we have to perform the following steps to configure passport's Twitter Strategy:

1. Creating and setting up a Twitter application. This will provide us with a consumer key (API Key) and a consumer secret (API Secret).
2. Adding a button to our login page that allows our users to **LOGIN WITH TWITTER**.
3. Adding the necessary routes.
4. Adding a middleware method to check authentication.
5. Redirecting the user to the home page after redirection and displaying the logged-in user's email in the top bar.

Let's dive into the details for each of the preceding steps.

Creating and setting up a Twitter app

Just as with Facebook Strategy, to be able to use the Twitter Strategy, we have to build a Twitter application as well. The developers' portal for Twitter is at `https://apps.twitter.com/`, where you will see a list of all of your applications. If this is new, you will see a button to create a new application—click on **Create your Twitter application**.

You will see a form, which will ask you to fill in the application name and other details. You can name the application whatever you want. For this application, we will name the application `movie_rating_app`. For the callback URL, we have provided `http://localhost:8081/login/twitter/return`, which we will have to define later:

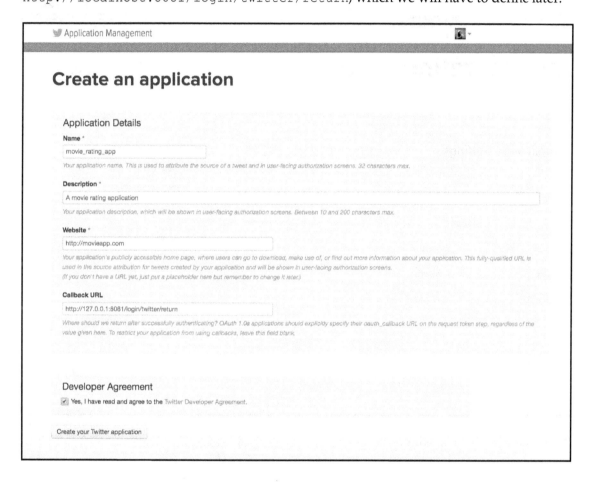

Upon successful creation of the application, you can see the API Key (Consumer Key) and API Secret (Consumer Secret) in the **Keys and Access Tokens** tab:

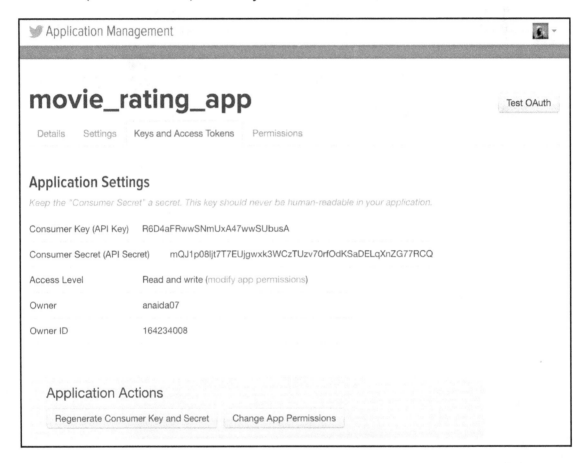

These tokens will be used for authentication in our application.

Adding a button to our login page that allows users to log in via Twitter

The next step is to add a **LOGIN WITH TWITTER** button in our login page, which we will link to our Twitter application that we just created.

In `Login.vue`, add a link to log in via Twitter with the following:

```
<template>
  <div>
    <div class="login">
      <a class="btn facebook" href="/login/facebook"> LOGIN WITH
FACEBOOK</a>
        <a class="btn twitter" href="/login/twitter"> LOGIN WITH TWITTER</a>
    </div>
    <v-form v-model="valid" ref="form" lazy-validation>
      <v-text-field
        label="Email"
        v-model="email"
        :rules="emailRules"
        required
      ></v-text-field>
...
```

The preceding code will add a **LOGIN WITH TWITTER** button. Let's run the following command:

```
$ npm run build
```

Now, if we visit the URL `http://localhost:8080/users/login`, we should see the following page:

Adding configurations for Twitter App

Now, the next step is to add the necessary routes for the Twitter login. For this, we will need to configure the settings and callback URL. Just like we did for the Facebook Strategy, let's create a separate file to set up our Twitter login. Let's create a new file inside the `controllers` directory called `twitter.js` and add the following contents:

```
const User = require('../models/User.js');
const passport = require('passport');
const config = require('./../config/Config');
const Strategy = require('passport-twitter').Strategy;

module.exports.controller = (app) => {
  // twitter strategy
  passport.use(new Strategy({
    consumerKey: config.TWITTER_APP_ID,
    consumerSecret: config.TWITTER_APP_SECRET,
    callbackURL: '/login/twitter/return',
    profileFields: ['id', 'displayName', 'email'],
  },
  (accessToken, refreshToken, profile, cb) => {
    // Handle twitter login
  }));
};
```

As we did in the Facebook Strategy, the first line imports the Twitter Strategy. The configuration takes the following three parameters: `clientID`, `clientSecret`, and a callback URL. The `consumerKey` and `consumerSecret` are the `App ID` and `App Secret` for your Twitter application app, respectively.

Let's add those secrets into our config file. In `config/Config.js`, add the `Facebook client ID` and `Facebook Client Secret`:

```
module.exports = {
  DB: 'mongodb://localhost/movie_rating_app',
  SECRET: 'movieratingappsecretkey',
  FACEBOOK_APP_ID: <facebook_client_id>,
  FACEBOOK_APP_SECRET: <facebook_client_secret>,
  TWITTER_APP_ID: <twitter_consumer_id>,
  TWITTER_APP_SECRET: <twitter_consumer_secret>
}
```

The callback URL is the URL that you want to route your application to after the successful transaction with Twitter.

The callback we have defined in the [preceding piece of code is
`http://localhost:8081/login/twitter/return`, which we have to define. The
configuration is followed by a function that takes the following four parameters:

- `accessToken`
- `refreshToken`
- `profile`
- `cb` (callback)

Upon a successful request, our application will get redirected to the home page.

Adding necessary routes for Twitter login

Now, let's add the necessary routes for when we click on the `Login` button and when we
receive the callback from Twitter. In the same file, `twitter.js`, add the following routes:

```
const User = require('../models/User.js');
const passport = require('passport');
const config = require('./../config/Config');
const Strategy = require('passport-twitter').Strategy;

module.exports.controller = (app) => {
  // twitter strategy
  passport.use(new Strategy({
    consumerKey: config.TWITTER_APP_ID,
    consumerSecret: config.TWITTER_APP_SECRET,
    callbackURL: '/login/twitter/return',
    profileFields: ['id', 'displayName', 'email'],
  },
  (accessToken, refreshToken, profile, cb) => {
    // Handle twitter login
  }));

  app.get('/login/google',
    passport.authenticate('google', { scope: ['email'] }));

  app.get('/login/google/return',
    passport.authenticate('google', { failureRedirect: '/login' }),
    (req, res) => {
      res.redirect('/');
    });
};
```

In the preceding code, we have added two routes: `/login/google` and `/login/google/return`. If you remember, in `Login.vue`, we have added a link to `http://localhost:8081/login/twitter`, which will be served by the first route that we defined here.

Now, the final thing to do is to actually log in the user using the strategy. Replace the contents of `twitter.js` with the following:

```
const User = require('../models/User.js');
const passport = require('passport');
const config = require('./../config/Config');
const Strategy = require('passport-twitter').Strategy;

module.exports.controller = (app) => {
  // twitter strategy
  passport.use(new Strategy({
    consumerKey: config.TWITTER_APP_ID,
    consumerSecret: config.TWITTER_APP_SECRET,
    userProfileURL:
'https://api.twitter.com/1.1/account/verify_credentials.json?include_email=
true',
    callbackURL: '/login/twitter/return',
  },
  (accessToken, refreshToken, profile, cb) => {
    const email = profile.emails[0].value;
    User.getUserByEmail(email, (err, user) => {
      if (!user) {
        const newUser = new User({
          fullname: profile.displayName,
          email,
          facebookId: profile.id,
        });
        User.createUser(newUser, (error) => {
          if (error) {
            // Handle error
          }
          return cb(null, user);
        });
      } else {
        return cb(null, user);
      }
      return true;
    });
  }));

  app.get('/login/twitter',
    passport.authenticate('twitter', { scope: ['email'] }));
```

```
app.get('/login/twitter/return',
  passport.authenticate('twitter', { failureRedirect: '/login' }),
  (req, res) => {
    res.redirect('/');
  });
};
```

We have to consider a few things here. Twitter does not allow us to access the user's email address by default. For that, we will need to check a field called **Request email addresses from users** while setting up the Twitter application, which can be found under the **Permissions** tab.

Before we do that, we also need to set the **Privacy Policy URL** and **Terms of Service URL** in order to request the user's access to their email address. This setting can be found under the **Settings** tab:

Fill in the privacy policy and terms of service URLs, and then under the **Permissions** tab, check the checkbox that says **Request email addresses from users** and click on **Update Settings**:

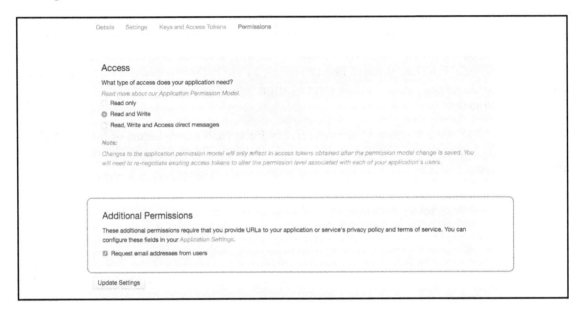

The last thing we also need is to specify the resource URL to be able to access the email address, which we do by adding the following in `twitter.js`:

```
...
passport.use(new Strategy({
    consumerKey: config.TWITTER_APP_ID,
    consumerSecret: config.TWITTER_APP_SECRET,
    userProfileURL:
    "https://api.twitter.com/1.1/account/verify_credentials.json?
    include_email=true",
    callbackURL: '/login/twitter/return',
  },
...
```

Now, everything is ready to go for the Twitter login. We should be able to log in successfully with the **LOGIN WITH TWITTER** button now.

Passport's Google strategy

The next strategy is the Passport's Google Strategy. Let's start with the installation of this strategy.

Installing Passport's Google strategy

Run the following command to install Passport's Google strategy:

```
$ npm install passport-google-oauth20 --save
```

The preceding command should add the package to your `package.json` file:

```
. . .
"node-sass": "^4.7.2",
"nodemon": "^1.14.10",
"passport": "^0.4.0",
"passport-google-oauth20": "^1.0.0",
. . .
```

Configuring Passport's Google strategy

The configuration for all the strategies is somewhat similar. For the Google strategy, the following are the steps we have to follow for configuration:

1. Creating and registering an application on Google. This will provide us with a consumer key (API key) and a consumer secret (API secret).
2. Adding a button to our login page that allows our users to log in via Google.
3. Adding the necessary routes.
4. Adding a middleware method to check authentication.
5. Redirecting the user to the home page and displaying the logged-in user's email in the top bar.

Let's dive into the details for each of the preceding steps.

Creating and setting up a Google app

Just as we did for the Facebook and Twitter strategies, to be able to use the Google Strategy, we have to build a Google application. The developers, portal for Google is at `https://console.developers.google.com/`.

Then, click on the drop-down list of the projects, which lies at the top-left corner of the page. A popup will show up. Then, click on the + icon to create a new application.

You just have to add the name of your application. We will name the application *movieratingapp*, as Google does not allow underscores or any other special characters:

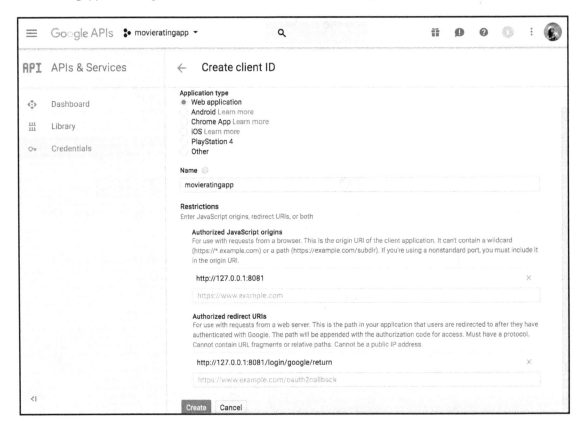

When the application gets created successfully, click on **Credentials** and `Create` and then on **OAuth Client ID** to generate the app tokens. To generate the tokens, we will first need to **Enable** the Google+ API via Developer Console at `https://console.developers.google.com/`.

It then takes us to the `Create Consent` page, where we need to fill in some information about our application. After that, on the **Credentials** page, we will be able to view our `Client ID` and `Client Secret`.

These tokens will be used to verify the authentication in our application:

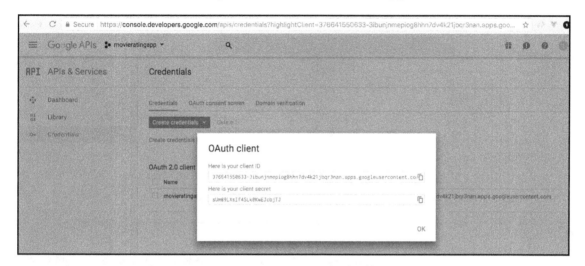

Adding a button to our login page that allows users to log in via Google

The next step is to add a **LOGIN WITH GOOGLE** button in our login page, which we will be linking to our Google application that we just created:

```
<template>
  <div>
    <div class="login">
      <a class="btn facebook" href="/login/facebook"> LOGIN WITH
FACEBOOK</a>
      <a class="btn twitter" href="/login/twitter"> LOGIN WITH TWITTER</a>
      <a class="btn google" href="/login/google"> LOGIN WITH GOOGLE</a>
    </div>
    <v-form v-model="valid" ref="form" lazy-validation>
      <v-text-field
        label="Email"
        v-model="email"
        :rules="emailRules"
        required
```

```
    ></v-text-field>
    <v-text-field
      label="Password"
      v-model="password"
      :rules="passwordRules"
      required
    ></v-text-field>
    <v-btn
      @click="submit"
      :disabled="!valid"
    >
      submit
    </v-btn>
    <v-btn @click="clear">clear</v-btn><br/>
  </v-form>
</div>
</template>
...
```

The preceding code will add a **LOGIN WITH GOOGLE** button:

Adding configurations for Google app

Let's configure the Google Strategy just as we did for the Facebook and Twitter strategies. We will create a separate file to handle Google login so that the code is simple. Let's create a file called `google.js` inside the `controllers` folder and add the following contents to it:

```
const User = require('../models/User');
const passport = require('passport');
const config = require('./../config/Config');
const Strategy = require('passport-google-oauth20').OAuth2Strategy;

module.exports.controller = (app) => {
  // google strategy
  passport.use(new Strategy({
    clientID: config.GOOGLE_APP_ID,
    clientSecret: config.GOOGLE_APP_SECRET,
    callbackURL: '/login/google/return',
  },
  (accessToken, refreshToken, profile, cb) => {
    // Handle google login
  }));
};
```

As we did in the Facebook and Twitter strategies, the first line imports the Google Strategy. The configuration takes the following three parameters: `clientID`, `clientSecret`, and callback URL. The `clientID` and `clientSecret` are the App ID and App Secret of the Google application we just created.

Let's add those secrets into our `config` file. In `config/Config.js`, add the `facebook_client_id` and `facebook_client_secret`:

```
module.exports = {
  DB: 'mongodb://localhost/movie_rating_app',
  SECRET: 'movieratingappsecretkey',
  FACEBOOK_APP_ID: <facebook_client_id>,
  FACEBOOK_APP_SECRET: <facebook_client_secret>,
  TWITTER_APP_ID: <twitter_client_id>,
  TWITTER_APP_SECRET: <twitter_client_secret>,
  GOOGLE_APP_ID: <google_client_id>,
  GOOGLE_APP_SECRET: <google_client_secret>
}
```

The callback URL is the URL that you want to route your application to after the successful transaction with Google.

The callback we just added is `http://127.0.0.1:8081/login/google/return`, which we have to define. The configuration is followed by a function that takes the following four parameters:

- `accessToken`
- `refreshToken`
- `profile`
- `cb` (callback)

Upon a successful request, our application will get redirected to the `profile` page, which we are yet to define.

Adding necessary routes for Google login

Now, let's go ahead and add the necessary routes, when we click on the login button and when we receive the callback from Google. In the same file, `google.js`, add the following routes:

```
const User = require('../models/User');
const passport = require('passport');
const config = require('./../config/Config');
const Strategy = require('passport-google-oauth20').OAuth2Strategy;

module.exports.controller = (app) => {
  // google strategy
  passport.use(new Strategy({
    clientID: config.GOOGLE_APP_ID,
    clientSecret: config.GOOGLE_APP_SECRET,
    callbackURL: '/login/google/return',
  },
  (accessToken, refreshToken, profile, cb) => {
    // Handle google login
  }));

  app.get('/login/google',
    passport.authenticate('google', { scope: ['email'] }));

  app.get('/login/google/return',
    passport.authenticate('google', { failureRedirect: '/login' }),
    (req, res) => {
      res.redirect('/');
    });
};
```

In the preceding code, we have added two routes. If you remember, in `Login.vue`, we have added a link to `http://localhost:8081/login/google`, which will be served by the first route that we defined here.

Also, if you recall, in the configuration setting, we have added a callback function, which will be served by the second route that we have defined here as well.

Now, the final thing to do is to actually log in the user using the strategy. Replace the contents of `google.js` with the following:

```
const User = require('../models/User');
const passport = require('passport');
const config = require('./../config/Config');
const GoogleStrategy = require('passport-google-oauth20').Strategy;

module.exports.controller = (app) => {
  // google strategy
  passport.use(new GoogleStrategy({
    clientID: config.GOOGLE_APP_ID,
    clientSecret: config.GOOGLE_APP_SECRET,
    callbackURL: '/login/google/return',
  },
  (accessToken, refreshToken, profile, cb) => {
    const email = profile.emails[0].value;
    User.getUserByEmail(email, (err, user) => {
      if (!user) {
        const newUser = new User({
          fullname: profile.displayName,
          email,
          facebookId: profile.id,
        });
        User.createUser(newUser, (error) => {
          if (error) {
            // Handle error
          }
          return cb(null, user);
        });
      } else {
        return cb(null, user);
      }
      return true;
    });
  }));

  app.get('/login/google',
    passport.authenticate('google', { scope: ['email'] }));
```

```
app.get('/login/google/return',
    passport.authenticate('google', { failureRedirect: '/login' }),
    (req, res) => {
      res.redirect('/');
    });
};
```

Passport's LinkedIn strategy

By now, you must understand quite well how to use each of the strategies provided by `passport.js`. Let's quickly revise these using the LinkedIn strategy. This is the last strategy we will be covering in this book. There are several other strategies that you can use according to your needs. You can find the list at `https://github.com/jaredhanson/passport/wiki/Strategies`.

Now, let's start with the installation of this strategy.

Installing Passport's LinkedIn strategy

Run the following command to install the LinkedIn strategy:

```
$ npm install passport-linkedin --save
```

The preceding command should add the following package to your `package.json` file:

```
...
"node-sass": "^4.7.2",
"nodemon": "^1.14.10",
"passport": "^0.4.0",
"passport-linkedin-oauth2": "^2.1.1",
...
```

Configuring Passport's LinkedIn strategy

The configuration for all the strategies is somewhat similar. So, the following are the steps we have to follow to configure this strategy:

1. Creating and registering an application on LinkedIn. This will provide us with a consumer key (API Key) and a consumer secret (API Secret).
2. Adding a button to our login page that allows users to log in via LinkedIn.

3. Adding the necessary routes.
4. Adding a middleware method to check authentication.
5. Redirecting the user to the home page and displaying the logged in user's email in the top bar.

Let's dive into the details for each of the preceding steps.

Creating and setting up a LinkedIn app

Just like we did for the Facebook and Twitter Strategies, to be able to use the Linkedin Strategy, we have to build a LinkedIn application. The developers, portal for LinkedIn is at `https://www.linkedin.com/developer/apps`. You will see a list of all of your applications there. You will also note a button to create a new application; click on **Create Application**.

We just have to add the name of our application. We can name the application whatever we want, but for our application, we will be naming it `movie_rating_app`:

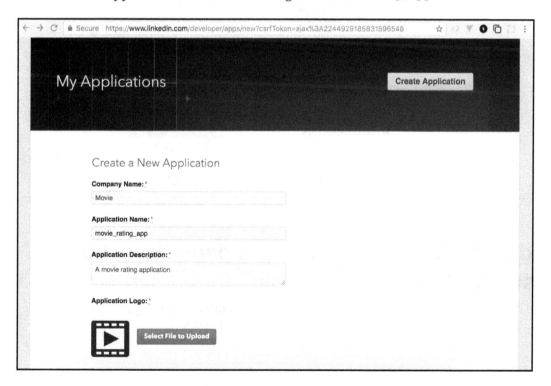

Upon successful creation of the application, you can see the API Key (`clientID`) and API Secret (client secret) in the **Credentials** tab.

These tokens will be used to verify the authentication in our application:

Adding a button to our login page that allows users to log in via LinkedIn

The next step is to add a **LOGIN WITH LINKEDIN** button in our login page, which we will be linking to our LinkedIn application that we just created.

In `Login.vue`, add the following code:

```
<template>
  <div>
    <div class="login">
      <a class="btn facebook" href="/login/facebook"> LOGIN WITH
FACEBOOK</a>
        <a class="btn twitter" href="/login/twitter"> LOGIN WITH TWITTER</a>
        <a class="btn google" href="/login/google"> LOGIN WITH GOOGLE</a>
        <a class="btn linkedin" href="/login/linkedin"> LOGIN WITH
LINKEDIN</a>
    </div>
    <v-form v-model="valid" ref="form" lazy-validation>
      <v-text-field
        label="Email"
        v-model="email"
        :rules="emailRules"
        required
      ></v-text-field>
      <v-text-field
        label="Password"
        v-model="password"
        :rules="passwordRules"
        required
      ></v-text-field>
      <v-btn
        @click="submit"
        :disabled="!valid"
      >
        submit
      </v-btn>
      <v-btn @click="clear">clear</v-btn><br/>
    </v-form>
  </div>
</template>
<script>
  import axios from 'axios';
  import bus from "./../bus.js";

  export default {
    data: () => ({
      valid: true,
      email: '',
      password: '',
      emailRules: [
        (v) => !!v || 'E-mail is required',
        (v) => /^\w+([\.-]?\w+)*@\w+([\.-]?\w+)*(\.\w{2,3})+$/.test(v) ||
```

```
'E-mail must be valid'
      ],
      passwordRules: [
        (v) => !!v || 'Password is required',
      ]
    }),
  methods: {
    async submit () {
      if (this.$refs.form.validate()) {
        return axios({
          method: 'post',
          data: {
            email: this.email,
            password: this.password
          },
          url: '/users/login',
          headers: {
            'Content-Type': 'application/json'
          }
        })
        .then((response) => {
          localStorage.setItem('jwtToken', response.data.token)
          this.$swal("Good job!", "You are ready to start!",
          "success");
          bus.$emit("refreshUser");
          this.$router.push({ name: 'Home' });
        })
        .catch((error) => {
          const message = error.response.data.message;
          this.$swal("Oh oo!", `${message}`, "error")
        });
      }
    },
    clear () {
      this.$refs.form.reset()
    }
  }
}
</script>
```

The preceding code will add a **LOGIN WITH LINKEDIN** button:

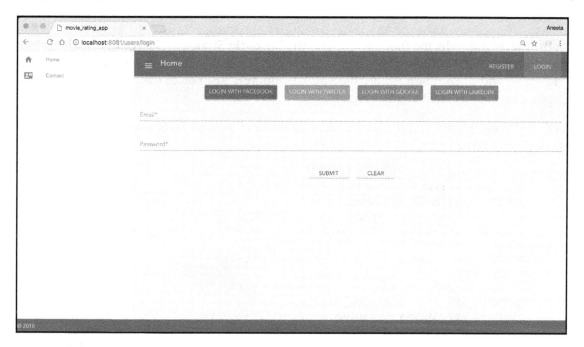

Adding configurations for LinkedIn app

Let's configure the LinkedIn strategy just as we did for all the other strategies. We will create a separate file to handle LinkedIn login so that the code is simple. Let's create a file called `linkedin.js` inside the `controllers` folder and add the following contents to it:

```
const User = require('../models/User.js');
const passport = require('passport');
const config = require('./../config/Config');
const Strategy = require('passport-linkedin').Strategy;

module.exports.controller = (app) => {
  // linkedin strategy
  passport.use(new Strategy({
    consumerKey: config.LINKEDIN_APP_ID,
    consumerSecret: config.LINKEDIN_APP_SECRET,
    callbackURL: '/login/linkedin/return',
    profileFields: ['id', 'first-name', 'last-name', 'email-address']
  },
  (accessToken, refreshToken, profile, cb) => {
```

```
    // Handle linkedin login
  }));
};
```

In the preceding code, the first line imports the LinkedIn Strategy. The configuration takes the following three parameters: `clientID`, `clientSecret`, and a callback URL. The `clientID` and `clientSecret` are the `App ID` and `App Secret` of the LinkedIn application we just created, respectively.

Let's add those secrets to our `config` file. In `config/Config.js`, add the `Facebook Client ID` and `Facebook Client Secret`:

```
module.exports = {
  DB: 'mongodb://localhost/movie_rating_app',
  SECRET: 'movieratingappsecretkey',
  FACEBOOK_APP_ID: <facebook_client_id>,
  FACEBOOK_APP_SECRET: <facebook_client_secret>,
  TWITTER_APP_ID: <twitter_consumer_id>,
  TWITTER_APP_SECRET: <twitter_consumer_secret>,
  GOOGLE_APP_ID: <google_consumer_id>,
  GOOGLE_APP_SECRET: <google_consumer_secret>,
  LINKEDIN_APP_ID: <linkedin_consumer_id>,
  LINKEDIN_APP_SECRET: <linkedin_consumer_secret>
}
```

The `callbackURL` is the URL that you want to route your application to after the successful transaction with LinkedIn.

The `callbackURL` that we have defined in the preceding code is `http://127.0.0.1:8081/login/linkedin/return`, which we have to define. The configuration is followed by a function that takes the following four parameters:

- `accessToken`
- `refreshToken`
- `profile`
- `cb` (callback)

Upon successful request, our application will get redirected to the profile page, which we are yet to define.

Adding necessary routes for LinkedIn login

Now, let's add the necessary routes for when we click on the **Login** button and when we receive the callback from LinkedIn:

```
const User = require('../models/User.js');
const passport = require('passport');
const config = require('./../config/Config');
const Strategy = require('passport-linkedin').Strategy;

module.exports.controller = (app) => {
  // linkedin strategy
  passport.use(new Strategy({
    consumerKey: config.LINKEDIN_APP_ID,
    consumerSecret: config.LINKEDIN_APP_SECRET,
    callbackURL: '/login/linkedin/return',
    profileFields: ['id', 'first-name', 'last-name', 'email-address']
  },
  (accessToken, refreshToken, profile, cb) => {
    // Handle linkedin login
  }));

  app.get('/login/linkedin',
    passport.authenticate('linkedin'));

  app.get('/login/linkedin/return',
    passport.authenticate('linkedin', { failureRedirect: '/login' }),
    (req, res) => {
      res.redirect('/');
    });
};
```

In the preceding code, we have added two routes. If you remember, in `Login.vue`, we have added a link to `http://localhost:8081/login/linkedin`, which will be served by the first route that we defined here.

Also, if you recall, in the configuration setting, we have added a callback function that will be served by the second route, which we have defined here as well.

Now, the final thing to do is to actually log in the user using the strategy. Replace the contents of `linkedin.js` with the following:

```
const User = require('../models/User');
const passport = require('passport');
const config = require('./../config/Config');
const Strategy = require('passport-linkedin').Strategy;
```

```
module.exports.controller = (app) => {
  // linkedin strategy
  passport.use(new Strategy({
    consumerKey: config.LINKEDIN_APP_ID,
    consumerSecret: config.LINKEDIN_APP_SECRET,
    callbackURL: '/login/linkedin/return',
    profileFields: ['id', 'first-name', 'last-name', 'email-address'],
  },
  (accessToken, refreshToken, profile, cb) => {
    const email = profile.emails[0].value;
    User.getUserByEmail(email, (err, user) => {
      if (!user) {
        const newUser = new User({
          fullname: profile.displayName,
          email: profile.emails[0].value,
          facebookId: profile.id,
        });
        User.createUser(newUser, (error) => {
          if (error) {
            // Handle error
          }
          return cb(null, user);
        });
      } else {
        return cb(null, user);
      }
      return true;
    });
  }));

  app.get('/login/linkedin',
    passport.authenticate('linkedin'));

  app.get('/login/linkedin/return',
    passport.authenticate('linkedin', { failureRedirect: '/login' }),
    (req, res) => {
      res.redirect('/');
    });
};
```

With this, everything is ready to go for the LinkedIn login. We should be able to log in successfully with the **LOGIN WITH LINKEDIN** button now.

Summary

In this chapter, we covered what OAuth is and how to integrate different varieties of OAuth with our application. We also covered Facebook, Twitter, Google, and LinkedIn strategies provided by `passport.js`. If you want to explore a different strategy, a good list of available packages is available
at `https://github.com/jaredhanson/passport/wiki/Strategies`.

In the next chapter, we will find out more about what `Vuex` is and how can we use `Vuex` to simplify our application.

8
Introducing Vuex

Vuex is a library that we can use with Vue.js to manage different states in an application. If you are building a small application that does not require much data exchange between its components, you are better off not using this library. However, as your application grows, complexities crawl along with it. There will be several components in the application, and, most obviously, you will need to exchange data from one component to another or share the same data across multiple components. That is when Vuex comes to the rescue.

Vue.js also provides an `emit` method to pass data between different components, which we used in previous chapters. As your application grows, you might also want to update data across several components when your data gets updated.

So, Vuex provides a centralized place to store all the pieces of data in our application. Whenever data changes, this new set of data will be stored in this centralized place. Also, all of the components that want to use that data will be fetched from the store. This means that we have a single source to store all the data, and all the components that we build will be able to access that data.

Let's first get acquainted with some of the terminology that come with Vuex:

- **State**: This is an object that contains the data. Vuex uses a single state tree, which means that it is a single object that contains all the pieces of data for the application.
- **Getters**: It is used to fetch data from the state tree.
- **mutations**: They are the methods that change the data in the state tree.
- **Actions**: They are the functions that perform mutations.

We will discuss each of these in this chapter.

Traditional multi-web page application

In traditional multi web page application, when we build a web application and open a website by navigating to the browser, it requests the web server to fetch that page and serve it to the browser. When we click on a button on the same website, it again requests the web server to fetch another page and again serve it. This process happens for every single interaction we do on the website. So, basically, the website gets reloaded on every single interaction, which consumes a lot of time.

The following is a sample diagram that explains how a multi-page application works:

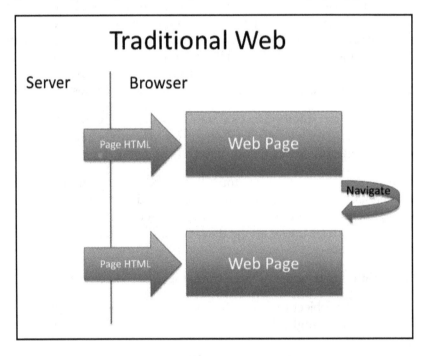

When a request is sent from the browser, the request is sent to the server. The server then returns the HTML content and serves a whole new whole page.

Multi Page Applications (MPA) can provide several benefits as well. It's not a matter of whether to choose MPA or a **Single Page Application (SPA)**, but it all depends on the content of your application. If your application contains a lot of user interaction, you should go for an SPA; however, if the only purpose of your application is to serve the users with the content, you can go with an MPA. We will explore more about SPAs and MPAs later in this chapter.

An introduction to SPAs

Contrary to the traditional MPAs, SPAs are designed specifically for web-based applications. The SPA fetches all the data when you first load the website in the browser. Once all the data is fetched, you don't need to fetch any more data. When any other interactions are done, that data is fetched over the internet, without having to send a request to the server and without reloading the page. This means that SPAs are much faster than the traditional MPAs. However, since SPAs fetch everything at once on the first load, the first page load time could be slow. Some applications that have SPA integration are Gmail, Facebook, GitHub, Trello, and so on. SPAs are all about making the user experience better by putting the content on one single page and not making the users wait for the information they want.

The following is a sample diagram of how SPAs work:

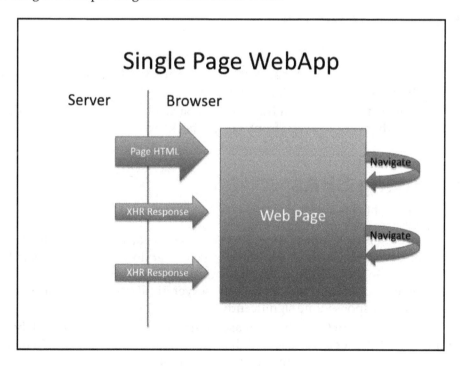

The website has all the content that it needs on the first page-load. When a user clicks on something, it just fetches the information for that particular area and refreshes only that part of the web page.

SPA versus MPA

SPA and MPA serve different purposes. You may want to use one over the other, depending on your needs. Before you start your application, ensure that you are clear about the kind of application that you want to build.

Pros of using MPAs

MPAs are the best approach if you want to make your application SEO friendly. Google can crawl different pages of your application by searching the keywords that you assign on each page, which is not possible in an SPA since it has only a single page.

Cons of using MPAs

There are a few cons of using MPAs:

- The development work for an MPA is much greater than for an SPA because the frontend and backend are tightly coupled.
- MPAs have tightly coupled frontend and backend, which makes it harder to separate the work between frontend and backend developers.

Pros of using SPAs

SPAs provides a lot of benefits:

- **Reduced server response time**: SPAs fetch all the data needed on the first load of the website. With such an application, the server does not need to reload the resources on the website. If new data needs to be fetched, it only fetches the updated piece of information from the server, unlike multi-page apps, decreasing the server response time significantly.
- **Better user interaction**: The decrease in server response time ultimately improves the user experience. With every interaction, the user gets a more quickly rendered page, which means *happy customers*.
- **Flexibility to change the UI**: SPAs do not have a coupled frontend and backend. This means that we can change the frontend and completely rewrite it without having to worry about breaking anything on the server side.

- **Data caching**: SPAs cache the data in the local storage. It only makes a single request the first time and saves the data. This makes the application available even when the internet is cut off.

Cons of using SPAs

There are few downsides of using SPAs as well:

- SPAs are not SEO friendly. Since everything is done on a single page, the crawlability is very low.
- You cannot share a particular piece of information with others since there is the only one link to the page.
- Security concerns are much greater with SPAs than in MPAs.

An introduction to Vuex

Vuex is a state management library that is specifically designed to work with applications built with Vue.js. It is centralized state management for Vuex.

Core concepts of Vuex

We got a glimpse of these core concepts in the introduction. Now, let's dive into a little bit more detail on each of these concepts:

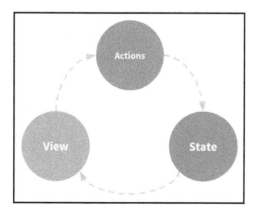

The preceding diagram is a simple diagram that explains how Vuex works. Initially, everything is stored in a state, which is the single source of truth. Every view component fetches data from this state. Whenever something needs to be changed, actions perform mutations on the data and store it back in the state:

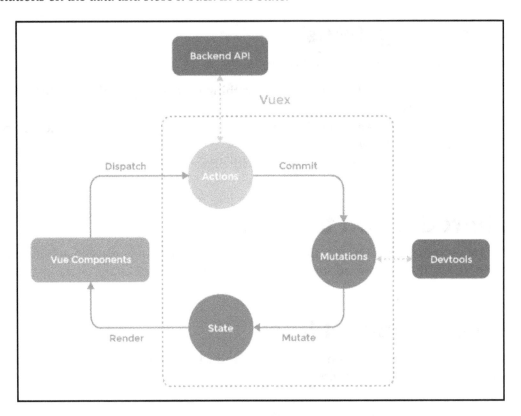

When we open our application in the browser, all the Vue components will be loaded. When we click on a button to fetch certain information from a component, that component dispatches an action that performs mutations on the data. When the mutation is successfully done, the state object is updated and new values are used. Then, we can use the new state for our components and display it in the browser.

Creating a simple Vuex application

We will start a fresh new application to learn the basics of Vuex. Let's get started.

Let's first create a new application:

```
$ vue init webpack vuex-tutorial
```

The preceding code snippet will ask you few questions about the application setup. You can choose what you want to keep. I will go with the following configuration:

```
~/Projects git:master >>> vue init webpack vuex-tutorial

  A newer version of vue-cli is available.

  latest:    2.9.3
  installed: 2.9.2

? Project name vuex-tutorial
? Project description A Vue.js project
? Author Aneeta Sharma <get.aneeta@gmail.com>
? Vue build standalone
? Install vue-router? No
? Use ESLint to lint your code? No
? Set up unit tests No
? Setup e2e tests with Nightwatch? No
? Should we run `npm install` for you after the project has been created? (recommended) npm

  vue-cli    Generated "vuex-tutorial".

# Installing project dependencies ...
# ========================
```

After the installation, navigate to the project directory:

```
$ cd vuex-tutorial
```

The next thing to do is to run the following command:

```
$ npm install
```

After that, run the following command:

```
$ npm run dev
```

The preceding command will spin up your server and open a port in `localhost:8080`.

Installing Vuex

The next step is to install `vuex`. To do that, run the following command:

```
$ npm install --save vuex
```

Setting up Vuex

Now, let's create a `store` folder to manage the `vuex` in our application.

Creating a store file

In the `src` directory, create a `store` folder and `store.js` file. Then, add the following to the `store.js` file:

```
import Vue from 'vue'
import Vuex from 'vuex'

Vue.use(Vuex)
```

In the preceding code block, the line `Vue.use(Vuex)` imports the Vuex library. Without this, we will not be able to use any of the `vuex` functionalities. Now, let's build a store object.

State

In the same `store.js` file, add the following lines of code:

```
import Vue from 'vue'
import Vuex from 'vuex'

Vue.use(Vuex)

const state = {
  count: 0
```

```
}

export const store = new Vuex.Store({
  state
})
```

In the preceding code, we set the default state for a variable called `count` as `0` and exported a Vuex state through the store.

Now, we will need to modify `src/main.js`:

```
// The Vue build version to load with the `import` command
// (runtime-only or standalone) has been set in webpack.base.conf with an
alias.
import Vue from 'vue'
import App from './App'
import { store } from './store/store'

Vue.config.productionTip = false

/* eslint-disable no-new */
new Vue({
  el: '#app',
  store,
  components: { App },
  template: '<App/>'
})
```

The preceding code imports the store file that we just created, and we can access this variable in our vue components.

Let's move on to creating a component that will fetch this store data. A default component is created when we create a new application with Vue. If we look into the `src/components` directory, we will find a file called `HelloWorld.vue`. Let's use the same component, `HelloWorld.vue`, or you can create a new one. Let's modify this file to access the `count`, which we defined in the state.

In `src/components/HelloWorld.vue`, add the following code:

```
<template>
  <div class="hello">
    <h1>{{ $store.state.count }}</h1>
  </div>
</template>

<script>
```

```
export default {
  name: 'HelloWorld',
  data () {
    return {
      msg: 'Welcome to Your Vue.js App'
    }
  }
}
</script>

<!-- Add "scoped" attribute to limit CSS to this component only -->
<style scoped>
</style>
```

The following is the final folder structure:

The preceding screenshot should print the default value of count in the `HelloWorld.vue` component. If you navigate to `http://localhost:8080/#/`, you should see the following screenshot:

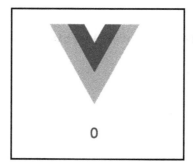

In the preceding screenshot, we accessed the count variable in the store directly using the `$` operator, which is not the preferred way of doing it. We have learned the fundamentals of using the state. Now, the proper way to access the variables is by using getters.

Getters

A `getter` is a function that is used to access the objects from the store. Let's create a `getter` method to fetch the count that we have in our store.

In `store.js`, add the following code:

```
import Vue from 'vue'
import Vuex from 'vuex'

Vue.use(Vuex)

const state = {
  count: 0
}

const getters = {
  fetchCount: state => state.count
}

export const store = new Vuex.Store({
  state,
  getters
})
```

In the preceding code, we added a method called `fetchCount`, which returns the current value of `count`. Now, to access this in our vue component—`HelloWorld.vue`, we will need to update the content with the following code:

```
<template>
  <div class="hello">
    <h1>The count is: {{ fetchCount }}</h1>
  </div>
</template>

<script>
import { mapGetters } from 'vuex'
export default {
  name: 'HelloWorld',
  computed: mapGetters([
    'fetchCount'
  ])
}
</script>

<!-- Add "scoped" attribute to limit CSS to this component only -->
<style scoped>
</style>
```

We have to import a module called `mapGetters` from Vuex, which is used to import the `fetchCount` method that we create as a `getter` method in `store.js`. Now, check the number by reloading the browser; this should also print the count as `0`:

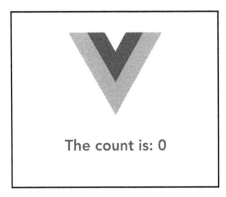

mutations

Let's move on to `mutations`. `mutations` are methods that perform modifications to the state of the store. We will define the `mutations` just as we defined `getters`.

In `store.js`, add the following lines:

```
import Vue from 'vue'
import Vuex from 'vuex'

Vue.use(Vuex)

const state = {
  count: 0
}

const getters = {
  fetchCount: state => state.count
}

const mutations = {
  increment: state => state.count++,
  decrement: state => state.count--
}

export const store = new Vuex.Store({
  state,
  getters,
  mutations
})
```

We added two different `mutation` functions in the preceding code. The `increment` method increments the count by 1, whereas the `decrement` method decreases the count by 1. This is where we introduce actions.

Actions

Actions are the methods that dispatch mutation functions. Actions perform `mutations`. Since `actions` are asynchronous and `mutations` are synchronous, it's always a good practice to use `actions` to mutate the state. Now, just like `getters` and `mutations`, let's define the `actions` as well. In the same file, that is, `store.js`, add the following lines of code:

```
import Vue from 'vue'
import Vuex from 'vuex'
```

```
Vue.use(Vuex)

const state = {
  count: 0
}

const getters = {
  fetchCount: state => state.count
}

const mutations = {
  increment: state => state.count++,
  decrement: state => state.count--
}

const actions = {
  increment: ({ commit }) => commit('increment'),
  decrement: ({ commit }) => commit('decrement')
}

export const store = new Vuex.Store({
  state,
  getters,
  mutations,
  actions
})
```

In the preceding code, we added two different functions for incrementing and decrementing. Since these methods commit the `mutations`, we will need to pass a parameter to make the `commit` method available.

Now we need to use the previously defined `actions` and make them available in our vue component, in `HelloWorld.vue`:

```
<template>
  <div class="hello">
    <h1>The count is: {{ fetchCount }}</h1>
  </div>
</template>

<script>
import { mapGetters, mapActions } from 'vuex'
export default {
  name: 'HelloWorld',
  computed: mapGetters([
    'fetchCount'
  ]),
```

```
methods: mapActions([
    'increment',
    'decrement'
  ])
}
</script>

<!-- Add "scoped" attribute to limit CSS to this component only -->
<style scoped>
</style>
```

To invoke these actions, let's create two buttons. In `HelloWorld.vue`, let's add the following lines of code:

```
<template>
  <div class="hello">
    <h1>The count is: {{ fetchCount }}</h1>
    <button class="btn btn-primary" @click="increment">Increase</button>
    <button class="btn btn-primary" @click="decrement">Decrease</button>
  </div>
</template>
...
```

The preceding lines of code add two buttons, which, when clicked, call a method to increment or decrement the count. Let's also import Bootstrap for CSS. In `index.html`, add the following code:

```
<!DOCTYPE html>
<html>
  <head>
    <meta charset="utf-8">
    <meta name="viewport" content="width=device-width,initial-scale=1.0">
    <!-- Latest compiled and minified CSS -->
    <link rel="stylesheet"
href="https://maxcdn.bootstrapcdn.com/bootstrap/3.3.7/css/bootstrap.min.css
" integrity="sha384-
BVYiiSIFeK1dGmJRAkycuHAHRg32OmUcww7on3RYdg4Va+PmSTsz/K68vbdEjh4u"
crossorigin="anonymous">
    <title>vuex-tutorial</title>
  </head>
  <body>
    <div id="app"></div>
    <!-- built files will be auto injected -->
  </body>
</html>
```

That's it. Now, if you reload the browser, you should be able to see the following result:

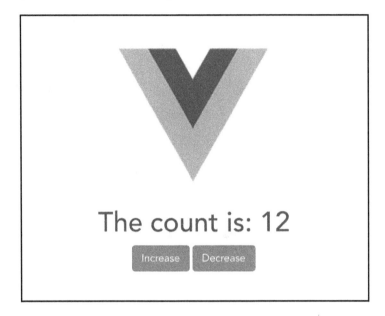

The count should increase or decrease when you click on the relevant button. This gives you a basic idea about how to implement Vuex in an application.

Installing and using Vuex in a movie application

We covered the basics of Vuex—how it works in an application and the core concepts. We covered how to create a store and mutations and how to use actions to dispatch them, and also discussed how to use getters to fetch information from the store.

We built an application in the previous chapters for a movie listing page. We will use the same application for Vuex. We will be doing the following actions:

- We will define a store where all the movies will be stored
- When a new movie is added, we will automatically display that to the movie listing page without reloading the page

Let's open the application and run the frontend and backend servers:

```
$ cd movie_rating_app
$ npm run build
$ nodemon server.js
```

Also, run the mongo server with the following command:

```
$ mongod
```

The movie listing page should look like this:

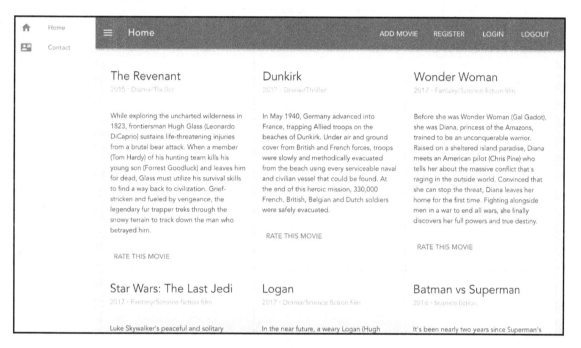

Let's start by installing vuex:

```
$ npm install --save vuex
```

Check your `package.json` file; vuex should be listed on the dependencies:

```
...
"vue-router": "^3.0.1",
    "vue-swal": "0.0.6",
    "vue-template-compiler": "^2.5.14",
    "vuetify": "^0.17.6",
    "vuex": "^3.0.1"
  },
...
```

Now, let's create a file, where we will be able to put all our `getters`, `mutations`, and `actions` that we will define as we go forward.

Defining a store

Let's create a folder named `store` inside the `src` directory, and a new file called `store.js` inside the `store` directory, and add the following lines of code to it:

```
import Vue from 'vue';
import Vuex from 'vuex';
import axios from 'axios';

Vue.use(Vuex);

export const store = new Vuex.Store({
})
```

Just like we did in the preceding sample application, let's add a `state` variable to store the current state of the application for movies listing page.

In `store.js`, add the following lines of code:

```
import Vue from 'vue';
import Vuex from 'vuex';
import axios from 'axios';

Vue.use(Vuex);

export const store = new Vuex.Store({
  state: {
    movies: []
  },
})
```

This means that the initial state of the application will have an empty movie listing.

Now, we need to import this `store` into `main.js` so that it is accessible throughout the components. Add the following lines of code in `src/main.js`:

```
// The Vue build version to load with the `import` command
// (runtime-only or standalone) has been set in webpack.base.conf with an
alias.
import 'bootstrap/dist/css/bootstrap.min.css';
import 'bootstrap-vue/dist/bootstrap-vue.css';

import BootstrapVue from 'bootstrap-vue';
import Vue from 'vue';
import Vuetify from 'vuetify';
import VueSwal from 'vue-swal';
import App from './App';
import router from './router';
import { store } from './store/store';

Vue.use(BootstrapVue);
Vue.use(Vuetify);
Vue.use(VueSwal);

Vue.config.productionTip = false;

/* eslint-disable no-new */
new Vue({
  el: '#app',
  store,
  router,
  components: { App },
  template: '<App/>',
});
```

Now, we will need to fetch the movies when we open the location `http://localhost:8081/` in the browser. Here is what we will do:

1. Modify `Home.vue` to call the action that fetches the movies
2. Create an action that will fetch all the movies
3. Create a mutation to store the fetched movies in the movies store
4. Create a getter method to fetch the movies from the state to display on the home page

Modifying Home.vue

Let's start this section by modifying our `Home.vue` component. Update the `script` part of the file with the following lines of code:

```
<script>
export default {
  name: 'Movies',
  computed: {
    movies() {
      return this.$store.getters.fetchMovies;
    }
  },
  mounted() {
    this.$store.dispatch("fetchMovies");
  },
};
</script>
```

In the preceding code, in the `mounted()` method, we have dispatched an action called `fetchMovies`, which we will define in our action.

When the movies are fetched successfully, we will use the `computed` method, which will be mapped to the `movies` variable, which we will use in our template:

```
<template>
  <v-layout row wrap>
    <v-flex xs4 v-for="movie in movies" :key="movie._id">
      <v-card>
        <v-card-title primary-title>
          ...
```

Creating an action

Let's move on to add an action to the `store.js` file:

```
import Vue from 'vue';
import Vuex from 'vuex';
import axios from 'axios';

Vue.use(Vuex);

export const store = new Vuex.Store({
  state: {
    movies: []
```

```
    },
    actions: {
      fetchMovies: (context, payload) => {
        axios({
          method: 'get',
          url: '/movies',
        })
          .then((response) => {
            context.commit("MOVIES", response.data.movies);
          })
          .catch(() => {
          });
      }
    }
  })
```

In the preceding code, we have moved the `axios` part from the component. When we get a successful response, we will commit a mutation called MOVIES, which then mutates the value of the `movies` in the state.

Creating a mutation

Let's go on and add a mutation as well. In `store.js`, replace the contents with the following code:

```
import Vue from 'vue';
import Vuex from 'vuex';
import axios from 'axios';

Vue.use(Vuex);

export const store = new Vuex.Store({
  state: {
    movies: []
  },
  mutations: {
    MOVIES: (state, payload) => {
      state.movies = payload;
    }
  },
  actions: {
    fetchMovies: (context, payload) => {
      axios({
        method: 'get',
        url: '/movies',
```

```
      })
        .then((response) => {
          context.commit("MOVIES", response.data.movies);
        })
        .catch(() => {
        });
    }
  }
})
```

The preceding `mutations` mutate the state of the movies of the application.

We now have the `action` and the `mutation`. Now, the last part is to add a `getter` method, which gets the value of the `movies` from the state.

Creating a getter

Let's add the `getter` method in `store.js` that we created to manage the state of our application:

```
import Vue from 'vue';
import Vuex from 'vuex';
import axios from 'axios';

Vue.use(Vuex);

export const store = new Vuex.Store({
  state: {
    movies: []
  },
  getters: {
    fetchMovies: state => state.movies,
  },
  mutations: {
    MOVIES: (state, payload) => {
      state.movies = payload;
    }
  },
  actions: {
    fetchMovies: (context, payload) => {
      axios({
        method: 'get',
        url: '/movies',
      })
        .then((response) => {
```

```
            context.commit("MOVIES", response.data.movies);
        })
        .catch(() => {
        });
    }
  }
})
```

That's it. When we navigate to `http://localhost:8081/movies/add`, we should have a functional Vuex implementation that fetches the movies to the home page.

Let's move on to implement the store when we add a movie to the application. We will follow the same process as we did earlier:

1. Modify `AddMovie.vue` to call the action to create the movie
2. Create an `action` that calls the POST API to create movies
3. Create a `mutation` to `store` the added new movie to the `movies` store

Replace the `script` contents in `AddMovie.vue` with the following code:

```
<script>
export default {
  data: () => ({
    movie: null,
    valid: true,
    name: '',
    description: '',
    genre: '',
    release_year: '',
    nameRules: [
      v => !!v || 'Movie name is required',
    ],
    genreRules: [
      v => !!v || 'Movie genre year is required',
      v => (v && v.length <= 80) || 'Genre must be less than equal to
      80 characters.',
    ],
    releaseRules: [
      v => !!v || 'Movie release year is required',
    ],
    select: null,
    years: [
      '2018',
      '2017',
      '2016',
      '2015',
```

```
      ],
    }),
  methods: {
    submit() {
      if (this.$refs.form.validate()) {
        const movie = {
          name: this.name,
          description: this.description,
          release_year: this.release_year,
          genre: this.genre,
        }
        this.$store.dispatch("addMovie", movie);
        this.$refs.form.reset();
        this.$router.push({ name: 'Home' });
      }
      return true;
    },
    clear() {
      this.$refs.form.reset();
    },
  },
};
</script>
```

Then, add the `action` and `mutations` to the `store.js` file:

```
import Vue from 'vue';
import Vuex from 'vuex';
import axios from 'axios';

Vue.use(Vuex);

export const store = new Vuex.Store({
  state: {
    movies: []
  },
  getters: {
    fetchMovies: state => state.movies,
  },
  mutations: {
    ADD_MOVIE: (state, payload) => {
      state.movies.unshift(payload);
    },
    MOVIES: (state, payload) => {
      state.movies = payload;
    }
  },
  actions: {
```

```
addMovie: (context, payload) => {
  return axios({
      method: 'post',
      data: payload,
      url: '/movies',
      headers: {
        'Content-Type': 'application/json',
      },
  })
    .then((response) => {
      context.commit("ADD_MOVIE", response.data)
      this.$swal(
        'Great!',
        'Movie added successfully!',
        'success',
      );
    })
    .catch(() => {
      this.$swal(
        'Oh oo!',
        'Could not add the movie!',
        'error',
      );
    });
},
fetchMovies: (context, payload) => {
  axios({
    method: 'get',
    url: '/movies',
  })
    .then((response) => {
      context.commit("MOVIES", response.data.movies);
    })
    .catch(() => {
    });
  }
 }
})
```

Finally, run the following command to build our static files for Vue components:

```
$ npm run build
```

Now, when we log in and add a movie with the admin user, the movie should be added to the database and also be listed on the home page.

Using Vuex in a small application such as this is overkill. The best use of Vuex is in large-scale applications where data needs to be transferred and shared among several components. This gives you an idea of how Vuex works and how to implement it.

Summary

In this chapter, we discussed what Vuex is—the core concepts of Vuex state, getters, mutations, actions, and how to use them in an application. We discussed how to structure our application to implement Vuex and the benefits it adds when the application grows larger.

In the next chapter, we will cover how to write unit tests and integration for Vue.js and Node.js application.

Testing an MEVN Application

9

Let's do a quick recap of what we have done so far in previous chapters:

- We created different Vue components for different pages
- We implemented Vuex—centralized state management for Vue.js applications, and defined state, getters, mutations, and actions for the components
- We created controllers and models to interact with the Node.js backend

In this chapter, we will discuss how to write test code to make sure that everything in the application works well. Writing test code is an integral part of any application. It helps to ensure that the functionalities that we have written do not break, and maintains the quality of the code we write.

Different practices can be followed while writing tests. It's always a good practice to write test code first, before writing the actual code. Writing tests ensures that our application will not break and everything will work as expected.

This helps us to write better code and also helps to reveal the potential problems before they arise.

Benefits of writing tests

Writing test code when developing an application has a lot of benefits. Some of them are as follows:

- **Ensures code works as expected**: It helps to ensure that each piece of functionality that we have written in our application works exactly as expected.
- **Improves the quality of code**: It improves the quality of code. Since writing test code helps to pre-empt defects that may arise, before we write actual code, it improves the quality of the code.

- **Identifies bugs beforehand**: It helps to identify bugs in the early stages. Since test code is written for every functionality, bugs and issues can be identified early.
- **Serves as documentation for new developers**: Test code is like documentation. If we need new developers to start work on the same application, test code helps them to understand how the application works instead of going through all the application code.
- **Application development is faster with test code**: If we write code without the test code, we will code faster. However, if we skip the process, we will later spending most of our time later fixing the bugs that will start to crawl in, which could have been identified earlier with the test code.
- **Application doesn't need to be run**: Writing test code and running it doesn't require the application to be up and running. It also doesn't require the application to be built either. This reduces the development time significantly.

So, in this chapter, we will discuss the following topics:

- Learn why and how to write unit tests and end-to-end tests
- Learn about the technologies for writing test code for a Vue.js and Node.js application
- Modify our application's structure to implement unit and end-to-end code
- Write test code for Vue components

Introduction to unit tests

Unit testing is a software development process in which the smallest functionality of the application is tested and examined to check whether it works as expected or not. A unit is the smallest part of any application. Every test code written for a unit of an application is independent of each other. The goal of unit testing itself is to perform an individual tests and make sure that each piece is correct.

Convention for writing unit tests

If you follow certain guidelines and principles while writing unit tests, it makes your code maintainable and readable. The following are a few techniques that we can use while writing unit tests for any application:

- Unit testing should be carried out in small units—for a single class or a method.
- Unit testing should be carried out in isolation, meaning that a unit test should not be dependent on any other classes or methods, which is achieved by mocking such dependencies.
- Since unit testing is done in smaller parts, these should be very lightweight, which makes the tests run faster.
- A unit test should test the behavior of a unit of an application. It should expect a certain value and return a certain output.
- Since unit tests are done in isolation, the ordering of tests for different units does not create a problem.
- Follow **Do not Repeat Yourself** (**DRY**); the code should not be repeatable.
- Add comments explaining where you can, which explains the why part of the test so that it is understandable.

An introduction to end-to-end test

End-to-end testing is the testing of our application from start to finish. Where as unit testing tests whether the functionalities of your application work independently or not—end-to-end testing checks whether the flow of the application is performing as expected or not. Usually, the end-to-end testing makes sure that all the user interactions are carried out the way as expected. End-to-end testing ensures that the flow of the application is working as expected.

Convention for writing end-to-end tests

There are certain guidelines to be followed when writing the end-to-end tests:

- Test cases should be written considering the end users and considering the real scenario
- Multiple test cases should be created for different scenarios
- The requirements should be gathered for all the software or applications that are involved
- For each requirement, gather as many conditions or scenarios as possible
- Write separate test cases for each scenario

Technologies we will be using

Here are some of the packages that we will be working with to write the tests for our application:

- **Mocha**: A JavaScript test framework to write unit testing (`https://mochajs.org/`)
- **Chai**: An assertion library for the Node.js framework (`http://chaijs.com/`)
- **Sinon**: `sinon` is for test spies, stubs, and mocks (`http://sinonjs.org/`)
- **Nightwatch**: A JavaScript library for writing end-to-end tests (`http://nightwatchjs.org/`)
- **Karma**: `karma` is the test runner for JavaScript (`https://karma-runner.github.io/2.0/index.html`)

We will discuss each of these technologies as we go along.

Introducing Mocha

Let's create a separate working directory to learn to write tests. Create a folder called `test_js` and switch to the `test_js` directory:

```
> mkdir test_js
> cd test_js
```

Let's also create a separate folder for `test` inside the `test_js` folder:

```
> mkdir test
```

To access `mocha`, you have to install it globally:

```
$ npm install mocha -g --save-dev
```

Let's write a simple test code in `mocha`. We will write a test for a simple function, which takes two arguments and returns the sum of the arguments.

Let's create a file called `add.spec.js` inside the `test` folder and add the following code:

```
const addUtility = require('./../add.js');
```

Then, run the following command from the `test_js` folder:

```
$ mocha
```

This test will fail, and we will require a utility called `add.js`, which does not exist. It displays the following error:

```
~/P/test_js git⊧master ⟩⟩⟩ mocha
module.js:472
    throw err;
    ^

Error: Cannot find module './add.js'
    at Function.Module._resolveFilename (module.js:470:15)
    at Function.Module._load (module.js:418:25)
    at Module.require (module.js:498:17)
    at require (internal/module.js:20:19)
    at Object.<anonymous> (/Users/aneetasharma/Projects/test_js/test/add.spec.js:1:80)
    at Module._compile (module.js:571:32)
    at Object.Module._extensions..js (module.js:580:10)
    at Module.load (module.js:488:32)
    at tryModuleLoad (module.js:447:12)
    at Function.Module._load (module.js:439:3)
    at Module.require (module.js:498:17)
    at require (internal/module.js:20:19)
    at /usr/local/lib/node_modules/mocha/lib/mocha.js:219:27
    at Array.forEach (native)
    at Mocha.loadFiles (/usr/local/lib/node_modules/mocha/lib/mocha.js:216:14)
    at Mocha.run (/usr/local/lib/node_modules/mocha/lib/mocha.js:468:10)
    at Object.<anonymous> (/usr/local/lib/node_modules/mocha/bin/_mocha:403:18)
    at Module._compile (module.js:571:32)
    at Object.Module._extensions..js (module.js:580:10)
```

Let's go ahead and write just enough code to pass the test. Create a file called add.js in the root of the test_js project and run the code again, which should pass:

```
~/P/test_js git⊭master ››› mocha


  0 passing (3ms)

~/P/test_js git⊭master ››› |
```

Let's go ahead and add the logic to the test code to check our add function. In add.spec.js, add the following lines of code:

```
var addUtility = require('./../add.js');

describe('Add', function(){
  describe('addUtility', function(){
    it('should have a sum method', function(){
      assert.equal(typeof addUtility, 'object');
      assert.equal(typeof addUtility.sum, 'function');
    })
  })
});
```

Now comes the assert library. The assert library helps to check whether the passed expression is right or wrong. Here, we will use the built-in assertion library for Node.js.

To include the assert library, let's add the following lines of code in add.spec.js:

```
var assert = require("assert")
var addUtility = require("./../add.js");

describe('Add', function(){
  describe('addUtility', function(){
    it('should have a sum method', function(){
      assert.equal(typeof addUtility, 'object');
      assert.equal(typeof addUtility.sum, 'function');
    })
  })
});
```

Let's rerun `mocha`. This should again fail, because we haven't added a method to our module. So, let's go ahead and do that. In `add.js`, let's add the following code:

```
var addUtility = {}

addUtility.sum = function () {
   'use strict';
   return true;
}

module.exports = addUtility;
```

Let's rerun `mocha`. The spec should pass now:

```
×  ...ects/test_js
~/P/test_js git⊮master ››› mocha


  Add
    addUtility
      ✓ should have a sum method


  1 passing (8ms)

~/P/test_js git⊮master ››› |
```

Now, let's add the functional part to the sum method. In `add_spec.js`, add the following code:

```
var assert = require("assert")
var addUtility = require("./../add.js");

describe('Add', function(){
  describe('addUtility', function(){
    it('should have a sum method', function(){
      assert.equal(typeof addUtility, 'object');
      assert.equal(typeof addUtility.sum, 'function');
    })

    it('addUtility.sum(5, 4) should return 9', function(){
      assert.deepEqual(addUtility.sum(5, 4), 9)
```

```
    })
  })
});
```

Then, take a look at the test; it fails. Then, add the logic to our module:

```
var addUtility = {}

addUtility.sum = function (a, b) {
  'use strict';
  return a + b;
}

module.exports = addUtility;
```

Then, rerun `mocha` and the test should pass. That's it!:

```
~/P/test_js git:master >>> mocha


Add
  addUtility
    ✓ should have a sum method
    ✓ addUtility.sum(5, 4) should return 9


2 passing (14ms)

~/P/test_js git:master >>> |
```

You can go on adding a few more cases to the test to ensure that nothing breaks.

Introducing chai

Let's discuss `chai`. `chai` is an assertion library, used with `mocha`. We could also use the native `assertion` library , but `chai` adds a lot of flexibility.

`chai` makes it a lot easier to write test definitions. Let's install `chai` and modify the preceding test to make it look more simple and easy to understand:

```
$ npm install chai -g
```

We passed the `-g` option to install it globally, since we do not have a `package.json` configuration.

Let's use `chai` in our previous test. In `add.spec.js`, add the following lines of code:

```
var expect = require('chai').expect;
var addUtility = require("./../add.js");

describe('Add', function(){
  describe('addUtility', function(){
    it('should have a sum method', function(){
      expect(addUtility).to.be.an('object');
      expect(addUtility).to.have.property('sum');
    })

    it('addUtility.sum(5, 4) should return 9', function(){
      expect(addUtility.sum(5, 4)).to.deep.equal(9);
    })

    it('addUtility.sum(100, 6) should return 106', function(){
      expect(addUtility.sum(100, 6)).to.deep.equal(106);
    })
  })
});
```

We have replaced the `assertion` library with, `chai expect()` method, which makes the code very much simpler and understandable.

Introducing sinon

`sinon` is used to test spies, stubs, and mocks for JavaScript tests. To learn about these, let's move on to the movie rating application we have in our `controller` file, `controller/movies.js`:

```
const Movie = require("../models/Movie");
const passport = require("passport");

module.exports.controller = (app) => {
  // fetch all movies
  app.get("/movies", function(req, res) {
    Movie.find({}, 'name description release_year genre', function
    (error, movies) {
      if (error) { console.log(error); }
      res.send({
        movies: movies
      })
    })
  })
```

```
// add a new movie
app.post('/movies', (req, res) => {
  const movie = new Movie({
    name: req.body.name,
    description: req.body.description,
    release_year: req.body.release_year,
    genre: req.body.genre
  })

  movie.save(function (error, movie) {
    if (error) { console.log(error); }
    res.send(movie)
  })
})
}
```

In the preceding code, each API call needs a request and a response object, which we need to mock. For this purpose, we have sinon. sinon provides us with a mechanism to stub and mock the requests.

The three major methods that sinon provides are spies, stubs, and mocks:

- **Spies**: Spies helps to create fake functions. We can use spies to track whether the functions are executed or not.
- **Stubs**: Stubs helps us to make functions return whatever we want. This is useful when we want to test different scenarios for the given function.
- **Mocks**: Mocks are used to fake network connections. They help to create a dummy class instance, which helps to set the predetermined expectations.

Let's write a test for a get call in the movies controller:

```
// fetch all movies
app.get("/movies", function(req, res) {
  Movie.find({}, 'name description release_year genre', function
  (error, movies) {
    if (error) { console.log(error); }
    res.send({
      movies: movies
    })
  })
})
```

Let's create a new file, called `movies.spec.js`, inside the `test/units` folder:

```
var movies = require("./../../../controllers/movies.js");
var expect = require('chai').expect;

describe('controllers.movies.js', function(){
  it('exists', function(){
    expect(movies).to.exist
  })
})
```

This test code simply checks whether the `controller` exists or not, which should pass when we run the following command:

```
$ mocha test/unit/controllers/movies.spec.js
```

This command runs the tests for our `controller/movies.js` and should pass with the following output:

```
~/P/movie_rating_app git▸test_spec ››› mocha test/unit/controllers/movies.spec.js


  controllers.movies.js
    ✓ exists


  1 passing (13ms)

~/P/movie_rating_app git▸test_spec ›››
```

Let's first write a test for a simple method. Let's create a request that responds with just an object with a name. In `movies.js,` let's add the following code to create a dummy API:

```
const Movie = require("../models/Movie");
const passport = require("passport");

module.exports.controller = (app) => {
  // send a dummy test
  app.get("/dummy_test", function(req, res) {
    res.send({
      name: 'John'
    })
  })
})
```

In the preceding code, we have a simple method that returns an object.

Let's move on to add the functional test part. We will be writing the test for the `/dummy_test` method.

In `movies.spec.js`, let's add the following lines of code:

```
var controller = require("./..//../../controllers/movies.js");
let chaiHttp = require('chai-http');
let chai = require('chai');
var expect = chai.expect;
var should = chai.should();
var express = require("express");
let server = require('./..//../../server.js');
var app = express();
chai.use(chaiHttp);


function buildResponse() {
   return http_mocks.createResponse({eventEmitter:
require('events').EventEmitter})
}

describe('controllers.movies', function(){
   it('exists', function(){
      expect(controller).to.exist
   })
})

describe('/GET dummy_test', () => {
   it('it should respond with a name object', (done) => {
      chai.request(server)
         .get('/dummy_test')
         .end((err, res) => {
            res.should.have.status(200);
            res.body.should.be.an('object');
          done();
        });
   });
});
```

In the preceding code, we have added a new package called `chai-http`, which is used to mock the request. Let's install this package, as follows:

```
$ npm install chai-http --save
```

Let's now run the test with the following command:

```
$ mocha test/unit/controllers/movies.spec.js
```

The preceding command should give us the following output:

```
~/P/movie_rating_app git:test_spec >>> mocha test/unit/controllers/movies.spec.js                    ⬡ ✦ ✧ ✧

(node:74122) DeprecationWarning: `open()` is deprecated in mongoose >= 4.11.0, use `openUri()` instead, or set the
`useMongoClient` option if using `connect()` or `createConnection()`. See http://mongoosejs.com/docs/connections.ht
ml#use-mongo-client
api running on port 8081
  controllers.movies
    ✓ exists
Connection has been made

  /GET dummy_test
::ffff:127.0.0.1 - - [17/Mar/2018:09:23:38 +0000] "GET /dummy_test HTTP/1.1" 200 15 "-" "node-superagent/2.3.0"
    ✓ it should respond with a name object (47ms)


  2 passing (96ms)
```

Writing tests for Node.js server

Let's start writing the tests for the application we built for the backend part of the node server.

We will be using the following folder structure:

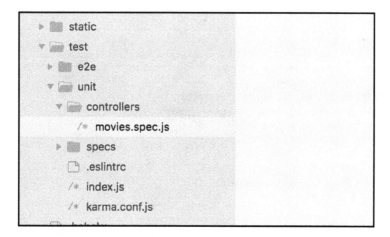

There are two folders inside the `test` folder. One for unit testing, called `unit`, and another for end-to-end testing, called `e2e`. We will start by writing the unit tests, which go under the `unit` directory. The naming convention is appending the `.spec` part to the filename for every file we will be writing tests for.

Writing tests for controllers

Let's get started with writing tests for the controllers we added. Create a folder called `controllers` inside the `test/unit/specs` and create a new file inside it called `movies.spec.js`. This will be the naming convention that we will follow while creating the test files for any components: controllers, models, or Vue components—the actual filename followed by `.spec.js`. This helps to maintain the readability of the code.

Let's first recap what we have in our `movies.js` file:

```
var Movie = require("../models/Movie");

module.exports.controller = (app) => {
  // fetch all movies
  app.get("/movies", function(req, res) {
    Movie.find({}, 'name description release_year genre', function
    (error, movies) {
      if (error) { console.log(error); }
      res.send({
        movies: movies
      })
    })
  })

  // add a new movie
  app.post('/movies', (req, res) => {
    const movie = new Movie({
      name: req.body.name,
      description: req.body.description,
      release_year: req.body.release_year,
      genre: req.body.genre
    })

    movie.save(function (error, movie) {
      if (error) { console.log(error); }
      res.send(movie)
    })
  })
}
```

This controller has two methods—one GET request and a POST request. The GET request is for fetching all the movies from the database, and the POST request saves the movies with the given parameters to the database.

Let's move on to adding the spec for the GET request first. Add the following contents in the `movies.spec.js` file that we just created:

```
const controller = require("./../../../../controllers/movies.js");
const Movie = require("./../../../../models/Movie.js");
let server = require('./../../../../server.js');
let chai = require('chai');
let sinon = require('sinon');
const expect = chai.expect;
let chaiHttp = require('chai-http');
chai.use(chaiHttp);
const should = chai.should();
```

The first two lines required the corresponding controller and model for the `Movie` component, which we will need later. We will also require the server file.

The other packages, such as `chai`, `sinon`, `expect`, and `should`, are needed for the assertions.

The next thing that we will need to make requests to the server is a package called `chai-http`. This package will be used for HTTP request assertions. So, let's install this package first with the following command:

```
$ npm install chai-http --save
```

Now, we can get ahead with adding the first test. Replace the contents in `movies.spec.js` with the following code:

```
const controller = require("./../../../../controllers/movies.js");
const Movie = require("./../../../../models/Movie.js");
let server = require('./../../../../server.js');
let chai = require('chai');
let sinon = require('sinon');
const expect = chai.expect;
let chaiHttp = require('chai-http');
chai.use(chaiHttp);
const should = chai.should();

describe('controllers.movies', function(){
  it('exists', function(){
```

```
        expect (controller) .to.exist
    })
  })
```

The preceding method describes the `movies` controller. It simply checks whether the controller we are describing exists or not.

To make sure we have the connection of our `node` server, let's export the server from `server.js`. Add the following code into `server.js`:

```
...
const port = process.env.API_PORT || 8081;
app.use ('/', router);
var server = app.listen(port, function() {
  console.log(`api running on port ${port}`);
});
```

```
module.exports = server
```

Now, let's run the test using the following command:

```
$ mocha test/unit/specs/controllers/movies.spec.js
```

The test should pass.

Let's move on to adding the test for the GET request. In `movies.js`, we have the following code:

```
var Movie = require("../models/Movie");

module.exports.controller = (app) => {
  // fetch all movies
  app.get("/movies", function(req, res) {
    Movie.find({}, 'name description release_year genre', function
    (error, movies) {
      if (error) { console.log(error); }
      res.send({
        movies: movies
      })
    })
  })
  ...
}
```

Since this method fetches all the existing movies from the database, we will first need to build the mock movies here to actually test it. Let's replace the contents of `movies.spec.js` with the following code:

```js
const controller = require("./../../../../controllers/movies.js");
const Movie = require("./../../../../models/Movie.js");
let server = require('./../../../../server.js');
let chai = require('chai');
let sinon = require('sinon');
const expect = chai.expect;
let chaiHttp = require('chai-http');
chai.use(chaiHttp);
const should = chai.should();

describe('controllers.movies', function(){
  it('exists', function(){
    expect(controller).to.exist
  })

  describe('/GET movies', () => {
    it('it should send all movies', (done) => {
      var movie1 = {
        name: 'test1',
        description: 'test1',
        release_year: 2017,
        genre: 'test1'
      };
      var movie2 = {
        name: 'test2',
        description: 'test2',
        release_year: 2018,
        genre: 'test2'
      };
      var expectedMovies = [movie1, movie2];
      sinon.mock(Movie)
        .expects('find')
        .yields('', expectedMovies);
      chai.request(server)
        .get('/movies')
        .end((err, res) => {
          res.should.have.status(200);
          res.body.should.be.an('object');
          expect(res.body).to.eql({
            movies: expectedMovies
          });
          done();
        });
    });
```

```
    });
  });
})
```

Let's learn step by step what we did here:

- We created a couple of movies with `sinon` mocks
- We created an HTTP GET request using `chai`
- We had three expectations:
  - The status of the request should be `200`
  - The request response should be an object
  - The response should contain the list of movies that we created with the mock

Let's run the test again with the following command:

```
$ mocha test/unit/specs/controllers/movies.spec.js
```

The tests should pass.

Let's now move on to add the tests for the POST request for `movies.js`. In `movies.js`, here is what we have so far:

```
var Movie = require("../models/Movie");

module.exports.controller = (app) => {
  ...

  // add a new movie
  app.post('/movies', (req, res) => {
    const movie = new Movie({
      name: req.body.name,
      description: req.body.description,
      release_year: req.body.release_year,
      genre: req.body.genre
    })

    movie.save(function (error, movie) {
      if (error) { console.log(error); }
      res.send(movie)
    })
  })
}
```

The POST method takes the preceding four attributes of the movie and saves them to the database. Let's add the test for this POST request. Replace the contents of `movies.spec.js` with the following code:

```
const controller = require("./../../../../controllers/movies.js");
const Movie = require("./../../../../models/Movie.js");
let server = require('./../../../../server.js');
let chai = require('chai');
let sinon = require('sinon');
const expect = chai.expect;
let chaiHttp = require('chai-http');
chai.use(chaiHttp);
const should = chai.should();

describe('controllers.movies', function(){
  it('exists', function(){
    expect(controller).to.exist
  })

  describe('/GET movies', () => {
    it('it should send all movies', (done) => {
      var movie1 = {
        name: 'test1',
        description: 'test1',
        release_year: 2017,
        genre: 'test1'
      };
      var movie2 = {
        name: 'test2',
        description: 'test2',
        release_year: 2018,
        genre: 'test2'
      };
      var expectedMovies = [movie1, movie2];
      sinon.mock(Movie)
        .expects('find')
        .yields('', expectedMovies);
      chai.request(server)
        .get('/movies')
        .end((err, res) => {
          res.should.have.status(200);
          res.body.should.be.an('object');
          expect(res.body).to.eql({
            movies: expectedMovies
          });
          done();
        });
    });
```

```
    });
  });

  describe('POST /movies', () => {
    it('should respond with the movie that was added', (done) => {
      chai.request(server)
      .post('/movies')
      .send({
        name: 'test1',
        description: 'test1',
        release_year: 2018,
        genre: 'test1'
      })
      .end((err, res) => {
        should.not.exist(err);
        res.status.should.equal(200);
        res.body.should.be.an('object');
        res.body.should.include.keys(
          '_id', 'name', 'description', 'release_year', 'genre'
        );
        done();
      });
    });
  });
})
```

Here, in the preceding code block, what we have done is, for the POST request:

- We are sending the POST request with movie parameters: name, description, release_year, and genre
- We had three expectations:
    - The status of the request should be 200
    - The request response should be an object
    - The response should contain all four attributes, along with the ID of the movie

Now if we run the tests again, they should all pass.

Similarly, we can add tests for other controllers as well.

Writing tests for models

Let's move on to adding the tests for the models that we have defined. Let's create a folder called `models` inside `test/unit/specs` and create a test file for our `Movie.js` model. So, the name of the spec file would be `Movie.spec.js`.

Let's first take a look at what we have in our `Movie.js`:

```
const mongoose = require('mongoose');
const Schema = mongoose.Schema
const MovieSchema = new Schema({
  name: String,
    description: String,
    release_year: Number,
    genre: String
})

const Movie = mongoose.model('Movie', MovieSchema)
module.exports = Movie
```

We just have a `Schema` defined here, which defines the data type for the `Movie` collection.

Let's add the specs for this model. Add the following contents to the `Movie.spec.js`:

```
var Movie = require("./../../../../models/Movie.js");
let chai = require('chai');
var expect = chai.expect;
var should = chai.should();
```

We do not need all the components that we added to the controller test here. We just have simple assertion tests here, so we will need the `Movie` model and the `chai` methods.

Let's add the test for the `Movie` existence just like we did for the controller. Replace the contents in `Movie.spec.js` with the following code:

```
var Movie = require("./../../../../models/Movie.js");
let chai = require('chai');
var expect = chai.expect;
var should = chai.should();

describe('models.Movie', function(){
  it('exists', function(){
    expect(Movie).to.exist
  })
})
```

This test checks whether the `Model` we are describing exists or not. Let's run the test using the following command:

```
$ mocha test/unit/specs/models/Movie.spec.js
```

The test should pass with the following output:

```
~/P/movie_rating_app git▸refactor >>> mocha test/unit/specs/models/Movie.spec.js


  models.Movie
    ✓ exists


  1 passing (18ms)

~/P/movie_rating_app git▸refactor >>> |
```

Let's move on to add a test when we send the `release_year` attribute of the `Movie` a string. Since we have a validation for the `release_year` attribute, sending a string value to it should throw an error.

Replace the contents in `Movie.spec.js` with the following code:

```javascript
var Movie = require("./../../../../models/Movie.js");
let chai = require('chai');
var expect = chai.expect;
var should = chai.should();

describe('models.Movie', function(){
  it('exists', function(){
    expect(Movie).to.exist
  })

  describe('Movie', function() {
    it('should be invalid if release_year is not an integer',
    function(done) {
      var movie = new Movie({
        name: 'test',
        description: 'test',
        release_year: 'test',
        genre: 'test'
      });

      movie.validate(function(err){
```

```
        expect(err.errors.release_year).to.exist;
        done();
      })
    })
  })
})
```

Here, we have prepared a movie object with `release_year` with an invalid value. The expectation we have here is that, when validating the model, it should send an error.

Let's run the test, and it should pass with the following output:

```
~/P/movie_rating_app git⊮master ››› mocha test/unit/specs/models/Movie.spec.js


 models.Movie
  ✓ exists
  Movie
     ✓ should be invalid if release_year is not an integer


 2 passing (30ms)

~/P/movie_rating_app git⊮master ››› |
```

Similarly, we can add tests for other models as well.

Writing tests for Vue.js components

Let's move on to write the test specs for our Vue.js components. We will start with the simplest component, which is the `Contact.vue` page.

This is what we have in our `Contact.vue` page so far:

```
<template>
  <v-layout>
    this is contact
  </v-layout>
</template>
```

Let's modify the component a little bit to make the tests more understandable. Replace the contents in `Contact.vue` with the following code:

```
<template>
  <div class="contact">
    <h1>this is contact</h1>
  </div>
</template>
```

Now, let's first create the necessary folder and file to write our tests. Create a file called `Contact.spec.js` inside the `test/unit/specs` directory and add the following contents to it:

```
import Vue from 'vue';
import Contact from '@/components/Contact';

describe('Contact.vue', () => {
  it('should render correct contents', () => {
    const Constructor = Vue.extend(Contact);
    const vm = new Constructor().$mount();
    expect(vm.$el.querySelector('.contact h1').textContent)
      .to.equal('this is contact');
  });
});
```

In the preceding code, we have added a test to check whether the vue component `Contact.vue` renders the correct contents or not. We expected to have a `div` element with the `contact` class, and inside it, there should be an `h1` tag, which should contain the `this is contact` content.

Now, to make sure that our tests run, let's verify that we have the correct script set up to run the unit test in `package.json`:

```
...
"scripts": {
    "dev": "webpack-dev-server --inline --progress --config
build/webpack.dev.conf.js",
    "start": "nodemon server.js",
    "unit": "cross-env BABEL_ENV=test karma start test/unit/karma.conf.js -
-single-run",
    "e2e": "node test/e2e/runner.js",
    "test": "npm run unit && npm run e2e",
    "lint": "eslint --ext .js,.vue src test/unit test/e2e/specs",
    "build": "node build/build.js",
    "heroku-postbuild": "npm install --only=dev --no-shrinkwrap && npm run
build"
```

```
  },
  ...
```

Now, let's run the test with the following command:

```
$ npm run unit
```

The test should pass with the following output:

```
Contact.vue
  ✓ should render correct contents

Chrome 65.0.3325 (Mac OS X 10.13.3): Executed 1 of 1 SUCCESS (0.015 secs / 0.002 secs)
TOTAL: 1 SUCCESS


============================= Coverage summary =============================
Statements    : 10.98% ( 9/82 )
Branches      : 0% ( 0/25 )
Functions     : 0% ( 0/38 )
Lines         : 10.98% ( 9/82 )
============================================================================
~/P/movie_rating_app git:master >>>
```

Let's move on to add specs for the component called AddMovie.vue. Create a file called AddMovie.spec.js inside test/unit/specs and add the following contents:

```
import Vue from 'vue';
import AddMovie from '@/components/AddMovie';

describe('AddMovie', () => {
  let cmp, vm;

  beforeEach(() => {
    cmp = Vue.extend(AddMovie);
    vm = new cmp({
      data: {
        years: ['2018', '2017', '2016', '2015']
      }
    }).$mount()
  })

  it('equals years to ["2018", "2017", "2016", "2015"]', () => {
    console.log(vm.years);
```

```
        expect(vm.years).to.eql(['2018', '2017', '2016', '2015'])
      })
    })
```

This test states that the `years` variable should have the given values, which is `['2018',
'2017', '2016', '2015']`.

Let's add another test to check whether the required methods exist in our `vue`
component, `AddMovie.js`, or not. Replace the contents in `AddMovie.spec.js` with the
following code:

```
import Vue from 'vue';
import AddMovie from '@/components/AddMovie';

describe('AddMovie', () => {
  let cmp, vm;

  beforeEach(() => {
    cmp = Vue.extend(AddMovie);
    vm = new cmp({
      data: {
        years: ['2018', '2017', '2016', '2015']
      }
    }).$mount()
  })

  it('equals years to ["2018", "2017", "2016", "2015"]', () => {
    console.log(vm.years);
    expect(vm.years).to.eql(['2018', '2017', '2016', '2015'])
  })

  it('has a submit() method', () => {
    assert.deepEqual(typeof vm.submit, 'function')
  })

  it('has a clear() method', () => {
    assert.deepEqual(typeof vm.clear, 'function')
  })
})
```

Now, let's run the tests with the following command:

```
$ npm run unit
```

The tests should pass.

Finally, to run all the tests, we can simply run the following command:

```
$ npm run test
```

Writing e2e testing

The vue.js applications created with `vue-cli` command contains the support for end-to-end testing which uses `Nightwatch`. `Nightwatch` is a very easy framework to write end-to-end test. `Nightwatch` uses `Selenium` commands to run the JavaScript.

Installing Nightwatch

If you haven't set up the application for `e2e`, then let's first install the package needed to run the `e2e` tests:

```
$ npm install nightwatch --save
```

Configuring Nightwatch

Now, we need a configuration file to run the test. Create a folder called `e2e` inside the `test` folder. Add the `nightwatch.conf.js` file and add the following contents to it:

```
require('babel-register')
var config = require('../../config')

// http://nightwatchjs.org/gettingstarted#settings-file
module.exports = {
  src_folders: ['test/e2e/specs'],
  custom_assertions_path: ['test/e2e/custom-assertions'],

  selenium: {
    start_process: true,
    server_path: require('selenium-server').path,
    host: '127.0.0.1',
    port: 4444,
    cli_args: {
      'webdriver.chrome.driver': require('chromedriver').path
    }
  },
```

```
    test_settings: {
      default: {
        selenium_port: 4444,
        selenium_host: 'localhost',
        silent: true,
        globals: {
          devServerURL: 'http://localhost:' + (process.env.PORT ||
config.dev.port)
        }
      },

      chrome: {
        desiredCapabilities: {
          browserName: 'chrome',
          javascriptEnabled: true,
          acceptSslCerts: true
        }
      },

      firefox: {
        desiredCapabilities: {
          browserName: 'firefox',
          javascriptEnabled: true,
          acceptSslCerts: true
        }
      }
    }
  }
}
```

In the preceding code, in the setting inside the `test_settings` attribute, we can see the different setups for different browsers. In this case, Chrome, Firefox, and the host and port settings for the development environment to run on the browser.

Also, in the preceding code, we have specified two folders: `specs` and `custom-assertions`.

- The `specs` folder contains the main test code for the application
- `custom-assertion` contains a script, which contains custom messages that get displayed when assertion tests are run on the command line

Let's first set up our `custom-assertions`. Create a file called `elementCount.js` inside `custom-assertions` and add the following contents to it:

```
// A custom Nightwatch assertion.
// The assertion name is the filename.
// Example usage:
```

```
//
// browser.assert.elementCount(selector, count)
//
// For more information on custom assertions see:
// http://nightwatchjs.org/guide#writing-custom-assertions

exports.assertion = function (selector, count) {
  this.message = 'Testing if element <' + selector + '> has count: ' +
count
  this.expected = count
  this.pass = function (val) {
    return val === this.expected
  }
  this.value = function (res) {
    return res.value
  }
  this.command = function (cb) {
    var self = this
    return this.api.execute(function (selector) {
      return document.querySelectorAll(selector).length
    }, [selector], function (res) {
      cb.call(self, res)
    })
  }
}
```

If you checked the e2e option when creating this application, you should also have the test/e2e/specs/test.js file. If not, go ahead and create this file and add the following contents into it:

```
// For authoring Nightwatch tests, see
// http://nightwatchjs.org/guide#usage

module.exports = {
  'default e2e tests': function test(browser) {
    // automatically uses dev Server port from /config.index.js
    // default: http://localhost:8080
    // see nightwatch.conf.js
    const devServer = browser.globals.devServerURL;
    console.log(devServer);

    browser
      .url(devServer)
      .waitForElementVisible('#app', 5000)
      .assert.elementPresent('.hello')
      .assert.containsText('h1', 'Welcome to Your Vue.js App')
      .assert.elementCount('img', 1)
```

```
        .end();
    },
};
```

This is the main file, where we will add our test cases for the application.

The end-to-end testing makes sure that all the the flow of our application is performing as expected or not. When we run the `e2e` test, we want certain parts of our application to be clicked and behave the way it should. This can be described as testing the behavior of the application.

To be able to run the `e2e` tests, we will need to start a `selenium-server`. If we take a look at the `test/e2e/nightwatch.conf.js` file, we can find a line that says:

```
...
selenium: {
    start_process: true,
    server_path: require('selenium-server').path,
    host: '127.0.0.1',
    port: 4444,
    cli_args: {
        'webdriver.chrome.driver': require('chromedriver').path
    }
},
...
```

This means that when we run the `e2e` test, a `selenium-server` is started automatically, and we don't have to run a separate server. The port defines which port to use for `selenium-server`. You can leave this as it is and run the test, or you can change the values and configure it yourself.

Finally, we need a `runner` file for `Nightwatch` to run the test. Create a file called `runner.js` inside the `e2e` folder and add the following contents:

```
// 1. start the dev server using production config
process.env.NODE_ENV = 'testing'

const webpack = require('webpack')
const DevServer = require('webpack-dev-server')

const webpackConfig = require('../../build/webpack.prod.conf')
const devConfigPromise = require('../../build/webpack.dev.conf')

let server

devConfigPromise.then(devConfig => {
```

```
    const devServerOptions = devConfig.devServer
    const compiler = webpack(webpackConfig)
    server = new DevServer(compiler, devServerOptions)
    const port = devServerOptions.port
    const host = devServerOptions.host
    return server.listen(port, host)
})
.then(() => {
    // 2. run the nightwatch test suite against it
    // to run in additional browsers:
    // 1. add an entry in test/e2e/nightwatch.conf.js under "test_settings"
    // 2. add it to the --env flag below
    // or override the environment flag, for example: `npm run e2e -- --env
chrome,firefox`
    // For more information on Nightwatch's config file, see
    // http://nightwatchjs.org/guide#settings-file
    let opts = process.argv.slice(2)
    if (opts.indexOf('--config') === -1) {
      opts = opts.concat(['--config', 'test/e2e/nightwatch.conf.js'])
    }
    if (opts.indexOf('--env') === -1) {
      opts = opts.concat(['--env', 'chrome'])
    }

    const spawn = require('cross-spawn')
    const runner = spawn('./node_modules/.bin/nightwatch', opts, { stdio:
'inherit' })

    runner.on('exit', function (code) {
      server.close()
      process.exit(code)
    })

    runner.on('error', function (err) {
      server.close()
      throw err
    })
})
```

We will use a stand-alone Selenium server and port 5555 for this application. For that, we will need to install the standalone server first:

```
$ npm install selenium-standalone
```

Let's run the package using the following command:

```
$ npx selenium-standalone start -- -port 5555
```

The `npx` is a command that runs the npm packages.
Since we are using the 5555 port, we will need to update it in the `nightwatch.conf.js` file as well.

Update the Selenium config in `nightwatch.conf.js` with the following code:

```
...
selenium: {
    start_process: false,
    server_path: require('selenium-server').path,
    host: '127.0.0.1',
    port: 5555,
    cli_args: {
       'webdriver.chrome.driver': require('chromedriver').path
    }
},

test_settings: {
  default: {
    selenium_port: 5555,
    selenium_host: 'localhost',
    silent: true,
    globals: {
      devServerURL: 'http://localhost:8081'
    }
  },
},
...
```

Since we are using the 8081 port to run the `node` server, make sure that you update the `devServerURL` attribute as well, as was done in the preceding piece of code.

Now, we are all set to run the tests with the following command:

```
$ npm run e2e
```

The test should fail with the following output:

```
~/P/movie_rating_app git feature-add_e2e_test ... npm run e2e

> movie_rating_app@1.0.0 e2e /Users/aneetasharma/Projects/movie_rating_app
> node test/e2e/runner.js


[Test] Test Suite
********************************

Running:  default e2e tests
http://localhost:8081
  Element <#app> was visible after 72 milliseconds.
  ✘ Testing if element <.hello> is present.            "present" but got: "not present"
      at Object.test [as default e2e tests] (/Users/aneetasharma/Projects/movie_rating_app/test/e2e/specs/test.js:15:15)
      at _combinedTickCallback (internal/process/next_tick.js:131:7)


FAILED:  1 assertions failed and 1 passed (6.467s)


  ---------------------------------------------------

  TEST FAILURE:  1 assertions failed, 1 passed. (24.351s)

  ✘ test

    - default e2e tests (6.467s)
    Testing if element <.hello> is present.            "present" but got: "not present"
        at Object.test [as default e2e tests] (/Users/aneetasharma/Projects/movie_rating_app/test/e2e/specs/test.js:15:15)
        at _combinedTickCallback (internal/process/next_tick.js:131:7)
npm ERR! code ELIFECYCLE
npm ERR! errno 1
npm ERR! movie_rating_app@1.0.0 e2e: `node test/e2e/runner.js`
npm ERR! Exit status 1
npm ERR!
npm ERR! Failed at the movie_rating_app@1.0.0 e2e script.
npm ERR! This is probably not a problem with npm. There is likely additional logging output above.

npm ERR! A complete log of this run can be found in:
npm ERR!     /Users/aneetasharma/.npm/_logs/2018-04-21T13_52_32_079Z-debug.log
~/P/movie_rating_app git feature-add_e2e_test ... |
```

The tests are failing because we do not have the element present with the .hello class in our application. So, to make the tests pass, we first need to add an identifier to the elements, which we will be doing as a part the e2e tests by following the below steps.

Here are the things that we want to capture with the e2e test:

1. Open the browser using http://localhost:8081
2. Check whether the element with the #inspire ID exists. We have defined that in App.vue with the following code:

```
<template>
  <v-app id="inspire">
    <v-navigation-drawer
      fixed
      v-model="drawer"
      app
    >
```

3. Check that the sidebar consists of the Home and Contact page links
4. Click on the Contact page
5. The contact page should contain the text this is contact
6. Click on the login page to make sure that the login works fine
7. Add a movie to our application
8. Rate the movie
9. Finally, add the ability for users to log out of the application

These are the important parts of our application. So, we will need to add an identifier to all of preceding components. The best practice for adding an identifier to the elements is to define a class or an id while building the application itself. However, we will assign an identifier to the now.

In App.vue, update the highlighted parts with the following code:

```
<template>
  <v-app id="inspire">
    <v-navigation-drawer
      fixed
      v-model="drawer"
      app
    >
      <v-list dense>
        <router-link v-bind:to="{ name: 'Home' }" class="side_bar_link">
          <v-list-tile>
            <v-list-tile-action>
              <v-icon>home</v-icon>
            </v-list-tile-action>
            <v-list-tile-content id="home">Home</v-list-tile-content>
          </v-list-tile>
        </router-link>
        <router-link v-bind:to="{ name: 'Contact' }" class="side_bar_link">
          <v-list-tile>
            <v-list-tile-action>
              <v-icon>contact_mail</v-icon>
            </v-list-tile-action>
            <v-list-tile-content id="contact">Contact</v-list-tile-content>
          </v-list-tile>
        </router-link>
      </v-list>
    </v-navigation-drawer>
    <v-toolbar color="indigo" dark fixed app>
      <v-toolbar-side-icon id="drawer" @click.stop="drawer = !drawer"></v-toolbar-side-icon>
```

```
        <v-toolbar-title>Home</v-toolbar-title>
        <v-spacer></v-spacer>
        <v-toolbar-items class="hidden-sm-and-down">
          <v-btn id="add_movie_link" flat v-bind:to="{ name: 'AddMovie' }"
            v-if="current_user && current_user.role === 'admin'">
            Add Movie
          </v-btn>
          <v-btn id="user_email" flat v-if="current_user">{{
current_user.email }}</v-btn>
          <v-btn flat v-bind:to="{ name: 'Register' }" v-if="!current_user"
id="register_btn">
            Register
          </v-btn>
          <v-btn flat v-bind:to="{ name: 'Login' }" v-if="!current_user"
id="login_btn">Login</v-btn>
          <v-btn id="logout_btn" flat v-if="current_user"
@click="logout">Logout</v-btn>
        </v-toolbar-items>
      </v-toolbar>
      <v-content>
        <v-container fluid>
          <div id="app">
            <router-view/>
          </div>
        </v-container>
      </v-content>
      <v-footer color="indigo" app>
        <span class="white--text">&copy; 2017</span>
      </v-footer>
    </v-app>
</template>

<script>
import axios from 'axios';

import './assets/stylesheets/main.css';
import bus from './bus';

export default {
  name: 'app',
  data: () => ({
    drawer: null,
    current_user: null,
  }),
  props: {
    source: String,
  },
  mounted() {
```

```
          this.fetchUser();
          this.listenToEvents();
        },
      methods: {
        listenToEvents() {
          bus.$on('refreshUser', () => {
            this.fetchUser();
          });
        },
        async fetchUser() {
          return axios({
            method: 'get',
            url: '/api/current_user',
          })
            .then((response) => {
              this.current_user = response.data.current_user;
            })
            .catch(() => {
            });
        },
        logout() {
          return axios({
            method: 'get',
            url: '/api/logout',
          })
            .then(() => {
              bus.$emit('refreshUser');
              this.$router.push({ name: 'Home' });
            })
            .catch(() => {
            });
        },
      },
    };
</script>
```

Also, let's update the `id` in `AddMovie.vue`:

```
<template>
  <v-form v-model="valid" ref="form" lazy-validation>
    <v-text-field
      label="Movie Name"
      v-model="name"
      :rules="nameRules"
      id="name"
      required
    ></v-text-field>
    <v-text-field
```

```
          name="input-7-1"
          label="Movie Description"
          v-model="description"
          id="description"
          multi-line
        ></v-text-field>
        <v-select
          label="Movie Release Year"
          v-model="release_year"
          required
          :rules="releaseRules"
          :items="years"
          id="release_year"
        ></v-select>
        <v-text-field
          label="Movie Genre"
          v-model="genre"
          id="genre"
          required
          :rules="genreRules"
        ></v-text-field>
        <v-btn
          @click="submit"
          :disabled="!valid"
          id="add_movie_btn"
        >
          submit
        </v-btn>
        <v-btn @click="clear">clear</v-btn>
      </v-form>
    </template>
```

Also, in `Login.vue`, let's add corresponding `id` for the form fields:

```
<template>
  <div>
    <div class="login">
      <a href="/login/facebook">Facebook</a>
      <a href="/login/twitter">Twitter</a>
      <a href="/login/google">Google</a>
      <a href="/login/linkedin">Linkedin</a>
    </div>
    <v-form v-model="valid" ref="form" lazy-validation>
      <v-text-field
        label="Email"
        v-model="email"
        :rules="emailRules"
        id="email"
```

```
        required
      ></v-text-field>
      <v-text-field
        label="Password"
        v-model="password"
        :rules="passwordRules"
        id="password"
        required
      ></v-text-field>
      <v-btn
        @click="submit"
        :disabled="!valid"
        id="login"
      >
        submit
      </v-btn>
      <v-btn @click="clear" id="clear_input">clear</v-btn><br/>
    </v-form>
  </div>
</template>
```

In `Movie.vue`, **update the** `id` for `Rate this Movie` **with:**

```
<template>
  <v-layout row wrap>
    <v-flex xs4>
      <v-card>
        <v-card-title primary-title>
          <div>
            <div class="headline">{{ movie.name }}</div>
            <span class="grey--text">{{ movie.release_year }} · {{
movie.genre }}</span>
          </div>
        </v-card-title>
        <h6 class="card-title" id="rate_movie" v-if="current_user"
@click="rate">
          Rate this movie
        </h6>
        <v-card-text>
          {{ movie.description }}
        </v-card-text>
      </v-card>
    </v-flex>
  </v-layout>
</template>
```

We have added the necessary identifier to all of the components. Now, let's add the e2e tests for the previously mentioned scenarios.

Replace the contents of test/e2e/specs/test.js with the following code:

```
// For authoring Nightwatch tests, see
// http://nightwatchjs.org/guide#usage

module.exports = {
  'default e2e tests': function test(browser) {
    // automatically uses dev Server port from /config.index.js
    // default: http://localhost:8080
    // see nightwatch.conf.js
    const devServer = browser.globals.devServerURL;
    console.log(devServer)

  browser
    .url(devServer)
    .waitForElementVisible('#inspire', 9000)
    .assert.elementPresent('.list')
    .assert.elementPresent('.list .side_bar_link')
    .assert.elementPresent('.side_bar_link #home')
    .assert.elementPresent('.side_bar_link #contact')
    .click('#drawer')
    .pause(1000)
    .click('#contact')
    .pause(1000)
    .assert.elementPresent('#inspire .contact')
    .assert.containsText('#inspire .contact h1', 'this is contact')
    .pause(1000)
    .click('#login_btn')
    .pause(1000)
    .assert.elementCount('input', 2)
    .setValue('input#email', 'get.aneeta@gmail.com')
    .setValue('input#password', 'secret')
    .pause(1000)
    .click('#login')
    .pause(1000)
    .click('.swal-button--confirm')
    .pause(1000)
    .assert.containsText('#user_email', 'GET.ANEETA@GMAIL.COM')
    .click('#add_movie_link')
    .pause(2000)
    .assert.elementCount('input', 3)
    .assert.elementCount('textarea', 1)
    .setValue('input#name', 'Avengers: Infinity War')
    .setValue('textarea#description', 'Iron Man, Thor, the Hulk and the
```

```
rest of the Avengers unite
      to battle their most powerful enemy yet -- the evil Thanos. On a
mission to collect all six
      Infinity Stones, Thanos plans to use the artifacts to inflict his
twisted will on reality.')
      .click('.input-group__selections')
      .pause(1000)
      .click('.list a ')
      .setValue('input#genre', 'Fantasy/Science fiction film')
      .click('#add_movie_btn')
      .pause(1000)
      .click('.swal-button--confirm')
      .pause(1000)
      .click('.headline:nth-child(1)')
      .pause(1000)
      .assert.containsText('#rate_movie', 'Rate this movie')
      .click('#rate_movie')
      .pause(1000)
      .click('.vue-star-rating span:nth-child(3)')
      .pause(1000)
      .click('.swal-button--confirm')
      .pause(1000)
      .click('.swal-button--confirm')
      .pause(1000)
      .click('#logout_btn')
      .end();
  },
};
```

To run the e2e script, make sure that we have set up the correct command in package.json:

```
...
"scripts": {
    "dev": "webpack-dev-server --inline --progress --config
build/webpack.dev.conf.js",
    "start": "nodemon server.js",
    "unit": "cross-env BABEL_ENV=test karma start test/unit/karma.conf.js -
-single-run",
    "e2e": "node test/e2e/runner.js",
    "test": "npm run unit && npm run e2e",
    "lint": "eslint --ext .js,.vue src test/unit test/e2e/specs",
    "build": "node build/build.js",
    "heroku-postbuild": "npm install --only=dev --no-shrinkwrap && npm run
build"
  },
...
```

After adding the `e2e` script, we should be able to run the test with the following command:

```
$ npm run e2e
```

Now, all the tests should pass, and the output should look like this:

```
> movie_rating_app@1.0.0 e2e /Users/aneetasharma/Projects/movie_rating_app
> node test/e2e/runner.js


[Test] Test Suite
========================

Running: default e2e tests
http://localhost:8081
  ✔ Element <#inspire> was visible after 65 milliseconds.
  ✔ Testing if element <.list> is present.
  ✔ Testing if element <.list .side_bar_link> is present.
  ✔ Testing if element <.side_bar_link #home> is present.
  ✔ Testing if element <.side_bar_link #contact> is present.
  ✔ Testing if element <#inspire .contact> is present.
  ✔ Testing if element <#inspire .contact h1> contains text: "this is contact".
  ✔ Testing if element <input> has count: 2
  ✔ Testing if element <#user_email> contains text: "GET.ANEETA@GMAIL.COM".
  ✔ Testing if element <input> has count: 3
  ✔ Testing if element <textarea> has count: 1
  ✔ Testing if element <#rate_movie> contains text: "Rate this movie".

OK. 12 assertions passed. (28.438s)

~/P/movie_rating_app git/feature-add_e2e_test >>> |
```

Summary

In this chapter, you learned how to write unit tests and we discussed the different technologies you can use to write them, such as `chai`, `mocha`, and `sinon`. You also learned to write tests for controllers, models, and Vue component.

In the next chapter, you will learn about continuous integration and how to deploy your apps to Heroku using GitHub.

10
Going Live

In the previous chapter, we learned how to write tests for the Node.js and Vue.js components for our application. We learned what technologies we can use for testing MEVN applications.

In this chapter, we will learn about what **Continuous Integration** (CI) is, how it makes our lives easier, and how we can deploy our application in Heroku.

Continuous integration

CI is a practice in the software development process where each member of the team is makes continuous small changes in the code and integrates them back into the original codebase. After each change, the developer pushes it to GitHub and the tests run automatically in that change. This helps to check whether there are any bugs or issues in the changed code.

Consider a scenario where multiple developers are working on the same application. Each developer is working on a different feature on separate branches. They all build the features and write the test code for the features they build. Everything is going well. Then when the features are completed, they try to integrate all the features, and all of a sudden everything breaks. The tests also fail and many bugs start to creep out.

If the application is small, it wouldn't be a very big deal because the bugs could be fixed easily. But if it's a large project, then it would be very hard just to figure out what went wrong, let alone fix it all. That is where CI originated.

CI came into practice to mitigate such risks while integrating software. The rule for CI is to integrate early and often, which helps to identify the bugs and problems early in the process of adding new functionalities to the existing codebase. So instead of waiting for the completion of every component, CI encourages us to build the codebase and run the test suites on every single change that is committed to the codebase.

Workflow for CI

Here is a diagram that explains how CI works:

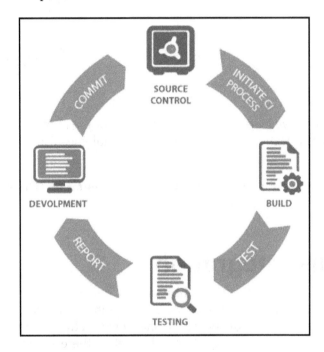

In a real-world scenario, multiple developers work on the same application. They work separately on their own machines. When they make changes to the codebase, they push it to the repository in the version control system that they are using.

Now, this change triggers the CI process that we have integrated into our application to run the test suites automatically and do the quality checks for the code that we have changed.

If the test suite passes, then it goes to the further process for testing the full application and is handed over to the QAs.

But, if the tests fail, then the developers or the whole team working on that application are notified. Then the developer working on that change makes the necessary changes to fix the bug, makes a commit, and pushes the fixed code changes to the repository. Again, the same process is repeated until the tests pass. Hence, if there are any bugs, they are identified early on and fixed early on.

Benefits of CI

Now that we are aware of what CI is and why we should use it, let's look into some of the benefits it gives:

- **Build and test applications automatically**: While it is expected that a developer builds the application and runs the tests before pushing the changed code into the repository, sometimes the developer might just forget. In such cases, integrating a Continuous Integration process helps make the process automatic.
- **Gives the confidence to deploy**: Since CI checks the test suites and we can configure it to check the quality of the code in our codebase, we don't need to worry about forgetting to run the tests before pushing the code to GitHub.
- **Easy configuration**: CI is very easy to configure. We only need to create a single file with all the configurations.
- **Error reporting**: This is one of the powerful features of CI. When something breaks while building or running the tests, the team gets a notification. It can also provide information about who made what changes, which is awesome.

Introduction to Travis CI

Now that we know about CI, we need to start using it in our application as well. There are several technologies that can be used to follow the CI process for any application. There are a lot of tools and each has their own benefits of use; the one that we are going to choose for our application is **Travis CI**.

Travis CI is a technology used to build a CI server. Travis CI is used heavily with GitHub. There are a few other tools as well. Some of them are:

- Circle CI
- Jenkins
- Semaphore CI
- Drone

If you want to learn more about each of the options, here is a good read for that: `https://blog.github.com/2017-11-07-github-welcomes-all-ci-tools/`.

Travis CI is used to build for every push that is made to GitHub and it is very easy to set up.

Setting up Travis in the app

Let's move on to the setup part. The first thing to do here is to check out the official website for Travis CI at `https://travis-ci.org/`.

Activating the repository

We need to sign up first, which can be done easily using **Sign in with GitHub**. When you are done, you should see the list of your existing repositories. Select the application that you want to set up the Travis CI with and you will be able to see the following page:

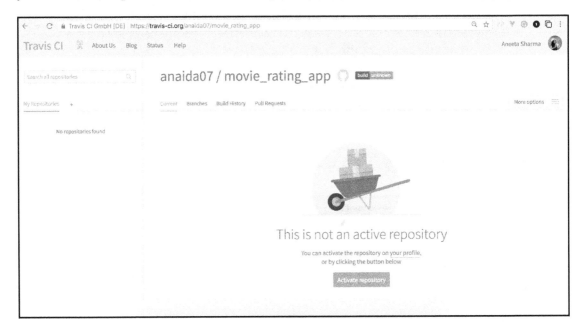

Specifying the Node.js version

Now, activate the repository in which you want to add Travis CI. We can see the list of our repositories in our profile. Select the application and click on the check mark to activate Travis CI in the repository. Now the next part is to add the configuration details. The first thing is to specify the `node` version that we will be using for the application.

Create .travis.yml file in the application in the root:

```
// travis.yml
language: node_js
node_js:
  - "10.0.0"
```

Now, this code block tells that this is a Node.js project and that the version of Node.js for this project is 10.0.0. You have to specify the Node.js that is installed in your application. You can check the version with the following:

```
$ node -v
```

You can specify the same version in the .travis.yml file as well.

If the specified version is not a standard or available version of Node.js, then an error is raised.

We can also specify the version of Node.js that we want to use to build the project in a file called .nvmrc. The travis.yml file reads the content of this file if the version is not specified in the .travis.yml file itself.

Building the script

Now the next part is to tell Travis to run the test suites. This part is specified in the script key in the .travis.yml file. The default build script for a Node.js project is npm test. But let's first start with adding a single command to run in a single file so that it's quick. Update the content of the .travis.yml file with the following:

```
language: node_js
node_js:
  - "10.0.0"
script: npm run unit
```

This tells the script to run the unit tests when any change is made to the repository.

Managing the dependencies

The next part is to install the dependencies. By default, no dependencies are added by Travis CI. The following command tells Travis CI to download the dependencies before building the `script`. It uses npm to install the dependencies, so let's add a `script` to install such dependencies:

```
language: node_js
node_js:
  - "10.0.0"
before_script:
  - npm install
script: npm run unit
```

That's it. We have successfully configured Travis CI for our application.

Now, let's commit and push this file to GitHub. When you do, check the branches on `travis.org` to view all the builds:

Here, the **master** is the branch where we added the Travis CI build and the build is passing. You can view the details for for `master` branch by clicking on the build.

While this is a good approach to view the builds, the best approach is to create a pull request for each branch and see the build pass or fail in that pull request itself. So, let's create a new pull request to see how we can make the best use of Travis CI to make our lives easier.

Let's create a branch called `setup_travis` (you can name your branch anything, but make sure it indicates a particular change so that it's easier to identify what changes that branch can expect) with the following command:

```
$ git checkout -b setup_travis
```

Let's make a simple change to the application so that our pull request contains some differences.

Update the `README.md` file with the following content:

```bash
# movie_rating_app

> A Vue.js project

## Build Setup

``` bash
# install dependencies
npm install

# serve with hot reload at localhost:8080
npm run dev

# build for production with minification
npm run build

# build for production and view the bundle analyzer report
npm run build --report

# run unit tests
npm run unit

# run e2e tests
npm run e2e

# run all tests
npm test
```
```

Then, make a `commit` for the changes with the following command:

```
$ git add README.md
$ git commit -m 'Update readme'
```

Finally, push the changes to GitHub with the following command:

```
$ git push origin setup_travis
```

Now, if we go to our GitHub repository page for this application, we should be able to see the following:

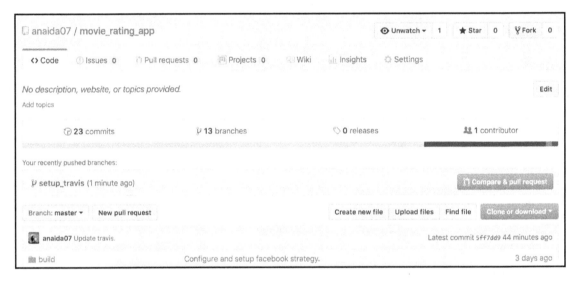

Click on the **Compare & pull request** button. Then add the necessary description and hit the **Create pull request** button.

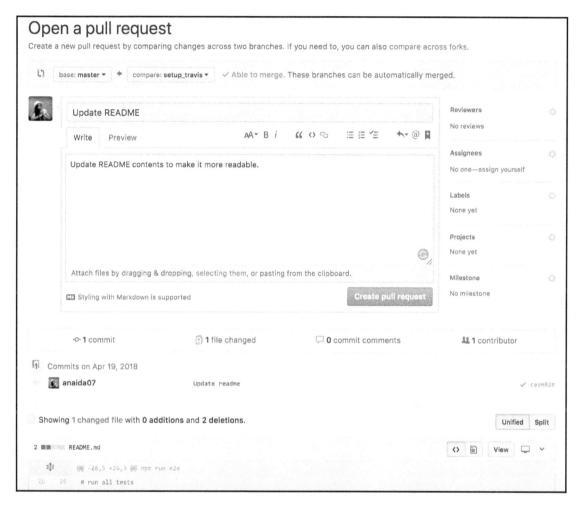

As soon as you create a pull request, Travis CI will start to build the application, and as you go on to add more commits and push changes to, Travis CI will build the application for every commit.

While it is a good practice to run the tests before we push any changes to GitHub, Travis CI build helps to notify if something breaks by building the application for every single commit.

We can also add settings to notify us via email or any other mechanism when the build fails or succeeds as well. By default, Travis CI will notify us via email notifications, as in the following screenshot:

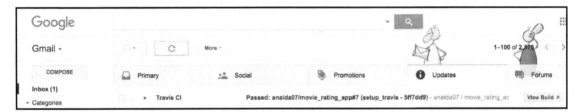

You can see here that Travis CI has been successfully integrated and that the tests are also passing:

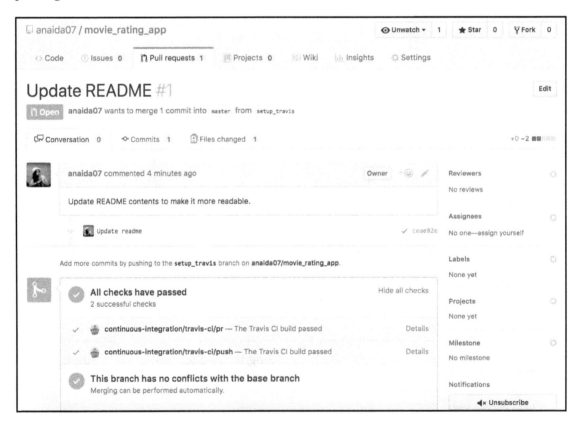

When we click on **Details**, we can see the detailed log for the build as well:

Once we are confident with the changes, we can merge the pull request to the **master** branch:

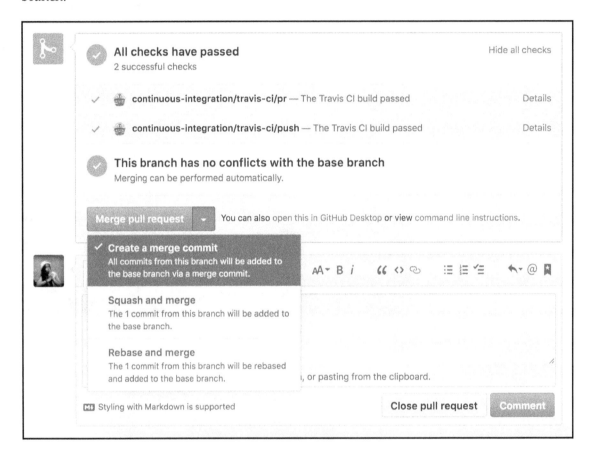

Introduction to Heroku

The last and most important part of developing an application is to deploy it. Heroku is a cloud platform as a service. It is a cloud platform where we can host our applications. Heroku is an easy and elegant way to deploy and manage our applications.

With Heroku, we can deploy our applications written in Node.js, and many other programming languages as well, such as Ruby, Java, and Python. Regardless of the programming language, the setup required for the Heroku application is the same across all languages.

There are several ways to deploy our application using Heroku, such as using Git, GitHub, Dropbox, or via API. We will be focusing on deploying our application with a Heroku client in this chapter.

Setting up a Heroku account

To get started with app deployment in Heroku, we first need to create an account. You can create yours directly from `https://www.heroku.com/`. If you want to learn more about different types of apps, you can check out the official documentation at `https://devcenter.heroku.com/`.

Once you create your account, you should be able to see your own dashboard:

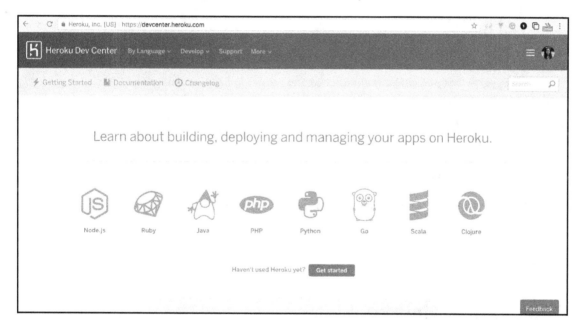

Creating a Node.js app

Heroku provides a lot of options for the application that we will build. It supports Node.js, Ruby, Java, PHP, Python, Go, Scala, and Clojure. Let's go ahead and choose Node.js from the dashboard.

This documentation itself will guide you when you follow each step. Let's go ahead and deploy our own app in Heroku.

Installing Heroku

The first and foremost thing to do is to install Heroku.

Installing Heroku in Windows

We can install Heroku in Windows simply by downloading the installer from the official page, `https://devcenter.heroku.com/articles/heroku-cli#download-and-install`, and running the installer.

Installing Heroku in Linux

Heroku can be installed in Linux with just a single command:

```
$ wget -qO- https://cli-assets.heroku.com/install-ubuntu.sh | sh
```

Installing Heroku in macOS X

We can install Heroku in macOS using `homebrew`:

```
$ brew install heroku/brew/heroku
```

We can check whether `Heroku` is installed using the following command:

```
$ heroku -v
```

This should print the version of Heroku that we just installed.

Deploying to Heroku

Once Heroku is installed, let's go to `https://dashboard.heroku.com/apps`, where we will be creating a Heroku application for our project. Click on the **Create New App** button and enter the application name that you want to provide to your application. We will be naming it `movie-rating-app-1` for our application:

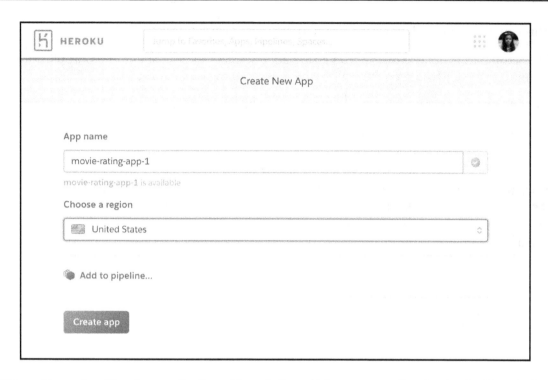

This will create a Heroku application. Now, let's switch to our application in the Terminal and run the following:

```
$ cd movie_rating_app
$ heroku login
```

This command will prompt you to enter your email and password:

```
~/P/movie_rating_app git⟩deploy ››› heroku login
This is the legacy Heroku CLI. Please install the new CLI from https://cli.heroku.com
Enter your Heroku credentials:
Email: get.aneeta@gmail.com
Password: ***************
Logged in as get.aneeta@gmail.com
~/P/movie_rating_app git⟩deploy ›››
```

Now, if you have already initialized a Git repository in your application, you can skip the `git init` part in the following code snippet:

```
$ git init
$ heroku git:remote -a movie-rating-app-1
```

This command will link our application to the Heroku application that we just created.

The setup part is done. Now, we can go ahead and make some changes in our application. Commit to the GitHub repo the way we have been doing so far and push the changes.

Now, the simple command to deploy to the Heroku app is to run the following command:

```
$ git push heroku master
```

There are a couple of things that we need to take care of here.

Since we are serving the Vue.js components by converting them to static files using the `serve-static` package in `server.js`, we need to update the start script in `package.json` to run the `node` server. Let's update the start script with the following line in `package.json`:

```
"scripts": {
    "dev": "webpack-dev-server --inline --progress --config
build/webpack.dev.conf.js",
    "start": "nodemon server.js",
    "unit": "cross-env BABEL_ENV=test karma start test/unit/karma.conf.js -
-single-run",
    "e2e": "node test/e2e/runner.js",
    "test": "npm run unit && npm run e2e",
    "lint": "eslint --ext .js,.vue src test/unit test/e2e/specs",
    "build": "node build/build.js",
    "heroku-postbuild": "npm install --only=dev --no-shrinkwrap && npm run
build"
    },
```

Also, in the `config/Config.js` file we have the following:

```
module.exports = {
  DB: 'mongodb://localhost/movie_rating_app',
  SECRET: 'movieratingappsecretkey',
  FACEBOOK_APP_ID: <facebook_client_id>,
  FACEBOOK_APP_SECRET: <facebook_client_secret>,
  TWITTER_APP_ID: <twitter_consumer_id>,
  TWITTER_APP_SECRET: <twitter_consumer_secret>,
  GOOGLE_APP_ID: <google_consumer_id>,
  GOOGLE_APP_SECRET: <google_consumer_secret>,
  LINKEDIN_APP_ID: <linkedin_consumer_id>,
  LINKEDIN_APP_SECRET: <linkedin_consumer_secret>
}
```

Here, we are specifying the local MongoDB URL that will not work when we host our application in Heroku. For this, we can use a tool called **mLab**. mLab is a Database as a service tool for MongoDB. mLab allows us to create as many databases as we want for a sandbox database.

Let's go ahead and create an account on `https://mlab.com/`. Once you are logged in, click on the **Create new** button to create a new database:

We can choose any cloud provider we want. Choose the plan type as **Sandbox** and click on **CONTINUE**. Choose any region and then click on **CONTINUE** and add the database name you want for the application. Finally, click on **Submit Order:**

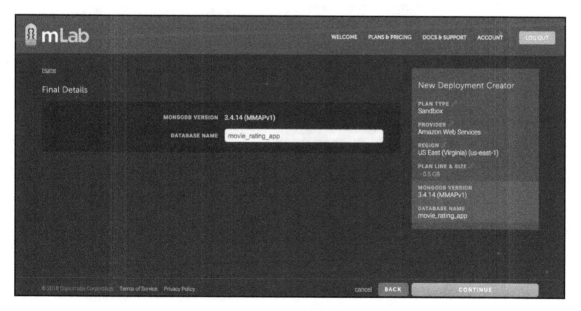

Now, if we click on the database name, we can see the link to the MongoDB URL provided by mLab. We also need to create a database user to be able to authenticate the database.

Go to the **Users** tab, click on **Add Database User**, provide the username and password, and hit **Create**.

We should be able to see the MongoDB URL in the database profile page:

Let's update the MongoDB URL in our `config/Config.js`:

```
module.exports = {
    mongodb://<dbuser>:<dbpassword>@ds251849.mlab.com:51849/movie_rating_app
    SECRET: 'movieratingappsecretkey',
    FACEBOOK_APP_ID: <facebook_client_id>,
    FACEBOOK_APP_SECRET: <facebook_client_secret>,
    TWITTER_APP_ID: <twitter_consumer_id>,
    TWITTER_APP_SECRET: <twitter_consumer_secret>,
    GOOGLE_APP_ID: <google_consumer_id>,
    GOOGLE_APP_SECRET: <google_consumer_secret>,
    LINKEDIN_APP_ID: <linkedin_consumer_id>,
    LINKEDIN_APP_SECRET: <linkedin_consumer_secret>
}
```

The last thing we need to change is the port of the application. The Heroku application automatically assigns a port when deploying an application. We should only be using port `8081` of the development environment only. So, let's verify that our `server.js` has the following code:

```
const port = process.env.PORT || 8081;
app.use('/', router);
var server = app.listen(port, function() {
  console.log(`api running on port ${port}`);
});

module.exports = server
```

Now, let's commit and push the changes to the `master` and then deploy again:

```
$ git add package.json config/Config.js server.js
$ git commit 'Update MongoDB url and app port'
$ git push origin master
$ git push heroku master
```

The application should be successfully deployed to Heroku and we should be able to view our application at `https://movie-rating-app-1.herokuapp.com/`:

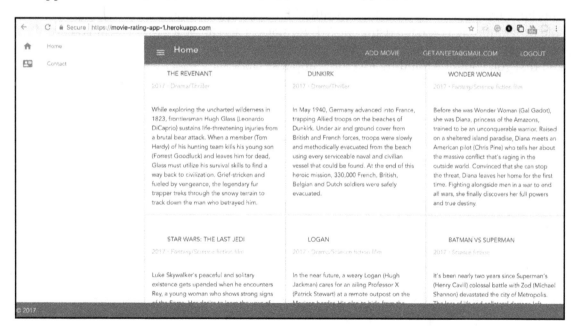

Heroku error logs

If something goes wrong when we are deploying in Heroku, we can also look into the error logs that Heroku provides with the following command:

```
$ heroku logs -t
```

Summary

In this chapter, we learned what CI is and how to use it to make the build automatic in the application. We also learned about how to deploy apps using Heroku integration. Overall, we learned how to build a full-stack web application using the Vue.js and Node.js technologies, we integrated a different authentication mechanism, and we also learned how to write tests for the application and make deployments for the application. Congratulations!

This is just the beginning of the journey that you will be taking forward. You should now be able to make small-to-large scale applications with all the technologies that we have learned about here.

This book has provided you with the skills to build an application using JavaScript as the sole programming language using the MEVN stack. This can be a great start if you are planning on building your own complete application. I hope you enjoyed reading the book and that you continue building awesome applications!

Other Books You May Enjoy

If you enjoyed this book, you may be interested in these other books by Packt:

Full-Stack Vue.js 2 and Laravel 5
Anthony Gore

ISBN: 978-1-78829-958-9

- Core features of Vue.js to create sophisticated user interfaces
- Build a secure backend API with Laravel
- Learn a state-of-the-art web development workflow with Webpack
- Full-stack app design principles and best practices
- Learn to deploy a full-stack app to a cloud server and CDN
- Managing complex application state with Vuex
- Securing a web service with Laravel Passport

Vue.js 2 Design Patterns and Best Practices
Paul Halliday

ISBN: 978-1-78883-979-2

- Understand the theory and patterns of Vue.js
- Build scalable and modular Vue.js applications
- Take advantage of Vuex for reactive state management
- Create single page applications with vue-router
- Use Nuxt for FAST server-side rendered Vue applications
- Convert your application to a Progressive Web App (PWA) and add ServiceWorkers and offline support
- Build your app with Vue.js by following best practices and explore the common anti-patterns to avoid

Leave a review - let other readers know what you think

Please share your thoughts on this book with others by leaving a review on the site that you bought it from. If you purchased the book from Amazon, please leave us an honest review on this book's Amazon page. This is vital so that other potential readers can see and use your unbiased opinion to make purchasing decisions, we can understand what our customers think about our products, and our authors can see your feedback on the title that they have worked with Packt to create. It will only take a few minutes of your time, but is valuable to other potential customers, our authors, and Packt. Thank you!

Index

getter function 263, 264
installing 260
installing, in movie application 268, 269
mutations function 265
setting up 260
state function 260, 261, 263
store file, creating 260
using, in movie application 268, 270

W

writing tests
  benefits 279, 280

Y

Yarn
  reference link 106

www.ingramcontent.com/pod-product-compliance
Lightning Source LLC
Chambersburg PA
CBHW080614060326
40690CB00021B/4696